THE POLITICAL STRUCTURE
OF THE CHINESE COMMUNITY
IN CAMBODIA

LONDON SCHOOL OF ECONOMICS
MONOGRAPHS ON SOCIAL ANTHROPOLOGY
No. 42

THE POLITICAL STRUCTURE OF THE CHINESE COMMUNITY IN CAMBODIA

BY

W. E. WILLMOTT

UNIVERSITY OF LONDON
THE ATHLONE PRESS
NEW YORK: HUMANITIES PRESS INC.
1970

Published by
THE ATHLONE PRESS
UNIVERSITY OF LONDON
at 2 Gower Street London WCI
Distributed by Tiptree Book Services Ltd
Tiptree Essex

Australia and New Zealand
Melbourne University Press

Canada and U.S.A.
Humanities Press Inc.

UK SBN 0 485 19542 9
USA SBN 391 00114 0

65380

Printed in Great Britain by
WESTERN PRINTING SERVICES LTD
BRISTOL

PREFACE

In studying a community of over a hundred thousand persons, it is not possible, of course, to undertake fieldwork in the classical anthropological tradition of village studies. Rather, this study fits into the new tradition (if there can be such a thing) of what Professor Freedman has called the 'Chinese phase in social anthropology': the combined use of anthropological, sociological, and historical materials and techniques to provide a coherent description of a complex society (Freedman 1963, 13 ff.). This method does not rely on participant observation to the extent that is useful and possible in a village or on an island. I did not live in a Chinese household, nor was I a member of any Chinese association, these opportunities being respectively denied me by my family situation and my ethnicity.

Research for this study was undertaken primarily during the academic year 1962–63, when I spent thirteen months in Cambodia, twelve in Phnom-Penh and one in Siemréap, a small provincial capital in northwestern Cambodia. Besides travelling about the country generally, I made brief research visits to Kompong-Trach, Takhmau, Battambang, Sisophon, Pursat, Maung, and Mongkol-borei. Much of my material was gathered through interviews and conversations with Chinese leaders, ex-leaders, aspiring leaders, and many followers. Since most Chinese in Cambodia can speak Mandarin, Cantonese, French, or English, I needed an interpreter in only one interview, that with an elderly Hainanese from Kompong-Trach.

For a period of two months, I hired an assistant to do two tasks I could not do myself. One was the collection of about two hundred and fifty brief biographies of elderly men born in China. The second was to visit each of the major centres of Chinese population in the country to collect demographic and sociological information which could provide me with some basis for generalizations beyond my own experience. Since he had spent several years as a teacher in various Chinese schools, my assistant had ubiquitous contacts and was able to interview community leaders with relative ease.

While in Cambodia, I followed one Chinese and two French daily newspapers regularly, reading others occasionally and at times of specific interest. The fieldwork was further supplemented by library research in Phnom-Penh, Paris, and London.

The bulk of my expenses were borne by a generous grant from the Social Science Research Council of the United States, which I acknowledge with deep gratitude. Grants-in-aid were received from the Canada Council, the Central Research Fund of the University of London, the Leon and Thea Koerner Foundation of Vancouver, and the London-Cornell Project for East and Southeast Asian Studies, all of which bodies I wish to thank. Many Cambodian government officials supplied me with information and suggestions. I also wish to express my gratitude to the many Chinese who spent hours instructing me in the history and sociology of their community, in particular M. Chao Kon, whose pioneer work on the Chinese Hospital appears in the bibliography. *L'Ecole française d'extrême-Orient* was my host in Siemréap. M. and Mme Charles Meyer and M. Bernard-Philippe Groslier were particularly generous in helping me in many ways. In Paris, M. Ferreol de Ferry of the National Archives and Mlle Michèle t'Serstevens of the *Musée Guimet* helped me to use my limited time to full advantage.

The extent of my intellectual debt to Professor Maurice Freedman, who educated me in the anthropology of the Far East, is incalculable and will be recognized by anyone reading these pages. Parts of the manuscript were also read by Dr G. William Skinner, who provided helpful suggestions and corrections. None of the above are responsible for the book in its final form, the author alone taking full responsibility for all opinions and errors in style, presentation, or fact.

The Publications Centre, University of British Columbia, has graciously granted permission to reprint here some of the tables, appendices I and III, and the technical notes below, all of which originally appeared in my book, *The Chinese in Cambodia*.

TECHNICAL NOTES

The French words *congrégation* and *chef* are used throughout this book, the first because it is not translatable in the sense in which it was used in French Indochina, and the second because the English word 'chief' may for some anthropologists have connotations of leadership in primitive societies – connotations that I wish to avoid. The term *congréganistes*, meaning members of a *congrégation*, is occasionally used for brevity.

The French word *congrégation* is translated by the Chinese in Cambodia as *bang*, but this word is now falling out of conversational use. The term *bang-zhang* exactly translates *chef*, and is still used in the appellation of ex-*chefs*, e.g. *Huang Bang-zhang*. *Hui-guan*, on the other hand, refers to the association within the *congrégation*, which was not recognized by the French; it does not translate the word *congrégation*.

Some writers insist that the term *hui-guan* refers to a building rather than to an association (e.g. Katô 1932, 45), but in usage among overseas Chinese with whom I am acquainted, the term applies to the association and only secondarily to its *siège-social*. In this book, the term *hui-guan* is used consistently to apply to the association embracing all the members of a single speech group in Phnom-Penh, or all the members of a *congrégation* elsewhere.

I have tried to be consistent in using the term *congrégation* to apply only to the components of the system as defined in colonial law, or to the body of Chinese embraced by each component, that is, to all the Chinese of one speech group in Phnom-Penh; thus: the Teochiu *chef* was responsible for all the members of his *congrégation* and was aided in his tasks by the Teochiu *hui-guan*. The terms *congrégation* and *chef* are also used in describing the pre-French Annamese system of indirect rule because they exactly translate Vietnamese words and are current in French writings about that period.

The word *khmer* is the Cambodian adjective meaning 'Cambodian'. It is also used as a substantive to refer to the people or the language of Cambodia. I have reserved the term 'Khmer' to apply to the majority ethnic population of Cambodia, while the term 'Cambodian' applies to anything relating to the country as a whole. This parallels the distinction made between Malay and Malaysian to differentiate between the ethnic group of Malays and the citizens of the country. Thus, a Chinese may be a Cambodian if he is a citizen of the country, but he cannot be a Khmer.

The distinction becomes important in discussing assimilation, naturalization, and intermarriage. Sino-Khmer refers to descendants of a mixed marriage, while Sino-Cambodian refers to

Cambodian citizens of Chinese descent, who may or may not be Sino-Khmer and who may be more or less assimilated into the Khmer population.

There is as yet no official system for the romanization of Khmer. The few Khmer words in this book are romanized according to conventions usually followed in Phnom-Penh. The vowels have values approximately as in French. An *h* after a plosive stop indicates that it is aspirated; the absence of an *h* indicates that it is unaspirated. An *nh* indicates a palatalized sound equivalent to *ny* in ca*ny*on. Thus, the first *p* in Phnom-Penh is aspirated, the second is not, while the final *n* is palatalized.

Names of places in Cambodia are given in the form usual to Cambodian government publications.

Mandarin is transcribed according to the system of romanization now used in China. Spellings conform to the sixth edition of *Si-Jiao Hao-Ma Xin Ci-Dian*, published in 1958 (see list of works cited); the use of hyphens and capital letters is somewhat arbitrary.

To allow the use of forms familiar to Western social scientists only four exceptions have been made to this system of romanization: (1) names of places in China familiar to Western scholars, e.g. Fukien, Kwangtung; (2) names of famous individuals, e.g. Chou En-lai, Liu Shao-chi; (3) names of dynasties, e.g. Ch'ing; (4) the names of the five speech groups in Cambodia: Teochiu, Cantonese, Hokkien, Hakka, Hainanese. (Teochiu is preferred to Tiuchiu, Ch'ao-chou, and other forms because it most closely corresponds to the Teochiu pronunciation of the word.)

The characters for all Chinese words in italics are provided at the end of the book, where they are arranged according to the alphabetical listing of their romanizations.

The Cambodian riel was officially valued at 98 to the pound sterling in 1962–63, but the black-market rate fluctuated at a level considerably higher than this. The approximate value of 100 riels to the pound has been used in the few conversions given in this book because it gives a better indication of buying power for native products by natives of Cambodia than would a rate more realistic in terms of international finance and trade. The riel is officially indivisible, *centimes* having been withdrawn from circulation some years ago. Only paper money is used in Phnom-Penh.

CONTENTS

MAP
facing page 1

CAMBODIA IN 1963

I

Introduction

Near the small hill (*phnom* in Khmer) that gives the city its name,
the richer inhabitants of Phnom-Penh live in large villas, standing
in spacious grounds along quiet, shady streets. Just to the south of
the *phnom*, the city takes on a completely different aspect as one
moves into the business district. Walking through its streets, even
the most casual observer cannot help but be aware that a large
part of the city's population is Chinese. Rows of open-front
stores display in giant Chinese characters the names that are
traditional for Chinese firms: Abundant Blessing, Virtuous Profit,
Precious Joy, or Growing Wealth. Chinese restaurants and tea-
shops are at every street corner. There are Chinese lending
libraries where old men sit turning over much-thumbed copies
of Chinese novels. From store-front schools rise the repetitious
chants of school children learning Mandarin, hidden from the
pedestrian by a screen. Most of the newspapers sold on the streets
are Chinese, and during the long hot noon hour Chinese shop-
owners sit in front of their stores in singlets and shorts, reading
the world news, articles about China, or the latest instalments of
romantic novels – all in Chinese. Bookstores sell Chinese books
and magazines. In the shops or on the pavement, one hears the
various Chinese spoken languages almost as frequently as one
hears Khmer.

Phnom-Penh, capital and principal city of Cambodia, has a
population of half a million. In 1962–63, when I spent a year
there, one in three of its citizens was Chinese. Many of them have
spent their entire lives in Phnom-Penh; others came as shirtless
immigrants as recently as 1950. Together – new immigrants and
established families – they form a community of overseas Chinese,
hua-qiao. This book is concerned with the political structure of that
community.

When one reads the literature on overseas Chinese, one is
struck by the many similarities between the communities in

various countries. One feels a sense of familiarity with each new area examined, as if it had all been said before. In adding yet another study to this *corpus*, I have considered it insufficient simply to describe one more example of overseas Chinese society. I have therefore focused on the differences between this and other examples in order to advance the task of analysing just what is Chinese about these immigrant communities. The main historical difference between Indochina and other countries, so far as the Chinese are concerned, is the system of indirect rule that was in force over them during the period of French hegemony (and before). Accordingly, the primary focus of this book is the *congrégation* system and its effects upon Chinese social organization.

The *congrégation* system was developed, as explained in chapter 2, by the Nguyen emperors of Vietnam in their colonization of the Mekong delta. It was adopted by the French to govern the Chinese in their colony of Cochinchina and was spread by them to their other possessions in Indochina. It would therefore have been helpful to the present study if a detailed sociological study of the *congrégations* in Cochinchina had been available. Several books have, indeed, been written about the *congrégations* in Cochinchina, but all by students of jurisprudence (Nguyen, Dubreuil, Lafargue, Levasseur) who were concerned primarily with various legal aspects. This study therefore represents the first attempt, so far as I know, to describe the sociology of the system.

Indirect rule over Chinese was not, of course, unique to Indochina, let alone Cambodia, for Tahiti, Madagascar and other French colonies practised similar systems (e.g. Coppenrath 1967, 59; Tsien 1961, 174-6). The Dutch East Indies and Spanish Philippines also exhibited formal systems of governing the Chinese through their own elected leaders. In other places, less formal systems of indirect rule developed, with different amounts of power being vested in Chinese leaders by the indigenous or colonial administrations. In chapter 12 some of these systems will be compared with the situation in Cambodia.

Although this study relates primarily to political structure, it does not pretend to make much progress toward the formulation of political theory in anthropology except in the minor way of providing a case study and some discussion of political concepts in terms of it. Political anthropology as yet includes few agreed or well-defined concepts (cf. Eisenstadt 1959), and it may be that the idea of 'political' is one of those concepts that Professor Firth has suggested must be defined only vaguely to permit us to communicate about other concepts (Firth 1951, 29). The word includes at least two disparate and in many ways contradictory referents that might be labelled by the terms 'polity' and 'politics'. On the one hand it refers to the ordering of society through a hierarchy of positions of differential authority (polity); on the other hand, it suggests the disorder of power and conflict between equal units (politics). Classical anthropology has stressed the former to the exclusion of the latter. For example, all the essays in *African Political Systems* (Fortes and Evans-Pritchard 1940), with the possible exception of Evans-Pritchard's discussion of the Nuer and Fortes' analysis of political power among the Tallensi, refer to the ordering of society through government and law. The book does not provide us with a definition of 'political system', except for Radcliffe-Brown's laconic remarks on law and war in the introduction (Radcliffe-Brown 1940, xiv); one of the contributors elsewhere defines political organization as 'that aspect of the total organization which is concerned with the establishment and the maintenance of internal cooperation and external independence' (Schapera 1956, 218). While the preservation of independence implies conflict of some sort, this definition explicitly relegates it to outside the society: that is, it is limited to war.

The emphasis upon political order is also found in Middleton and Tait's *Tribes Without Rulers* (1958), which is a sequel in the same vein. This emphasis is also characteristic of the important study by political scientists entitled *The Politics of Developing Areas*, where the political system is defined by one of the co-editors as (Almond 1960, 70):

That system of interactions to be found in all independent societies which performs the functions of integration and adaptation (both internally and vis-à-vis other societies) by means of the employment, or threat of employment, of more or less legitimate physical compulsion. The political system is the legitimate, order-maintaining or transforming system in the society.

In an essay published in 1956, M. G. Smith clearly distinguished two aspects of political organization, calling them administration and politics. 'Administration consists in the authorized processes of organization and management of the affairs of a given unit'

(Smith 1956, 49), while politics refers to 'a competition for power over the policy-making process' (Smith 1960, 17). For Smith, the key distinction separating these categories is that between authority and power: 'Authority is the right to order certain actions, power is the ability to secure their performance' (Smith 1956, 50). 'As political action is defined by power competition, and is inherently segmentary, so administrative action is defined by authority, and is inherently hierarchic' (*ibid.*, 49; cf. Smith 1960, 15–20).[1]

At this point Smith's analysis becomes too precise to be useful, for the right to order certain actions means nothing unless that right includes some expectation that the actions will be carried out, that performance will be secured; in short, the concept of authority implies power, and it would therefore be more useful to consider it as a special kind of power. Following C. Wright Mills, I would prefer to speak of authority as 'power justified by the beliefs of the voluntarily obedient' (Mills 1959, 41), implying that the diacritical factor is lack of compulsion.

A further difficulty arises with Smith's categories. Because he has used the term politics to refer to what others usually consider a sub-category of politics, he proposes that the word government should refer to the sum of political and administrative actions (Smith 1956, 47 f.). This is contrary to common usage, for government usually means that aspect of political organization which Smith has termed administration. That both administration and competition for power should be included in the concept 'political behaviour' is not unnatural, for power competition usually occurs over positions of authority in the administrative structure: most men interested in power attempt to convert it into authority.

[1] Easton has attempted to advance the analysis begun by Smith by distinguishing five kinds of actions involved in the formulation and implementation of policy (Easton 1959, 227–9). His categorization of political activities implies a close relationship between the administrative and competitive spheres of action at the same time as it allows one to deal with either sphere in isolation by referring to different steps in the policy process. However, its usefulness seems limited to large-scale societies where power has to do primarily with policy; that is, where decisions usually have reference to a plurality of cases. Furthermore, the limitation in his scheme of adjudication to the area of criminal law, excluding civil disputes, makes this category artificial when applied to Chinese society.

Almond advances on Easton's categories by, among other things, dividing the first into two kinds of process: the articulation and the aggregation of interests (Almond 1960, 17).

In this book, I try to be consistent in using the words as follows: political organization refers to a system of behaviour that includes the polity (political structure) and politics (competition for power). In distinguishing between types of leaders in Chinese associations, however, where Smith's terminology appears useful, I use the adjective 'political' in a narrower sense, in contrast to 'administrative', to refer to those leaders having the power to make policy decisions affecting a significant segment of the Chinese community.

THE PLACE OF THE CHINESE IN CAMBODIAN SOCIETY

In a previous publication I have described in some detail the relationship between the Chinese community and the larger Cambodian society of which it forms a part (W. Willmott 1967). Because the present study is an attempt to describe the structure of the Chinese community itself, only a summary statement is necessary here.

The first problem confronting a student of overseas Chinese society is a definition that will be useful in distinguishing the Chinese population from the rest of the inhabitants of the region. While physical characteristics can serve in Europe, Africa, and the western hemisphere, they are of little use in Southeast Asia, despite the fact that racial stereotypes exist among the people themselves. Social scientists have used various definitions based on a variety of factors, but I have found none that is wholly satisfactory (W. Willmott 1967, xii). For this study, I define as Chinese any individual who supports or participates in some or all of the Chinese associations available to him. This definition has the advantage of being operational both for collecting estimates of Chinese population and for determining the ethnicity of any individual. My estimates come primarily from Chinese leaders, who are probably thinking in terms of associational membership and support in giving Chinese population figures.

There are about 425,000 Chinese in Cambodia, forming about 7 per cent of the total population in 1963.[1] Although this community has historical continuity over some four centuries, from

[1] Estimates of the Chinese population in Cambodia vary between wide extremes, reflecting the difficulty of obtaining accurate figures. See Table 1 in my book, *The Chinese in Cambodia* (W. Willmott 1967, 13), for a collection of differing estimates. The process by which I arrived at the estimate presented here is described in an appendix to that book (*ibid.*, 103–7).

the founding of Phnom-Penh as the capital, its greatest growth has occurred since the French occupation of Cambodia, and in particular since the end of the Sino-Japanese war in 1945. Estimates of the Chinese population over the last seventy years are provided in Table 1.

TABLE 1. Estimates of Chinese Migration to Cambodia since 1890

Period	Annual Entries	Annual Exits	Net Annual Immigration	Chinese Population at End of Period	Approximate Percentage of Total Population
1890				130,000	9.7
1891–1905*			2,500	170,000	8.9
1906–1920*			1,600	200,000	8.3
1921–1925*	14,500	9,100	5,400	230,000	7.9
1926–1930*	22,400	13,900	8,500	275,000	9.8
1931–1934*	14,400	17,500	–3,100	260,000	8.7
1935–1942			5,500	300,000	8.7
1943–1945	N	N	N	300,000	8.3
1946–1949	35,000	5,000	30,000	420,000	10.8
1950–1952	3,000	1,000	2,000	425,000	10.3
1953–1962	N	N	N	425,000	7.4
1963–1968	N	N	N	425,000	6.5

* Derived from Wang Wen-Yuan 1937, pp. 15–23. Estimates calculated as two-thirds of migrations to Cochinchina or one-third of migrations to all Indochina.

N: Negligible numbers of migrants.

The Chinese community of 135,000 in Phnom-Penh is just ten times that of Battambang, the next largest concentration in Cambodia. About 41 per cent of the Chinese in Cambodia live in rural areas, a substantially higher proportion than in most other Southeast Asian countries.

The Chinese in Cambodia originated from four different regions of southeastern China and speak five distinct Chinese languages (see Table 2). Probably the earliest Chinese settlers in Phnom-Penh were Hokkien, from the region of Amoy (*Xia-men*) in southern Fukien Province. Some of the richest families in Cambodia today are of Hokkien extraction. Numerically, however, the Cantonese became preponderant after the founding of Saigon-Cholon and its emergence as the principal trading centre for the Mekong basin in the early nineteenth century.

Cantonese, who today form the second largest grouping, are predominantly urban, the vast majority residing in Phnom-Penh,

TABLE 2. Chinese Population in Cambodia and Phnom-Penh
by Speech Group, 1962–63

Group	All Cambodia Number	All Cambodia Percentage	Phnom-Penh Number	Phnom-Penh Percentage
Teochiu	324,000	77	100,000	74
Cantonese	43,000	10	16,000	12
Hainanese	33,000	8	10,000	7
Hakka	14,000	3	4,000	3
Hokkien	10,000	2	4,500	3
Other	1,000	0	500	0
Totals	425,000	100	135,000	99

Battambang, and Kompong-Cham. Most of them come from the region of Kwangtung Province south and west of Canton City, and most came to Cambodia after first settling in Cochinchina for a time. Originally concentrated in labour and carpentry, today Cantonese are found in every occupation open to Chinese.

Teochiu, from the hinterland of Swatow in northeastern Kwangtung Province, comprise about three-quarters of the Chinese in Cambodia, but this numerical preponderance dates only from about 1935, after the economic crisis of 1930–31 had forced many bankrupt Cantonese out of the country. In the rural areas of Cambodia, nine of every ten Chinese are Teochiu, while in the cities the Teochiu constitute about seven of ten Chinese.

The history of the Hainanese, from Hainan Island, is clearer than that of any other Chinese group in Cambodia, for it is known that they came to the area of modern Kampot Province during the eighteenth century, when it formed part of a large fiefdom governed by a Hainanese family founded by Mac Cuu.[1] Today, although there is still a concentration in Kampot, many Hainanese have moved to Phnom-Penh, where they have almost monopolized the hotel and restaurant business.

The Hakka in Cambodia originated primarily in the extreme northeastern regions of Kwangtung Province, migrating with the Teochiu in recent times. Apart from Phnom-Penh there are concentrations of Hakka in Takéo Province and around Voeunsai in Rattanakiri. Many of the cobblers, herbalists, and street dentists in Phnom-Penh are Hakka.

[1] The history of Mac Cuu and his family is given briefly in W. Willmott 1966. Longer versions are available in Gaspardone 1952; W. Willmott 1964b, 41 f. and 442 f.; and Boudet 1942.

Although the Chinese form a distinct ethnic group in Cambodia, relations between Chinese and Khmer are relatively cordial when compared with those in other Southeast Asian countries. Part of the reason for this lack of animosity lies in the presence of another sizeable minority, the Vietnamese, who absorb much of the hostility Khmer feel toward resident foreigners. Because Cambodia has been the victim of Vietnamese aggression throughout four centuries, and because Vietnamese today are found in occupations where they compete directly with Khmer for valued resources (rice-growing and fishing), the 400,000 Vietnamese in Cambodia suffer from both formal and informal discrimination that at times includes violence.

The Chinese, on the other hand, have remained predominantly in commerce, an area where no Khmer competition has developed until very recently. Even before French times, the Chinese acted as the economic middle men between Khmer peasant and aristocrat, leasing monopoly farms from the king, collecting revenue from his subjects, and organizing the rice and fish trade from which the court obtained substantial income. Under French rule, their rôle continued to be that of economic intermediary, and today they still predominate among the merchants and small industrialists of the country. Cambodia has been a plural society, in which ethnic and class boundaries coincided to a large extent. Professor Wertheim has pointed out that in such societies, conflict arises not simply from cultural differences, but from the appearance in similar economic classes of different ethnic groups (Wertheim 1964, 76 ff.); because this did not occur in Cambodia between Khmer and Chinese, relations remain cordial between them. Intermarriage has been both the result and a further cause of this cordiality.

2

Origins of the *Congrégation* System

It has been assumed by almost all students of Indochina that the method of governing the Chinese through *congrégations* originated with the Annamese emperors, specifically with Gia-Long in 1814.[1] This assumption is partly due to a general bias of historians in regarding Annam as the focus of Indochina. While this is probably a correct view of Indochina in the late eighteenth and early nineteenth centuries, there is no doubt that prior to that, Cambodia was the main political power in the area. But because Cambodia appeared to the Europeans arriving in the nineteenth century as a hinterland of the Annamese Empire, they read this view back on to the history of the previous era.[2] In fact, the Chinese in Cambodia were under a system of indirect rule some two centuries and a half before the edict of Gia-Long.

In a letter from Barom Reachea V (1659–72) to the Franciscan missionaries in Malacca we learn that at the end of the seventeenth century foreigners in the Khmer kingdom were under the direct justice of the king (Groslier 1958, 155). With the growing foreign populations in Phnom-Penh, this system was probably found to be inadequate to govern groups as diverse from each

[1] Levasseur 1939, 99; 'Notice' 1909, 1066; Vigier 1936, 178; Dubreuil 1910, 6; Lafargue 1909, 23; Purcell 1951, 224, does not give a date; Purcell 1965, 189, attributes the *congrégation* system to Minh Mang.

[2] The view of Cambodia as the hinterland of Vietnam has not been dispelled from Western scholarship, even from disciplines, such as political studies, where Cambodia's importance is great. For example, Lucian Pye, writing about 'the politics of Southeast Asia', describes the traditional system of government in Indochina as 'Sinofied' [*sic*] and as participating in 'Confucian civilization' (Pye 1960, 95). Even more recently a British scholar on Southeast Asia has suggested that Cambodia's pro-Chinese neutralism ill-suits her for her 'rôle' as a 'buffer' (Fisher 1964, 572). Writing about the main cities of Indochina, Ginsburg mentions only Saigon and Hanoi (Ginsburg 1955, 457). To indicate that this is not solely a Western bias, I mention that a Chinese historian marks Cambodia as 'Siam' on a map in one of his recent books (Lo 1963).

other as they were different from the Khmer. It is therefore not surprising that toward the end of the seventeenth century, soon after Barom Reachea's reign, a system of indirect rule over the foreign communities was developed. The evidence for this is to be found in the Kram Srok, or 'law of the country', promulgated at Oudong in 1693 (Leclère 1898, 89). The Kram Srok may have been based on an earlier code, dated as much as two centuries before. Unfortunately, repeated Thai raids completely destroyed the Cambodian archives at Oudong, so the Kram Srok of 1693 is the earliest extant Cambodian code (see Monod 1931, 7–12).

The principal law touching foreigners in Cambodia is article 100 of the Kram Srok, which, according to the translation made in 1898 by the *Résident-Supérieur* to Cambodia, Adhémard Leclère, reads as follows (*ibid.*, 114):

Pour les étrangers, on doit choisir parmi eux leurs chefs (chautéa) et les chefs des jeux.

Qu'un chautéa laotien soit chargé de la direction des piroques laotiennes; qu'un chautéa annamite ait la direction de tous ses compatriotes; qu'un chautéa cham soit chargé de la surveillance des chams; qu'un chautéa malais soit chargé de la surveillance des chvéa (javanais, malais); qu'un chautéa chinois soit chargé de surveiller ses compatriotes; qu'un chautéa japonais soit chargé de surveiller les japonais.

Article 101 goes on to state that either a Japanese or Chinese métis may be placed in charge of European ships if he knows both Cambodian and the European language; if, however, a European knows the language and customs of the Cambodian kingdom, he may be named *chautéa* of the Europeans. Article 102 adds that supervision of Indian and Burmese ships will be done by a national of the ship if he knows Cambodian, otherwise by a Malay (*ibid.*, 115).

To a student of the Chinese, this law is interesting in its omissions. We should like to know whether or not the *chautéa* was also responsible for the collection of taxes from his countrymen. We should like to know his relationship to the Cambodian administration, to whom he reported, and upon what sanctions he could rely. We should like to know his term of office and his privileges as well as his duties. Most important of all, we should like to know how he was chosen – whether elected by his countrymen or appointed by the king – for this might tell us something of the internal structure of the Chinese community at the time.

None of these questions is answered by the law; but one thing is clear: the Cambodian kings instituted a system of indirect rule whereby one member of each foreign community was responsible for law and order among his countrymen. This is the essence of the *congrégation* system elaborated in the nineteenth century by Annamese emperors and, somewhat later, formalized further by the French.

Although we do not know for sure, it is likely that the Chinese community in Cambodia was itself internally organized before the Kram Srok of 1693. An edict of the Annamese emperor about 1675, forbidding associations of Chinese merchants of more than two hundred members, suggests that there were rather large associations in Cochinchina by the seventeenth century.[1] Furthermore, some organization must have existed after the Kram Srok was promulgated, for otherwise one leader could not have controlled the Chinese community, which numbered over 3000 at the time. We know nothing of the nature of this social organization.

Nguyen Quoc Dinh, who has written the only study treating specifically the Chinese *congrégations* in Indochina, argues that in fact the 1693 Kram Srok did not establish indirect rule over the Chinese. In a footnote explaining why he does not treat Cambodia prior to French occupation, he writes the following (Nguyen 1941, 21 n. 5):

Nous ne parlons que de la réglementation annamite en laissant de côté celle du pays cambodgien qui était peu compliquée. Avant l'occupation française, il n'y avait pas au Cambodge d'organisation de Chinois en groupements spéciaux comme en Annam. Ces immigrants y étaient considérés commes des régnicoles aux points de vue fiscal, juridictionnel et législatif: par rapport aux cambodgiens, ils étaient soumis aux mêmes impôts de capitation, acquittaient les mêmes taxes fiscales entre les mains des fermiers royaux, relevaient des mêmes juges et des mêmes lois en cas de crime, délit ou contravention. Tout juste, le code cambodgien contenait-il quelques dispositions sur les étrangers selon lesquelles ceux-ci étaient placés dans les localités où ils résidaient sous l'autorité d'un chef (Chautéa); chef laotien pour les Laotiens, chef chinois pour les Chinois, etc.

Nguyen has turned too quickly from the evidence. In stressing that the Chinese were legally subjects of the Cambodian king, he

[1] Nguyen 1941, 23. The terminology of Gia-Long's edict of 1814 suggests that it was legitimizing already existing Chinese locality associations. See below, pp. 14 f.

ignores the fact that the Kram Srok states explicitly (article 7) that the Chinese are to be considered as foreigners, that 'ils ne constituent point la force vive du royaume' (Levasseur 1939, 55). Levasseur, whose important legal study of the Chinese in Indochina does not appear among the references cited by Nguyen, goes so far as to say, referring to the eighth law of the Kram Srok, 'Les Chinois en particulier étaient organisées en communautés autonomes' (*ibid.*, 54).

The Cambodian system was far from clearly defined, for the law stated no more than that each foreign community should have a *chef*. Furthermore, there is a fundamental difference between this Cambodian system and the system of *bang* (*congrégations*) decreed by Gia-Long, in that the Cambodian system had only one *chef* for all the Chinese, while Gia-Long explicitly divided the Chinese into separate *bang* according to their places of origin. (It may be, of course, that all the Chinese in Phnom-Penh during the seventeenth century were of one speech group.)

Further doubt may be cast on Nguyen's bold statement that in every way the Chinese in Cambodia were treated as indigenous subjects. Tax farms, for instance, were run by Chinese, and one may assume that the Chinese farmers' relations with fellow Chinese were somewhat different from their relations with Khmer subjects. Gambling farms were by law let only to Chinese (Leclère 1898, 54). In matters of justice, there is one piece of evidence that cases arising between Chinese were tried by the Chinese themselves: when the French arrived in Kampot, they found that the leader of the Chinese, an ex-pirate of Fukienese extraction named Mun-suy, was highly respected and himself tried all cases arising between Chinese in that town (Leclère 1907, 839).

The system set down in the Kram Srok may have evolved into a lax arrangement of rule by notables before the French arrived. In 1880, over a decade before the Royal Ordinance by which the French established the Vietnamese *congrégation* system in Cambodia (see below), a visiting Frenchman noted that there were two Chinese '*congrégations*' in Phnom-Penh (De La Porte 1880, 31; italics in original):

Le trafic énorme qui se fait dans cette ville…est presque entièrement concentré entre les mains des commerçants originaires des provinces méridionales du Céleste-Empire. Cette espèce de colonie chinoise qui, unie, pourrait causer de graves embarras au gouvernment, est par bonheur divisée en deux *congrégations* rivales et sans cesse en dispute.

It may well be that these two '*congrégations*' were nothing more than secret societies, for we have no other information on them. Nevertheless, it is possible that they were locality associations for Cantonese and Hokkien, and that their leaders were used by the Cambodian administration to govern the Chinese indirectly.

We have established that, contrary to Nguyen, a system of indirect rule over the Chinese in Cambodia probably predates by two centuries the *congrégation* system in Annam. The Annamese system is important to us, however, for it is certainly that system, and not the Cambodian, that was adopted by the French, firstly for the colony of Cochinchina and eventually for the whole of Indochina.

The Chinese *congrégations* in Annam date from the edict of Gia-Long in the thirteenth year of his reign, 1814. This edict established a special administration for the Chinese, dividing them according to their place of origin into groups under the jurisdiction of Chinese leaders. But the system of *congrégations* in Annam had its beginnings long before this, according to Nguyen Quoc Dinh, in the attempts of succeeding Nguyen kings of Annam to control the unsettled and mixed population of Cochinchina (Nguyen 1941, 23 f.). The Nguyens were in the process of colonizing Cochinchina with people who would pay them tribute, thus increasing those loyal to the court at Hué who would eventually swamp the rather sparse but indigenous Khmer population.[1] Chinese émigrés played an important part in this colonization (cf. Willmott 1966, 24 f.). Until 1693, they lived and moved without restrictions, but in that year the Emperor Hieu-Minh decreed that the names of all Chinese be inscribed on the registers of the villages in which they lived. In his attempt to reorganize this territory following a Khmer popular revolt in 1691, he divided the population into villages and hamlets grouped into two provinces. To facilitate control of the Chinese, Hieu-Minh organized them in 1699 into two 'villages', one for each province, with the same structure and officers as the Annamese villages, but

[1] Boudet states that Cochinchina was inhabited by deserters, adventurers, colonizers, and soldiers who had been given land (Boudet 1942, 116). Compare Beauchataud, 12–17.

including all the Chinese in each province regardless of their actual place of residence.[1]

According to Nguyen, the Chinese found these groupings too large to serve the functions usually performed by their indigenous associations, and they therefore organized sub-divisions within them on the basis of speech groups, each of which had its leader, who was able to direct the activities of welfare and conciliation which the Chinese expected of any association. These associations developed throughout the eighteenth century (Nguyen 1941, 24–7).

In 1802 Gia-Long mounted the throne and proceeded to reorganize the administration in his kingdom. Feeling completely independent of Chinese suzerainty, he altered the administration of the Chinese living in the whole Annamese empire, from Tonkin to Cochinchina. Recognizing that they had locality associations that could be utilized to the advantage of the imperial administration, he decreed that they should have the right to form these associations, which he called *bang*, that each association should have a *chef*, and that this *chef* should henceforth be responsible for law and order and act as intermediary between his members and the administration in matters of communication and taxes. This right of association became an obligation if there were more than thirty Chinese in one locality (Levasseur 1939, 99).

The number of *bang* in each province depended on the number of Chinese. In some cases, all the Chinese in a province of Annam would be grouped together in a single *bang*; in cases where there was a larger Chinese population, the *bang* might be organized on a county level. Nguyen explains that the law was not explicit on this point; in Annam the Chinese were grouped into *congrégations* at one of three levels: the province, the 'Phu' (*fu*), or the 'Xuyen' (*xian*) (Nguyen 1941, 31). Each *bang* was under the leadership of a *chef*, called *bang-truong* in Vietnamese (*bang-zhang* in Mandarin), who was responsible to the head of the province for the personal taxes of all his members, to the local village head for their land taxes, and to the township head (mayor) for maintaining

[1] Nguyen 1941, 23–4. The Chinese 'village' in Gia-dinh Province was called Minh-Huong (*ming-xiang*); hence the word used later to designate Sino-Annamese (Nguyen *ibid.*, 24 n. 12). The Vietnamese city, unlike the village, was not administered as a commune (Vu 1955, 209).

law and order among them. In practice, disputes were usually settled within the *congrégation* itself.[1]

It is clear from the terminology of the edict that Gia-Long was incorporating already existing Chinese associations into the administrative system of his empire. It is also clear that these were locality associations, based on the different origins of the Chinese in Annam at the time. Gia-Long recognized seven possible groups: Cantonese, Hokkien, Teochiu, Hainanese, Hakka, Foochow, and Ch'iung Chou (Kiungchow).[2] In practice, then, a *bang* usually included all Chinese of one language, and if these were too many, it would be divided into sub-*congrégations*, Pho-Bang (*fu-bang*), to according place of origin (Nguyen 1941, 31).

In 1824 and 1829, Minh-Mang followed Gia-Long in issuing other edicts that clarified the structure and operation of the *bang*.[3] Minh-Mang laid down election procedures for the *chefs*: henceforth they were to be approved by the provincial administration following their election by the 'notables' among their constituents. The term 'notables', also used by the French until a sharper definition of the electorate was thought necessary, seems to include 'simply the rich and influential persons, mostly the wholesale merchants'.[4]

To facilitate the collection of taxes, Minh-Mang specified that there were to be two classes of Chinese: those who had just arrived and had not yet a secure position paid only half the personal tax, while those who were already established in their profession paid the full annual tax of almost seven strings of cash, equivalent to about one and a half ounces of silver.[5] In contrast

[1] 'Notice' 1909, 1066. The words *bang* and *congrégation* are used interchangeably by this anonymous author.

[2] Lafargue gives the following Franco-Vietnamese names for the seven groups: Canton, Phuoc-Kien, Trieu-Chau, Hainan, Akas, Phuoc-Chau, Quinh-Chau (Lafargue 1909, 207). According to him, Phuoc-Chau was joined to Phuoc-Kien and Quinh-Chau to Hainan in 1885 (*ibid.*, 208).

[3] Nguyen 1941, 30–42. Later edicts affected the system only in minor details, such as changes in tax rates or punishments. These edicts were: Minh Mang 1832, Trieu-tri 1842 (Nguyen gives 1812, obviously a misprint), Tu-duc 1849 and 1858 (Nguyen 1941, 30; 'Notice' 1909, 1068 and 1097).

[4] My translation from Nguyen, which reads as follows (p. 32):
  Les notables étaient simplement des gens riches et influents, pour la plupart des gros négociants.

[5] According to Nguyen, the tax was six and five-sixths strings, a string consisting of six hundred zinc 'sapèques', or cash (Nguyen 1941, 34). On p. 35, n. 19, Nguyen tells us that eight or nine strings equalled about two ounces of silver at the time.

to Cambodia, then, the Chinese in Annam were on a separate tax roll from the rest of the population before French control was established.

In matters of law and order, the *chef* was held personally responsible for all members of his *congrégation*. However, since members might live in several villages, everyday matters were usually handled by the Annamese local administrator. Nevertheless, it was up to the *chef* to keep a record of all members, to know their movements, and to make amends for any crimes they committed. Furthermore, the *chef* had a direct responsibility over immigration, his approval being necessary for any Chinese desiring to settle in a province of Annam. If the *chef* were negligent in any of these duties, he was subject to discharge and even to punishment by beating, the same sanctions applying to him as applied to the Annamese local officials. But there was no legal restriction whatsoever on the powers of the *chef* over the members of his *congrégation*. In this sense, rule over the Chinese was probably more completely indirect than during the French régime, when the powers of the *chef* over his *congrégation* were legally defined.

Prior to Minh-Mang, Annamese women who married Chinese were assimilated to their husbands' *congrégations*; their descendants, the Minh-Huong, were treated as Chinese. After 1827, however, the Minh-Huong and their Annamese mothers were considered as Annamese nationals.[1] As children, the Minh-Huong were now 'protected' from their Chinese fathers, who were subject to one hundred blows if they sent them to China. The same penalty was inflicted on the Chinese who took his Annamese wife to China without authorization; and if a Chinese married an Annamese woman without official permission, not only he, but the *chef* of his *congrégation*, the middle-man, and even the neighbours could be beaten. Mature Minh-Huong (over eighteen) were grouped into 'villages' that united all the Minh-Huong in each province under 'mayors' who had an equivalent status to the mayors of Annamese villages. Although similar in operation to the Chinese *congrégations*, these groupings were organized according to the terminology of the Annamese local administration, to emphasize the fact that they were considered by the emperor to be Annamese.

[1] Vigier 1936, 179, whose account of this edict is followed here.

The treatment of Minh-Huong as a separate grouping was in sharp contrast to the practice in Cambodia at the time. There, the descendants of mixed marriages were assimilated to the Cambodian population and became ordinary subjects without any difficulties ('Notice' 1909, 1068 f.).

3

The *Congrégation* System under the French

The French promulgated three basic laws defining the *congrégation* in Cambodia. These were the Royal Ordinance of 31 December 1891 (An. du Camb. 1892, 179–90), and the decrees of the Governor General of Indochina on 15 November 1919 (JOIF 1919, 2508–14), and 6 December 1935 (JOIF 1935, 4092–9). Although various decrees changed minor points between these acts, the basic pattern was established by the first. A comparison between the first and third laws – the one at the beginning and the other close to the end of effective French rule in Cambodia – shows that the system, as defined by law, changed little throughout the five decades that separate them. It therefore can be discussed generally without reference to dates; whenever a specific aspect is treated that does not span the entire period, mention will be made of its date of introduction. (Although this system was applied to other minorities in Cambodia – the Indians, Arabs, and Malays – our concern here is exclusively with the Chinese.)

Nguyen Quoc Dinh has described fully the legal aspects of the *congrégation*, and this chapter relies heavily on his work (Nguyen 1941, esp. chapters III and IV). Much of the material also comes from interviews with the ex-*chefs* who are still living in Phnom-Penh.

As far as the immigration authorities or local residents were concerned, the *congrégation* consisted of a membership, a *chef*, and a *sous-chef*. So long as he fulfilled the functions for which he was selected, the *chef* was left to organize his activities as he saw fit. The *sous-chef* had no statutory duties except to take the place of the *chef* when the latter was absent; in practice he also aided the *chef* at all times. The system therefore centred on the person of the *chef*, who was the only formal link between the members of a *congrégation* and the colonial authorities. Prior to the law of 1935, the *congrégation* as a body did not have a legal personality (*personnalité civile*), but even after the *congrégations* became corporations in law, the rôle and manner of selection of the *chefs* remained the heart of the system. Before examining these two questions, I shall make an estimate of the number of *congrégations* (hence *chefs*) in the country.

THE GEOGRAPHIC DISTRIBUTION OF 'CONGRÉGATIONS'

The Royal Ordinance of 1891 stipulated in article 6 that there were to be *congrégations* in each district (*circonscription*) of the country. There were nine districts at the time, grouping a total of thirty-seven provinces (*khet*), each district being under the administration of a Resident (JOIF 1897, 1528). In 1907, the territory of Battambang was returned to Cambodia, and the total number of provinces rose to sixty-five (Russier 1914, 139), grouped into fourteen districts (Recueil 1927, 1297–1300). Some districts had administrative posts other than the residency, and interviews indicated that there were independent *congrégations* at each administrative post.

The law stated that the number of *congrégations* for each district would depend on the size of the Chinese population. In Phnom-Penh, and somewhat later in Kompong-Cham, separate *congrégations* were established for each of the five speech groups. Elsewhere, speech groups with small numbers (less than 100 according to article 2 of the 1919 law) were combined to form composite *congrégations*. Thus, the city of Battambang had three *congrégations* (Cantonese, Hokkien, and Teochiu-Hainanese-Hakka), while Kampot had only two (Hainanese and Teochiu-Cantonese-Hokkien-Hakka). Most other cities and towns had only one *congrégation* for all the Chinese.[1]

The 1935 law also made provision for large speech groups to be split into *sous-congrégations* (article 1), but there is no indication that this ever happened in Cambodia.[2]

[1] The single *congrégation* in most provincial towns may have included all alien Asians prior to the distinction made between Chinese and other alien Asians in the 1935 and 1936 immigration acts. The ex-*chef* of the *congrégation* in Sisophon told me that Indians had been included under his responsibility, but he may have been speaking *en principe* rather than of actual persons, for no Indians live in Sisophon today.

[2] There is no evidence that there were any *sous-congrégations* even in Cholon prior to the war. The Chinese in Cholon spoke of the Chinese community as a

I found no record of the number of Chinese *congrégations*, but from various sources one can estimate that there were at least seventy in Cambodia by the end of French rule. The number of *congrégations* at the time of their demise in 1958 was culled from interviews and from the research of my assistant. On the assumption that elections occurred every four years, I examined the *Bulletin Administratif du Cambodge* over two periods of at least four years, 1922–26 and 1932–35, for decisions of the *Résident-Supérieur* on the appointment of *chefs*. Table 3 includes all those *congrégations* discovered from any of these sources. It is not likely

TABLE 3. Distribution of Known Chinese *Congrégations* in Cambodia, about 1935

Residency	All Chinese[a]	Teochiu	Cantonese	Hokkien	Hainanese	Hakka	Total
Phnom-Penh[b]	–	1	1	1	1	1	5
Battambang	6	1*	1	1	–	–	9
Kampot	3	2*	–	–	2	–	7
Kandal	7	–	–	–	–	–	7
K-Cham	2	1	1	1	1	1	7
K-Chhnang	6	–	–	–	–	–	6
K-Speu	–	2*	–	–	–	–	2
K-Thom	2	–	–	–	–	–	2
Kratié	2	–	–	–	–	–	2
Prey-veng	3	3*	1	–	–	–	7
Pursat	2	–	–	–	–	–	2
Siemréap	4	–	–	–	–	–	4
Stung-Treng	2	–	–	–	–	1*	3
Svay-Rieng	–	1*	2	–	–	–	3
Takéo	–	3*	–	–	–	1*	4
Totals	39	14	6	3	4	4	70

[a] *Congrégations* that united all Chinese in an area.

[b] There is evidence of *congrégations* for other foreign communities only in Phnom-Penh.

* Those figures marked with an asterisk include *congrégations* that unite more than one speech group but are known to consist almost exclusively of one speech group; they are listed under the appropriate speech groups.

whole as the *qi-fu* (seven districts), recognizing that the Cantonese came from three different districts (*fu* or *zhou*) of Kwangtung (*Guang-zhou*, *Hui-zhou*, and *Zhao-zhou*); together with the four other speech groups these formed a total of seven districts of origin among the Chinese. For another interpretation of the seven districts, see chapter 2, p. 15. A bronze incense urn in the *wu-bang* temple in Phnom-Penh, a gift from a benefactor in Canton, is inscribed *qi-fu gong-so*, but the term was not familiar even to my older informants in Phnom-Penh.

that the number changed much between 1914 and 1958, despite the tremendous increase in Chinese population during that time.

The law stipulated nothing about the relationship between *congrégations* in different regions, whether or not they were of the same speech group. Thus, the Cantonese *congrégations* in Kompong-Cham and Phnom-Penh had no relation with each other, the respective *chefs* operating independently and with no responsibilities beyond their own *congrégations*. In practice, the *chefs* in Phnom-Penh were considered *primi inter pares*, but this status was not defined by law and had nothing to do with the administration. There were therefore about seventy independent *chefs* throughout Cambodia during the French period.

RÔLE OF THE 'CHEF'

The *congrégations* were established with two main purposes in mind: the collection of revenue from, and the policing of, a foreign population whose alien culture and community solidarity made it difficult to tax and govern in a more direct way. The rôle of the *chef* may therefore be analysed under the two headings of collecting revenue and keeping order.

1. *Collecting Revenue*

Prior to 1884, the Chinese in Cambodia paid the same personal taxes as the Cambodians, although they were exempt from the corvée. This head tax (*impôt de capitation*) was collected through agents who were granted revenue farms by the king (W. Willmott 1967, 45). But the introduction in 1884 of a special tax on the Chinese necessitated the establishment of a system of control, and in fact the law was not applied to the Chinese until after the *congrégations* had been inaugurated and the revenue farms abolished on 1 January 1892 (Nguyen 1941, 147–8). The duty of the *chef* in the matter of revenue is spelled out in the following manner in article 9 of the Royal Ordinance of 31 December 1891:

La congrégation est pécuniairement responsable dans la personne de son chef, et au besoin, solidairement entre tous ses membres, de la totalité des contributions personnelles dûes par ses congréganistes.

Article 12 of the 1935 law is substantially the same, but includes this additional sentence (JOIF 1935, 4093):

Dans tous les cas où la responsabilité civile d'un chef de congrégation est ainsi engagée, elle est solidairement partagés par tous les membres de la congrégation pour la totalité des sommes dûes par l'un d'eux.

In the fiscal reforms of 1884, the Chinese were divided for tax purposes into three categories according to class of business licence: the first class paid sixty piastres, the second fifteen, and the third four.[1] These taxes were charged on males between the ages of fifteen and sixty, who also paid $5\frac{1}{2}$ piastres annual registration; women, children, invalids, and men over sixty were exempt, and men between fifteen and eighteen paid half the registration fee.[2] The tax rates for the three categories were raised in 1897 to 88, 33, and 7 piastres respectively. In addition, the Chinese were to provide each year to the Administration ten days' free labour, which they could avoid by paying thirty cents per day ('Notice' 1909, 1087–8). This law remained in force until 1914, when the idea of providing labour was dropped and the whole tax structure was changed with regard to the Chinese. From 1914 until the end of French rule, each Chinese paid a 'fixed tax' (*droit fixe*) and each merchant also paid a 'graduated tax' (*droit gradué*) at a rate equal to 100 per cent of the sum of his payments in business licences and land taxes.[3] Originally established at ten piastres, the

---

[1] Nguyen 1941, 147. Taxes in Cambodia favoured Chinese immigration, for they were lower than in Cochinchina. Nguyen gives the following rates for the other countries:

Cochinchina:	60	20	5 (p. 143 f., revised into five categories in 1897)
Tonkin:	60	20	4 (p. 149, after 1889)
Annam:	40	12	3 (p. 152)

Laos had no tax categories until 1910, when the principle of a *droit fixe* and a *droit gradué* was adopted (Nguyen 1941, 154).

[2] A law of 3 December 1919 (JOIF 1919, 2266) set at seven piastres the annual registration fee for alien Asians over eighteen years of age, and allowed the same exemptions, except that men over sixty were exempted only if they were known to be incapable of earning a living and had lived in the country at least fifteen years and had no business licence.

[3] The principle of dividing the tax into a *droit fixe* and a *droit gradué* was established in Cochinchina on 31 December 1898 (Nguyen 1941, 145). This law worked on the basis of subtracting the *droit fixe* from the *droit gradué*, so that its only purpose was to fix a minimum tax. In Cambodia, however, they were added together for everyone. The annual land tax in Phnom-Penh was established at 5 per cent of rentable value by a decision on 25 October 1910 (Recueil 1927, 934). The collection of direct taxes from the Chinese was pushed to further extremes in 1938, when an additional graduated tax was instituted, varying from 20 to 100 per cent of the combined business and land taxes already paid if those

fixed tax rose gradually by a series of decrees until it reached eighteen piastres in 1938 (Levasseur 1939, 128).[1]

The personal taxes of all the Chinese were collected by the *chef*, who then handed them over to the Immigration Bureau. Any discrepancy between the amount collected and the amount due according to the roster of Chinese in each *congrégation* had to be made good by the *chef* himself. From 1924, *chefs* were given a commission of 3 per cent on all taxes paid before 30 April of each year; outside Phnom-Penh this rebate was shared with the village headman (*mékhum*), but in the capital it went entirely to the *chef* (JOIF 1924, 2143). Furthermore, the *chef* and *sous-chef* were exempt from the personal tax, although they of course paid business taxes like everyone else. To check on the payment of taxes, the law stipulated that the *chef* keep a roster (in Chinese and French) of all his *congréganistes*, and report each month (after 1935, each quarter) on losses by emigration, death, or removal to another part of the country. Penalties were inflicted – including both fines and imprisonment – on any *chef* who was negligent in these duties.

There is some doubt as to whether the *chefs* were responsible for the collection of business taxes as well as personal taxes. Article 12 of the 1935 law mentions only personal taxes and fines, and an informant stated that business taxes in Kompong-Trach had not been collected by the *chef*, but were paid individually to the local *gendarme*, a Frenchman. However, one informant, who had been general secretary of a *congrégation* in Phnom-Penh, stated that the *chef* was responsible for all taxes. A spokesman of the Tax Office told me that the Chinese were first placed on the tax rolls in 1955; prior to that they had been on separate rolls of the *Service des Contributions* under the direct supervision of the provincial governors, and the taxes were collected by the *chefs*. That he was referring to business taxes is suggested by the fact

taxes were above a certain figure (JOIF 1938, 243 f.). This surtax was calculated according to the following formula (here simplified):

20 per cent of tax above $160 for Europeans in Phnom-Penh, above $80 for all others in Phnom-Penh (lower figures for provinces)

50 per cent of tax above $500 for everyone.

100 per cent of tax above $1000 for everyone.

[1] The actual formula for the *droit fixe* was more complicated, for a law of 27 November 1937 implies that the eighteen piastres is made up of a *droit fixe* of ten piastres, from which the *chefs* were exempt, and additional *prestations* of eight piastres, paid by everyone including *chefs* (JOIF 1938, 243).

that the personal tax was collected on issuance of the identity card and has always been paid directly to the Immigration Service, not to the Treasury. An ex-functionary of the Immigration Service explained that a special *Bureau des Contributions des Asiatiques Etrangers* was established in October 1944, when the Immigration Service was abolished for a time. This *Bureau* was in turn abolished in 1955.

It can be seen from the above that the fiscal power of the *chef* over his *congréganistes* was not great: his fiscal duties involved collecting taxes, but not setting the rates or assigning individuals to various tax categories. He made a commission from these responsibilities, but he also ran the risk of losses through negligence or delinquency in his *congrégation*. Tax-collection alone could not have provided much incentive for a Chinese merchant to seek the post of *chef de congrégation*. In order to ensure the collection of revenue, however, as well as the maintenance of law and order, the *chef* was given wide power over his *congréganistes*, and it is in the examination of these powers that one may see the advantages of the position of *chef*.

2. *Keeping Order*

Throughout the period of French rule from 1891, a Central Immigration Bureau in Phnom-Penh supervised all the aliens in the country. With respect to the Chinese, this supervision was delegated to the *chefs* of the various *congrégations*, who in Phnom-Penh reported directly to the Bureau and elsewhere reported to the district residency.

Article 11 of the 1935 immigration law states the following (JOIF 1935, 4093):

Le chef de congrégation est l'intermédiaire pour recevoir de l'Administration les communications adressées à la collectivité des individus composant le groupement. Les chefs et sous-chefs concourent avec les agents de l'Administration à la police de la congrégation; ils exercent une surveillance directe sur celle-ci et font appel au besoin à la protection des autorités pour assurer leur intervention dans l'intérêt de l'ordre public.

The *chef*'s rôle in these matters was therefore twofold: on the one hand he was the medium of communication from the Administration to his *congréganistes*, and on the other hand he was responsible to the Administration for their behaviour.

It is significant that the law permitted the *chef* at any time to call on local administrative authorities for protection or for aid in policing his *congrégation*. Although the *chef* himself did not have police authority, a police force outside the Chinese community was at his bidding. This gave him great powers within the *congrégation* as well. Nguyen points out that while the police were limited to intervening only when an illegal act had been committed, the *chef* could take action against one of his *congréganistes* merely on suspicion (Nguyen 1941, 131):

Alors que la police, telle qu'elle est exercée par les agents de l'Administration, ne sévit que contre les actes matériels qui sont de nature à troubler l'ordre public, et non contre les idées, si suspectes soient-elles, tant qu'elles ne se manifestent pas par des actes, le chef de congrégation lui, agit sans distinction dans les deux hypothèses. Il est de son devoir de se rendre compte de l'état d'esprit de ses ressortissants et de prévenir les autorités de la présence dans son groupement d'individus indésirables par leur moralité douteuse.

An individual who felt himself wronged by a *chef* could appeal to the courts, but in such cases, 'the judges [were] very harsh in the estimation of motives', for experience taught them that such actions were seldom the result of real damages, but rather matters of face (Nguyen 1941, 135). It is obvious that the Administration had everything to gain from supporting the authority of the *chef* at almost all times.

The sanctions available to the *chef* in the control of his *congrégation* included fines and commercial penalties backed by police force, and, most important, the ultimate sanction of deportation. If a *chef* declared to the Immigration Bureau that he would no longer take responsibility for someone, that individual was deported forthwith by the Administration. The only curbs on this sanction were the facts that the expenses of repatriation were borne by the *congrégation* in the person of its *chef* and that the deportee had the right to appeal to the council of *chefs* (see below, pp. 29 f.).

The power of a *chef* was established over an immigrant as soon as he arrived in the country. Since it was compulsory for every Chinese to belong to a *congrégation*, the *chefs* had the authority by law to accept or reject any immigrant, and an individual refused by the appropriate *congrégation* was not admitted to the country. (The only exception to this rule was for those Chinese who arrived on a contract to work for a European *colon*; in this case the *colon* assumed all responsibilities for his contracted workers. There were very few Chinese workers on contract to Europeans in Cambodia, and this exception may therefore be ignored in a study of the Chinese community as a whole.[1]) Because the *congrégations* were divided according to speech groups, an individual refused by one *chef* could not appeal to join another *congrégation*.

Just as an individual could not enter Cambodia without the explicit approval of the *chef* of his *congrégation*, so also he could not change residence within the country without the *chef*'s agreement. For a *laissez-passer* to move from one district to another, an individual needed a certificate of approval from the *chef* of his *congrégation*, and acceptance by the *chef* in the locality to which he wished to move was necessary for him to stay there.

Finally, in order to receive an exit visa to leave the country, it was necessary for the individual to accompany his *chef* to the Immigration Bureau and to bring with him a certificate signed by the *chef* stating that he was free of all obligations toward the national treasury and that there were no other hindrances to his leaving Cambodia. This stipulation was included in the law to ensure that a Chinese could not leave the country without paying his current taxes, but it incidentally gave the *chef* the power to avert the flight of individuals who had not settled their affairs within the Chinese community.

In sum, the authority of the *chef*, as defined by law, was sufficient to give him tremendous power over the members of his *congrégation*, from the moment they arrived in Cambodia to their ultimate departure. This power was based on the legal right of the *chef* to call in enforcing agents from outside the Chinese community and to effect the deportation of any Chinese. The authority was given him by the Administration in order that he maintain peace among his charges and collect direct taxes from them.

It would be wrong, of course, to think of the power of the *chef*

[1] W. Willmott 1967, p. 61. The law exempting the contract labour of European *colons* from the supervision of *congrégations* was promulgated 20 August 1898 (Recueil 1927, 435). It states that such workers were exempt from head-tax, personal tax, corvée, guard duty, etc., during their period of engagement. They received a special identification card, which included the name of the *colon* for whom they worked. The *colon* paid the Administration an annual registration fee of two piastres for each worker. The law states specifically that these contract workers were not considered as belonging to *congrégations* or villages.

as unlimited. Although the sanctions at his disposal were outside their control, his *congréganistes* were nevertheless able to exercise restraint through the system by which he was elected. Legitimation of his power came therefore from within the *congrégation* as well as from the French Administration.

SELECTION OF THE 'CHEF'

The rules of election for *chef de congrégation* differed somewhat in the three successive major laws relating to the *congrégations*. The question was dealt with summarily in article 7 of the 1891 law, which stipulated that the *chef* and *sous-chef* be appointed by the *Résident-Supérieur* meeting with the Council of Ministers, from lists of three nominations for each post. The nominees, to be of good reputation and resident in the district for at least two years, were elected by the members of the *congrégation* who had paid their head tax for that year (An. du Camb. 1892, 181).

In 1919 the electorate was limited to those members of the *congrégation* who held business licences, and nominations were restricted to members who, in addition to the two conditions above, held business licences in one of the top five classes.[1] The term of office is not mentioned in this law.

Finally, in 1935 the method of election was detailed in articles 4–10. The *chefs* were still to be appointed by the *Résident-Supérieur* from a list of three nominations for each post, but those eligible for nomination had to be thirty years of age, to have lived at least two years in the country, to lack a criminal record, and to pay a minimum of forty piastres in business licences in Phnom-Penh, thirty in other urban centres, or fifteen in rural areas. The electorate in Phnom-Penh was limited to those over eighteen who held business licences, but this restriction did not apply in other areas, where any adult *congréganiste* could vote. Elections were to be held every four years, during the second half of

---

[1] JOIF 1919, 2508 (article 2). I was unable to determine the nature of the various categories of business licences in Cambodia during the French period. A French expert at the Ministry of Justice in Phnom-Penh is making a study of this question, and it is hoped that a description of these categories will be available in the near future. One Chinese informant stated that there were three categories in Phnom-Penh before the war, depending on the area of the city in which the business was located: those on the main street (then Rue Orhier, now Ang Eng) paid the highest tax, those in the poorest alleys the lowest. This implies that the *chef* had no way of affecting the category of any individual.

November, and the new *chef* was to assume office the following 1 January. Elections for the *sous-chef* were to be held two years after those for the *chef* so that their terms could overlap. If a *chef* were away for less than three months, his duties would be assumed by the *sous-chef*, but if the absence were for longer, a new election was called. If the *congrégation* refused to elect, the *chef* was to be appointed by the head of the local administration.

Interviews and historical records suggest that the four-year term was in effect in Cambodia for some time before 1935, although I could find no earlier law relating to this matter. In any case, *chefs* usually served for at least two terms, occasionally longer. One *chef* led the Cantonese *congrégation* in Phnom-Penh for twenty-five years, and in Sisophon a *chef* served for forty years. In Phnom-Penh, the Teochiu, Hakka and Hainanese *chefs* appear to have changed more frequently than the Cantonese.

Although the *Résident* appointed the *chefs*, it was clear from interviews with men who had been *chefs* that in Phnom-Penh the Chinese merchants decided who would be *chef*, ensuring his appointment by including no other appropriate names among the three nominations. Since the Administration was concerned primarily with maintaining peace and ensuring revenue, the man chosen by the members of the *congrégation* was usually acceptable, and no record was found of a *Résident* refusing to appoint from the nominations provided. In districts with small Chinese populations, the power of the *Résident* might have been felt more directly. In Sisophon, for instance, a *chef* of Teochiu extraction remained in office for forty years despite strong opposition from among the Chinese, a majority of whom were Hainanese.

Interviews in Siemréap, Kompong-Trach, Sisophon, Battambang, and Pursat indicated that, despite the fact that the law enfranchised all members of the *congrégation*, the *chef* in these areas was elected by the merchants in the *congrégation*. Informants explained that since the *congrégation* had to do with money, it was only fair that those who had to pay should elect their representatives. Throughout Cambodia, as far as I know, the *chef* was elected by the body of merchants within his *congrégation*, who thereby exercised some control over his activities. In fact, of course, their control went far beyond elections, as will be explained in chapter 4, but within the strict limits of the law, this was their check on the *chef*.

The immigration law passed in 1919 introduced a photographic identity card for the more wealthy Chinese. Armed with this card, they were exempt from the more onerous formalities of visas and examinations in crossing borders.[1] The idea may have been suggested by the Chinese themselves, who considered finger-printing degrading and found that the difficulties of travel hampered their businesses. In any case, one result of this new card was the establishment of a legal and visible distinction between the Chinese of wealth and the workers and poorer merchants. It was clearly the former category who were expected to exercise influence within the *congrégation* and to ensure the selection of a competent *chef*.

THE COUNCIL OF 'CHEFS'

From quite early in the period of *congrégations*, the various speech groups in Phnom-Penh found it convenient for all the *chefs* to meet at regular intervals. A *conseil des congrégations réunies* had been created for Cochinchina in 1863 (Nguyen 1941, 122), but I found no law relating to its establishment in Cambodia. In Cochinchina, its main function was as an appeal court for deporta-tions, and the same appears to have been its formal rôle in Cambodia, for the only mention of this council in the law of Cambodia prior to the Sino-Japanese war is the following para-graph (article 9) of the 1919 immigration act (JOIF 1919, 2059):

Aucun Asiatique étranger ou assimilé, rejeté par une congrégation, ou qui refuse de continuer à faire partie d'une congrégation, ne pourra séjourner dans la colonie. Il sera, après avoir été entendu par le Congso ou Conseil des congrégations réunies, expulsé à ses frais, par les soins de l'Administration, ou, en cas d'insolvabilité, aux frais de sa con-grégation.

[1] JOIF 1919, 2511 f. (chapter iv). The photo-card was available after 1919 to those merchants whose business licences were in the top five classes or who paid equivalent land taxes, as well as to bank managers, compradores, and notables presented by their *chefs* and approved by the immigration authorities. With this card, a man could disembark freely with his family, could move freely throughout French Indochina, and could make verbal declarations of movements rather than applying for permits.

An Identity Service had been established in 1913 (decree of Gov. Gen., 2 July 1913), among whose duties was the photographing of notables who had been decorated or retired, and of criminals or deportees. No doubt this Service testified to the feasibility and usefulness of photographic identification compared to the cumbersome methods then employed.

The Chinese called this council the *wu-bang gong-so* (hence the term 'Congso' in the law quoted above); its operation can be treated more appropriately in the discussion of Chinese social organization in chapter 4.

In 1944, the council of *chefs* in Phnom-Penh was given formal recognition by the French, and a secretariat of the Five *Congrégations* was established with a staff of full-time secretaries led by a general secretary. This secretariat became known in Chinese as the *Zhong-hua hui-guan*, short for *Zhong-hua li-shi hui-guan*. The *chef* of the Teochiu *congrégation*, by then the largest, was designated *président des cinq chefs*, with responsibilities for communicating directives of the Administration aimed at all the Chinese. In 1947 the *congrégations* were officially renamed *Groupements Administratifs Chinois Régionaux*, and the council of *chefs* was accordingly called *le Conseil des Chefs de G.A.C.R.*

LEGAL RECOGNITION OF THE 'CONGRÉGATION' AS A CORPORATION

Although the *congrégations* did not become corporations in law until 1935, they had the right, after 1919, to levy a special tax 'in order to cover their general expenses' (JOIF 1919, 2510). The rate of this tax was subject to the approval of the *Résident-Supérieur*. According to one informant, it amounted to less than one piastre per year, plus an additional two piastres upon departure from the country. Since this tax was collected by the *chef* with the taxes for the Administration, its collection was assured by the same sanctions that assured the collection of government taxes. It therefore provided the *congrégations* with a steady income.

In 1935, besides endowing the *congrégations* with legal personality, the law provided that they could own whatever property was 'necessary to their functioning' (JOIF 1935, 4092). This gave legal recognition to a situation that had existed since their origins, namely that each *congrégation* had property under the supervision of its *chef*. In Phnom-Penh, each *congrégation* owned at least a temple and a cemetery. The temple served as the headquarters of the *congrégation* and usually also as a school. By the time of their demise, each of the *congrégations* in Phnom-Penh had substantial holdings of urban land, the income from which went into the coffers of the *congrégation* as a body; all or part of this property consisted of the land around the temple.

That the association of *congréganistes* was eventually recognized in law suggests that the French were well aware that the *chef* could not have carried out his duties without the support of a structure within the *congrégation*. This structure, called a *hui-guan*, in fact predated the *congrégation* in some cases in Phnom-Penh (Cantonese, Hokkien, and possibly Teochiu), but the French at first followed the pattern established by Gia-Long of virtually ignoring its existence in the law and making the *chef* personally responsible for the whole body of members.[1]

Chinese community organization in French Cambodia was moulded by the *congrégations*, for they gave form and power to the *hui-guan* that were the heart of Chinese social structure. In Battambang, to give a concrete example, there were three Chinese 'public' schools, one of them called the *Chao-Qiong-Ke* school because it combined Teochiu, Hainanese, and Hakka – a combination that cannot be explained by ethnic or linguistic considerations, but is based solely on the fact that these three speech groups were included in one *congrégation*. In Phnom-Penh, where there was one *congrégation* for each speech group, it was primarily the political structure that was determined by the *congrégations*. I turn now to an examination of Chinese social organization under the *congrégation* system.

---

[1] Among Chinese all over the world (including China) the term *hui-guan* refers to associations based on the criterion of locality or origin, while among the Chinese in North America, *gong-so* now refers only to clan associations. The Chinese in Cambodia use these two terms interchangeably. One friend explained that *gong-so* was more current during the French period because it is equivalent to the Vietnamese term, while *hui-guan* has become more popular since independence. But, as noted in chapter 4, the sign *Wu-bang Hui-guan* was raised over the gate of the temple belonging to all five *hui-guan* as early as the beginning of this century. Furthermore, the Teochiu temple carries the sign *Chao-zhao hui-guan*, which appears to be quite old.

4

Chinese Social Organization within the *Congrégation*

Until 1953, the city of Phnom-Penh comprised several distinct districts, each inhabited by a different ethnic group. Around the *phnom* stood the great villas of the French administrators, officers, and *colons*. To the north lay the Vietnamese quarter, commonly called '*le village catholique*'; and further north still, along the Tonlé-sap River, lived the community of Malay-Cham. To the south of the French quarter and separated from it by a small river, lay the Chinese quarter, which was also the commercial centre, with shops, banks, docks, business houses and markets; in this area lived almost all the Chinese until the sudden increase of population after the war forced many Chinese to move west into what was known as Chamcar Chen, the 'Chinese gardens', where previously Chinese had cultivated vegetables. Further south, behind the Royal Palace, along the Tonlé Bassac, and around the fringes of the whole city, lived the Khmer, who formed a small minority of the city's population.

Within the Chinese quarter, there were no clear geographic distinctions among the five speech groups. The membership of each *congrégation* was not confined to a ward but was dispersed throughout the Chinese quarter. Therefore, the *hui-guan* could not operate as territorial governments, but left such functions entirely to the French. Policing streets, supervising sanitation, and planning improvements were done by the municipal authorities or not at all.[1]

[1] The Municipal government of Phnom-Penh was under a *Résident-Maire*, responsible to the *Résident-Supérieur* in the same way as were the *résidents* in each district. A decree of the Governor General in Council in 1915 (Recueil 1927, 1557–62) established a Municipal Commission appointed by the *Résident-Supérieur* and composed of five French citizens nominated by the *Résident-Maire*, three Cambodians from a list of six nominated by the Council of Ministers and approved by the king, one Annamese nominated by the *Résident-Maire*, and one

THE 'HUI-GUAN' IN PHNOM-PENH

Although the speech groups in Phnom-Penh varied in size from several hundred to several tens of thousands of individuals, the formal structure of the *hui-guan* did not differ greatly. In the smaller *hui-guan* (Hainanese, Hakka, Hokkien), the *chef* had substantially more personal power, but in all of them some of his power was delegated to a council or executive, which in turn delegated specific responsibilities to committees. The structure of the Cantonese *hui-guan* serves admirably as an example, for, because of the preponderance of Cantonese in the early period of the system, this *hui-guan* was the most highly elaborated in its formal structure. The information in this section comes from interviews with two former officers of the Cantonese *hui-guan* and from some of the ex-*chefs* who still live in Phnom-Penh.

In Phnom-Penh, the Cantonese businessmen – those with business licences in the top categories – elected a council of eighty men biennially. This number did not meet as a body, but was distributed by the *chef* and *sous-chef* into the various committees that ran the business of the *hui-guan*. The main committee was the *bang-hui* (*congrégation* council), which acted as the executive of the *hui-guan*. This committee, which included both the *chef* and *sous-chef*, numbered about twenty and employed a full-time general secretary. Unlike the five other committees staffed from the council of eighty, the *bang-hui* was not limited to specific duties, but had power over all matters in the *hui-guan*. It supervised the work of the other committees, made policy decisions affecting the whole speech group, and acted as a consultative body for the *chef* in his dealings with the Administration. Clearly, in this committee resided the main power in the *hui-guan*.

The executive committees of the other *hui-guan* in Phnom-Penh were somewhat smaller, numbering about fifteen members; all of them included the *chef* and *sous-chef*. In the case of the Teochiu *hui-guan*, the over-all responsibility for the committee rotated each month among its members, probably because there was no full-time secretariat. The Teochiu, Hokkien, and Hakka

Chinese appointed from three nominations by the *chefs de congrégation* in the city. This council had no power to legislate; it merely advised the *Résident-Maire*. It received no funds from taxes on Asians.

bang-hui were elected every year, the Hainanese, like the Cantonese, every second year.

The Cantonese *hui-guan* structure comprised five other committees. In describing their duties, I shall indicate where other *hui-guan* differed from the Cantonese.

1. *Cemetery Committee*

Each *hui-guan* in Phnom-Penh administered its own cemetery through a cemetery committee. The Cantonese cemetery committee consisted of nine or ten persons from the elected council. Besides looking after the cemetery, this committee supervised the exhumation of bones, which was done five years after the first burial. According to a law promulgated in Cambodia in 1898 (Recueil 1927, 431), the permission of the district resident was necessary for each exhumation, and a functionary had to be present when graves were opened. The bones were to be placed in special wooden boxes, which could be stored only in a place designated by the Administration. These arrangements could obviously be made with much greater facility by a *chef* for the entire *congrégation* than by an individual. Indeed, it was extremely difficult for an individual to make private arrangements for the exhumation and shipment of bones to China. In some cases individuals accompanied the bones of their kinsmen to their home districts, and in a few cases the bones were first burned to allow for easier transport; most pots of bones, however, went in large shipments organized by the *hui-guan* every three years; in this they were assisted by the Cantonese locality associations (*tongxiang hui*), which will be discussed later (see pp. 48 ff.). The cemetery committee also organized transport and policed the cemetery for the family celebrations at Qing-Ming and Chong-Yang, on which festival days many Cantonese went to the graves of kinsmen to refurbish them and make sacrifices.

None of the other speech groups was as concerned as the Cantonese to ship bones to China. This may be an example of Cantonese emphasis upon Chinese tradition and ties with the homeland, for all informants agreed that the Cantonese were more concerned than the other groups with Chineseness. Or it may simply be a result of the Cantonese practice of double burial: Cantonese open graves and wash the bones after a period of about five years, then store the bones in a pot until they can be reburied in a permanent grave, a practice also followed by the Hakka in China.[1] In any case, the other cemetery committees had fewer responsibilities with regard to exhumation than did the Cantonese. All speech groups went to their respective cemeteries at *Qing-Ming*; the Cantonese, Hakka, and a few Hokkien also went at *Chong-Yang*, and only the Hainanese at *Dong-Jie* (see chapter 8 for the yearly cycle of festivals). The Teochiu cemetery committee was about the same size as the Cantonese, but each of the others consisted of seven persons.

2. *Temple Committee*

From its inception, the Cantonese *hui-guan*, like all other *hui-guan* in Phnom-Penh, conducted its business in a temple. Unlike the others, the Cantonese temple was torn down in 1928, when a large school was constructed on the temple site; after that the *hui-guan* had offices in the school. The temple was re-established in a ground-floor room of the new school building. The duties of the temple committee were greatly reduced, for its administrative functions over the temple property were assumed by the school committee. After that it did little but ensure that the room was tidy, that the idols were refurbished periodically, and that they entered the procession at *Yuan-Xiao* each year (see pp. 98 ff.). The temple committees of other *hui-guan* had similar duties but with more responsibility for the property itself.[2]

[1] In recent years (especially 1959–60) Cambodian government orders to move the Chinese cemeteries further from Phnom-Penh have forced all the groups to open graves and place the bones in pots to be buried in new cemeteries. These recent double burials do not lead to the shipment of bones because China has refused bones since 1949; indeed, no bones have been shipped from Cambodia since 1938.

[2] The gods represented in the *hui-guan* temples are the following:

Teochiu: *Guan Gong* (*Xie-tian Da Di*); lesser gods: *Rao-sheng Da Di*, *Tian-hou Sheng Mu*.
Cantonese: *Kang Zhen Jun*.
Hokkien: *Guan Gong* (*Guan-sheng Da Di*); lesser gods: *Ben-tou Gong*, *Zhu-sheng Niang-niang*.
Hainanese: *Sheng Mu*.
Hakka: *Tian-hou Sheng Mu*.

The temple built by all five *hui-guan* (see below, p. 40) has *Bei-ji Da Di* as the principal god, flanked by *Ben-tou Gong* and *Zhu-sheng Niang-niang*. A Hainanese friend told me that prior to the bombing of Phnom-Penh in 1945, the goddess in the Hainanese temple had been called *Shui-wei Sheng Mu*, who was, according to Skinner, 'the Hainanese deity par excellence' (Skinner 1958, 84), but this name had been changed because the Cantonese connotations of the term 'water-tail',

3. School Committee

Far more important was the school committee of the *hui-guan*. The Cantonese school was organized on a formal basis following the completion of school buildings in 1929, although there had been informal schooling in the temple prior to that date. The school committee was responsible for the appointment of a principal, for the hiring of the teachers, and for the financing of the school. School funds were separate from the general finances of the *hui-guan*, although subsidies were paid by the *hui-guan* to allow children of poor families to attend classes without paying tuition. Prior to the Sino-Japanese war, instruction was in the Cantonese language, and enrolment was therefore limited to Cantonese children.

Both Teochiu and Hokkien *hui-guan* had established 'public' schools before the Cantonese (1914 and 1927 respectively), but the Hainanese and Hakka *hui-guan* did not open schools until the war (1941 and 1942 respectively), by which time most schools were teaching in Mandarin. In all cases, the school boards were selected by the *hui-guan*, and the schools were public in the Chinese sense (*gong-li*) of being run by public subscription and for the benefit of the community.

4. Welfare Committee

The Cantonese *hui-guan* was the only one in Phnom-Penh to include a special committee to look after welfare problems. The twelve members of this committee dealt with indigence among the Cantonese, each of them acting as convener for one month of the year. This committee also nominated four of its members to the managing board of the Chinese Hospital after 1945 (see below, pp. 40 f.). In the other *hui-guan*, these matters were handled by the *bang-hui*.

5. Reconciliation Commission

The fifth committee of the Cantonese *hui-guan* was the reconciliation commission; like all the other committees, its members were appointed by the *chef* from among the elected council of

associated with bad fortune in business, kept many people from frequenting the temple: the phrase 'slow-water' is a Cantonese slang expression for 'business is slow', and the 'tail' implies slowness. The Hainanese temples in Sisophon and near Kompong-Trach are still dedicated to *Shui-wei Sheng Mu*.

eighty businessmen. It consisted of seven members, each one acting as convener for two months in turn. It was the convener's responsibility to investigate any dispute brought to him involving Cantonese, and to prepare a report for the commission, which would then attempt to solve the dispute. Stress was placed on the reconciliation of differing views rather than on abstract principles of justice: no law was invoked, no lawyers heard, but rather the commission attempted to *arranger à l'amicale* as one informant put it, or to *diao-jie* according to another.

Informants agreed that the reconciliation commission did not hear cases involving criminal charges under Cambodian law, such as theft, fraud, or assault. It mediated in all commercial disputes – bad debts and bankruptcies – as well as in marital disputes and in all kinds of personal fights involving only Cantonese.

It is interesting that neither *chef* nor *sous-chef* belonged to the reconciliation commission. This appears to have been the case for the Teochiu as well. The Hainanese reconciliation commission included the *chef*, however, and in the Hakka *hui-guan* there was no such commission, disputes being settled by the *bang-hui* itself, in which both *chef* and *sous-chef* sat as members. I do not know the situation in this regard in the Hokkien *hui-guan*.

LEADERSHIP IN THE 'HUI-GUAN'

From the outline of *hui-guan* structure presented above, it is apparent that two kinds of leadership operated within this association. Following Smith, I shall refer to them as political leadership and administrative leadership.[1] At the head of the *hui-guan* are one or more leaders who have the political power to initiate policy, while throughout the lower reaches there are various committee chairmen and secretaries who carry out policy in the administration of the membership. Although both kinds of leadership entail some kind of power, they are sufficiently different that we may speak of two kinds of leaders in the *hui-guan* system.

[1] Smith 1956, 47–50. D. Willmott uses the term 'administrative leadership' in very nearly the same sense in his analysis of the Chinese society in Semarang (D. Willmott 1960, 159). His use of the term 'political leadership', however, appears to me to be too narrow, referring only to the formulation of demands by the Chinese on the Dutch administration. His four categories of leadership – administrative, political, commercial, organizational – represent a classification of areas in which leadership operates rather than an analysis of the nature of the leadership processes involved.

1. *Political Leaders*

Political leadership of the *hui-guan* resided in the members of
the *bang-hui*, and principally, of course, in the person of the *chef*.[1]
It should be noted that in the Cantonese *hui-guan* the membership
of the *bang-hui* was to a large extent under the control of the *chef*,
for he had the power to assign elected members either to it or to
one of the committees that had little political power. In other
words, the Cantonese *chef* (with his *sous-chef*) could decide who
would be in positions of political power in the *hui-guan*, who
merely administrative leaders. This was not the case in any other
hui-guan, for in the other four the *bang-hui* was elected.

The prime requisite for achieving political power in the *hui-
guan* was wealth, not only because money could buy power, but
also because wealth was the principal index of prestige among the
Chinese in Phnom-Penh, as it was and is among most overseas
Chinese (cf. D. Willmott 1960, 117 f.; Skinner 1958, 80). More
important, a wealthy man could seek electoral support from within a wider circle of debtors, creditors, and business associates
than could a man of less means. It is not surprising, therefore,
that prior to the Sino-Japanese war all the *chefs* of whom I have
knowledge were among the richest men in their speech groups.

A secondary requisite for the position of *chef* was the willingness
to devote time (and money) to the welfare of the community.
Wealthy men could serve on the *bang-hui* without neglecting
their businesses, but the *chef* himself had to devote almost all his
time to the affairs of the *hui-guan* and the work of the Immigration
Service. Furthermore, the *chef* was expected to contribute from
his own funds to the same extent as other wealthy men.

Unlike the Kapitan China in Java, whose mandate depended
on fostering relations with the Dutch (D. Willmott 1960, 148–
150), the *chef* in Phnom-Penh was able to achieve and maintain his
position only by developing relations within the community of
his speech group. Furthermore, the motivations for taking the
position involved the possibility of enhancing one's prestige
within the Chinese community itself, not of transcending that
community. Men who became *chefs* were therefore oriented

---

[1] Since *bang-zhang* and *chef* have an identical meaning in the context of the
congrégation and *hui-guan*, the shorter term is used throughout this study. The
colloquial term 'ang-bang' (Mandarin *hong-bang*) used by Teochiu, Hokkien, and
Hainanese is discussed in chapter 5, p. 48, n. 1.

toward overseas Chinese society rather than toward the larger polity of Cambodia. All those for whom I have information were born in China (with the possible exception of one Hainanese). Few of them spoke French, and they exhibited little desire to assimilate to Khmer ways.

2. *Administrative Leaders*

The acquisition of administrative leadership in the *hui-guan* involved somewhat different requisites and motivations from those necessary for political leadership. Certainly, administrative positions were occasionally used as stepping stones to politically powerful positions, but there were many whose ambitions to leadership were satisfied with the power to organize people and events on the basis of policies initiated elsewhere. These leaders staffed the committees and ran the day-to-day affairs of the *hui-guan*. In the Cantonese *hui-guan* the highest administrative position was the general secretary, who was a full-time functionary of the *bang-hui* and as such dealt with all the committees that made up the *hui-guan* structure. In other *hui-guan*, these functions were sometimes assumed by the *sous-chef* (Chinese *fu-zhang*).

The administrative leaders were not necessarily wealthy. The main requisite for administrative positions was a willingness to work, to devote one's energies and time to the problems of the *hui-guan* and the speech group it governed. Furthermore, it was not necessary to develop a wide circle of supporters, for the patronage of a single political leader could assure one of such a position.

In the main, administrative leaders were oriented toward overseas Chinese society, but some activities demanded contact with French and Khmer authorities, and for these a different kind of person was necessary; he acted as an agent rather than a leader, for he undertook to expedite commercial and personal matters, such as visas and import permits. From interviews it appears that the functions of agent were often carried out by the general secretary or the *sous-chef*, but seldom by the *chef* himself. It was suggested by one ex-*chef* that the functions of the agent allowed one to amass considerable wealth through bribes and gifts, a possibility that was exemplified by one penniless man who possessed two motor-cars only two years after accepting the position of secretary of a *hui-guan*.

COOPERATION BETWEEN 'HUI-GUAN'

While each *hui-guan* in Phnom-Penh was entirely independent of the other four, there was cooperation among them for various purposes. This cooperation was evident even before the *congrégations* were established in Cambodia, for a temple was constructed by all the *hui-guan* in 1890, which became known as the *Wu-bang Hui-guan*. It was not a *hui-guan* in the same sense as those of the various speech groups, for it had no membership and no elected body nor leader. Nevertheless, when the temple was rebuilt in 1909, a sign was raised over the front gate on which were written the characters for *Wu-bang Hui-guan*. In conversation it was also known as the *Wu-bang Gong-so*. At this temple met the council of *chefs* which existed in Phnom-Penh from quite early in the French period despite the fact that its recognition in law was not so formal as in Cochinchina (see chapter 3, pp. 29 f.). The council consisted of the ten *chefs* and *sous-chefs*, who met regularly to discuss questions of concern to the Chinese community as a whole and to initiate projects that involved the cooperation of more than one *hui-guan*.

The temple was also the meeting place for the reconciliation commission, the *Wu-bang Diao-jie Wei-yuan Hui*, established to deal with all kinds of disputes between members of different speech groups.[1] It consisted of ten persons, two from each speech group; although the *chefs* themselves were excluded, its members owed their positions indirectly to their own *chefs*, since they were appointed by their *bang-hui*. It should be noted that the law specified that the council of *chefs* hear deportation cases, for this reconciliation commission was entirely extra-legal.

Prior to the Sino-Japanese war, the largest project undertaken by the five *hui-guan* acting together was the establishment of a Chinese hospital in 1906. An epidemic in Phnom-Penh caused the Chinese to request the visit of a doctor from the Tung Wah Hospital in Hongkong.[2] While the doctor was in Phnom-Penh,

[1] A friend told me of an unusual case heard by this commission, which gained considerable notoriety in the Chinese community because it involved a woman who wanted to sue her husband for divorce because his 'generating organ' was not long enough to satisfy her. The case was settled by the commission, but my friend did not know the nature of the solution.
[2] The Chinese name of the Tung Wah Hospital is *Dong-hua Yi-yuan*. I found no mention of an epidemic in 1906 elsewhere than in the official history of the

the five *hui-guan* agreed to establish a hospital and asked him to stay on to supervise it. In order to finance this project, each *hui-guan* agreed to contribute an annual amount in proportion to its membership. The original contributions totalled 6688.80 piastres, divided among the *hui-guan* as follows (Chau Kon 1961, 3; the total given does not correspond exactly to the sum of these figures): Cantonese: 3120.00; Teochiu: 2714.00; Hokkien: 378.40; Hakka: 335.20; Hainanese: 140.80. Some time later the rate was established at half a piastre and then one piastre per member. Medicines were donated by the richer merchants. The hospital was run by the council of *chefs* until 1945, when direction was transferred to a managing board, to which each *hui-guan* appointed a number of members in proportion to its total membership. It remained directly under the joint responsibility of the five *hui-guan* until 1956 (Chau Kon 1961, 5–9).

Another area of cooperation between *hui-guan* was the organization of an annual ritual parade of the temple idols at *Yuan-Xiao*, the fifteenth day of the first lunar month. This festival, marking the end of the Chinese New Year celebrations in Phnom-Penh, was observed by three nights of opera in front of the main temples (Cantonese, Teochiu, and Hokkien) and a great parade on the evenings of the fourteenth and fifteenth days of the month. While there was some rivalry between three *hui-guan* in staging opera, which was supported by private subscriptions and provided free to the public,[1] all five cooperated in the organization of the parade, known as *You-shen*, 'procession of gods'. It was a joyful and noisy event, with firecrackers, music, and shouting from dusk to dawn on two successive nights. The parade followed a route that took it down every street in the Chinese (i.e. business) section of the city, for it was thought to bring good fortune to the businesses and houses it passed. At the head of the procession were a large number of paper lanterns shaped as fish, flowers, birds, and lions, each mounted on a high pole and carried by one person. There followed orchestras, dragon and lion teams, opera troupes,

Chinese Hospital, from which comes the material presented here (Chau Kon 1961, 1–5). The earliest law relating to epidemics in Indochina was one promulgated in Cochinchina in 1914 (Recueil 1927, 1417–18). For the importance of the Tung Wah Hospital to overseas Chinese, see Wickberg 1965, 216–17.

[1] The opera at *Yuan-Xiao* is played 'for the gods', and is therefore presented free to the public. The stage is constructed facing the door of the temple so that the idols may 'see' the performance.

and finally the idols of the various temples, each carried in an ornate sedan chair by four or eight men and preceded by an orchestra and a flock of people from that speech group carrying banners and flags and tossing lighted firecrackers into the air, on to the street, and into the crowds that lined the pavements.[1]

This parade demanded considerable cooperation among the five *hui-guan*. Permission from the municipality was necessary in order to hold such a noisy and disrupting public celebration, and the five *hui-guan* together paid for this licence. Furthermore, the preparation of the lanterns and banners at the head of the procession was a joint responsibility. Finally, the *hui-guan* had to reach agreement on the route of the parade and on the order of the various groups and idols included in the procession. All these questions were decided by the council of *chefs*.

To sum up, one can state that the areas of cooperation between the *hui-guan* in Phnom-Penh included a reconciliation commission, a Chinese hospital, and the organization of one annual ritual event.[2] Furthermore, there existed a council of *chefs*, tacitly recognized by the Administration, which undertook these various activities and supervised a temple. From the point of view of the individual Chinese, however, the areas of cooperation were far less important than those aspects of his life directly affected by the *hui-guan* of his own speech group.

THE 'HUI-GUAN' AND ECONOMIC ORGANIZATION

From the brief outline of the various bodies that made up the Cantonese and other *hui-guan* in Phnom-Penh and from the

[1] This description is based on Hepp 1928, 234–6. From his book one gathers that Hepp was fascinated by the exotic, and it is therefore significant that he does not mention any spirit possession in relation to this procession, for mediums have become its most important feature in recent years (see chapter 8, pp. 98 ff.)

[2] During the Sino-Japanese war but before the fall of France, the various *hui-guan* cooperated in a campaign to support the Chungking war effort. This may have continued throughout the war, but officially, of course, there was no such activity while the Japanese occupied Indochina. It is possible that the creation of an official Secretariat of the Five *Congrégations* in 1944 was an attempt by the *chefs* to extricate themselves from the embarrassing position of being held responsible for an 'enemy' community.

In 1944 the Secretariat opened an anti-trachoma clinic at its headquarters, run by the secretary-general, Mr Chau Kon, who had completed a course of training in anti-trachoma techniques. Mr Chau Kon was decorated at this time with the Order of *Mérite du Monisaraphon*, for he had served the Chinese community in various capacities for fifteen years, part of the time as secretary of the Cantonese *hui-guan*.

discussion of the areas of cooperation between *hui-guan*, it can be seen that these associations fulfilled many functions for their members. Welfare matters were looked after by the *hui-guan*. Public education was, until the Sino-Japanese war, mainly in the hands of the larger *hui-guan*. Extra-familial ritual was undertaken by the *hui-guan*, and the familial ritual of attending the graves was organized and supervised by them. Disputes were settled by the *hui-guan*, singly or in cooperation as the case demanded. In the most general sense, power and leadership were matters of *hui-guan* organization. And finally, the transport of bones to China was the responsibility of the *hui-guan* in those speech groups where stress was placed on double burial. The question of the economic functions of the *hui-guan* now deserves more detailed consideration.

It is in the economic sphere that the artificiality of treating Cambodia in isolation from the rest of Indochina is most apparent. During the period of French rule, Saigon-Cholon was the commercial centre not only for Cochinchina, but for Cambodia and much of Laos as well. Economically, Phnom-Penh was a satellite of Cholon, and there is little doubt that the major Chinese companies in Phnom-Penh had close ties with either parent or associated companies there, for both rice and imports moved through Cholon to and from Phnom-Penh. This fact affected the degree of control the *hui-guan* in Phnom-Penh could exercise over the commerce of their members. There was considerable variation between speech groups in this regard, the extremes being represented by the Hainanese and Cantonese *hui-guan*.

For several reasons, the Hainanese *hui-guan* probably had considerable control over the economic activities of its members during the French period. First, there were only a few hundred Hainanese in Phnom-Penh. Second, the Hainanese were almost all in the restaurant business, which they dominated; the *hui-guan* could therefore operate as a guild of restaurateurs, setting standards and maintaining them, acting as a clearing house for personnel, and ensuring that competition remained within limits. Finally, the restaurant business did not involve relations with more powerful companies elsewhere but was relatively self-contained in Phnom-Penh and in Cambodia.

The Cantonese *hui-guan*, on the other hand, had little control over the commerce of its members beyond the collection of taxes for the government and the mediation of whatever commercial disputes Cantonese cared to bring it. There were many Cantonese enterprises, their business was highly diversified, and they were associated with larger companies in Cholon who were not subject to the sanctions available to the *hui-guan* in Phnom-Penh.

None of the other speech groups exhibited the same degree of economic specialization as the Hainanese in Phnom-Penh. Hakka and Hokkien *hui-guan* controlled as small numbers of individuals as the Hainanese, but they were involved in diverse trades, and these *hui-guan* could not be considered guilds. Agreement on occupational specialization according to speech group was indicated by several informants:

Teochiu: dry goods, groceries, import-export, pharmaceutics, vegetable farming, street peddling.

Cantonese: carpentry, mechanics, transportation, construction work, wine.

Hokkien: import-export, banking, hardware, foodstuffs.

Hakka: dentistry, traditional pharmaceutics, shoe-making.

Hainanese: restaurants and hotels, pepper, tailoring, shirt stores.

In the case of all but the Hainanese, many individuals were to be found in occupations other than those listed.

The *hui-guan* probably all served as employment agencies for the businesses and workers in each speech group, although there is no direct evidence to prove this point. None of them provided capital loans, however, for none of them was rich enough as a corporation to become involved in extending credit.[1]

With the probable exception of the Hainanese *hui-guan*, then, the economic functions of the *hui-guan* in Phnom-Penh were not general, but limited to settling disputes, welfare, and the informal allocation of personnel.

It is worth mentioning that no Chinese chamber of commerce has existed in Phnom-Penh, for such associations are often present in overseas Chinese communities. One informant explained that the Chinese had 'threatened' to organize such a chamber at one time, but the French had persuaded them to desist because they were afraid it would undermine their *Chambre Mixte de Commerce*

---

[1] Contrast the locality and clan associations in North America, which included among their functions the provision of capital for members starting business (W. Willmott 1964a, 36).

et d'Agriculture du Cambodge, which had been established in 1922 (JOIC 1923, 170–2). This official Chamber of Commerce was composed of ten French, two 'alien Asians' (probably Chinese), one Vietnamese, and one Cambodian; it was obviously beyond the control of the Chinese merchants and represented primarily the interests of the French *colons* and commercial houses.

5

Alternative Centres of Power

Throughout the period of *congrégations*, the *hui-guan* held an almost total monopoly of political power within the Chinese community. A brief examination will show that other possible centres of power – secret societies, locality associations, and kin groups – either worked within the structure of the *hui-guan* or else had little power.

I. SECRET SOCIETIES

The presence of secret societies during at least the first half of the period of French rule was attested by various sources, but the information is scant, and there are few clues as to the extent of their power. Dr Virginia Thompson has the following to say about the function of Chinese secret societies in French Indochina (Thompson 1937, 170 f.):

Secret societies are the cement of the congregation, and its real head, not the official figurehead, is unknown to the administration. This seems to the French especially dangerous since such groups, notably the Society of Heaven and Earth, are affiliated with the mother organisations in China.

Although Thompson may have had more direct information on secret societies than is available to me, it seems probable that she is referring here to the *hui-guan* operating within the *congrégations* – associations that may well have appeared secret to the French she interviewed in Vietnam before the war. I have no reason to believe that the *chefs* were not the most powerful leaders in the Chinese community at that time.

The only two societies mentioned by informants in Cambodia were the *Hong-men Hui* and the *San-he Hui*, which appear to have operated as separate associations, although both names refer to Triad Societies that elsewhere are sometimes associated in some kind of federation. *San-he Hui* seems to have been in more

common use in China than within the diaspora (Blythe 1941, iii[1];
Wynne 1941, 112; Comber 1957, 2), while *Hong-men Hui* is
common among Chinese in North America. Cordier writes that
the *San-he Hui* can be traced back to the Sung dynasty, evidently
using the term as a generic name for all Triad Societies (Cordier
1888, 64). Although Ward and Sterling make no mention of this
name, they translate 'Sam-ho-hui' as 'The Society of the Three
Rivers' (Ward and Sterling 1925–26, 7 n. 2), a name I have seen
nowhere else in the literature on Chinese secret societies. Perhaps
they have here mistaken one character of *San-he Hui*, for the
two terms have identical sounds in Mandarin. Morgan gives both
San-he Hui ('Sam Hop Wui') and *Hong-men* ('Hung Mun') in his
list of Triad Societies (Morgan 1960, 284 and 286). It is possible
that in Cambodia the *San-he Hui* was confined to the Cantonese
while the *Hong-men Hui* drew its membership from among the
Teochiu. A Cantonese informant asserted that the *San-he* was
nothing but a criminal association, while the *Hong-men* followed
the original high ideals of fellowship for protection and welfare.

Another Cantonese informant stated that prior to the establishment of the *congrégations* the Cantonese *hui-guan* had been 'really
a secret society' which owed allegiance to a higher lodge in
Cholon; he did not distinguish between the *San-he* and the
Hong-men, asserting that they were the same thing. But there is
written evidence of the presence of the *Hong-men Hui* within the
Teochiu *hui-guan* at the beginning of this century; it comes from
a history of the Teochiu 'public' school (*Mian-Hua Qiao-jiao*
1957, 123–4; my translation):

Before 1907, the *Duan-hua* Public Middle School was a private school.
In 1914 some of the older generation of overseas Chinese [lists five
names] and the Chinese apothecary were impressed by the importance
of education and therefore established a school at the Teochiu *hui-guan*
in order to provide a place for poor children to seek knowledge. Some
time before, there was in the Teochiu *hui-guan* the *Hong-men Tuan-ti*,
called the Yangtse Club Gong and Drum Class [*Chang-jiang Ju Luo
Ban Gu*]. At that time the Father of the Country [Sun Yat-sen] started
the revolution, and all the older generation responded to his call to
abolish the *Hong-men* association and reformed it into a cultural organ,
as well as responding to Sun's appeal to support the revolution.

[1] In his later book, which is too recent to have been consulted in the preparation
of my account, Blythe mentions that 'Sam Hop Wui' was the name of the first
secret society for which we have an historic record in Malay (Blythe 1969, 46 n.).

The suppression of the secret societies was described to me by another Cantonese informant, who told me how his great-uncle had put an end to the two secret societies in Phnom-Penh some time in the 1920s after the French commissioner of police had sought his aid. According to this informant, the two societies were constantly fighting each other, disturbing the peace and interrupting business, to the growing disgust of the Chinese community. Finally the *chef* of the Cantonese *congrégation* (the great-uncle of my informant) was empowered by the police to arrest the leaders so that they might be deported. Since this move apparently received support from the Chinese community in the city, it is likely that by this time the power of the secret societies had waned.

From these few sources, one can deduce that secret societies operated within at least the two largest *hui-guan* during the early years of the *congrégations*.[1] The extent of their power over the affairs of the *hui-guan* cannot be determined, but there is a strong suggestion that it decreased sharply following the establishment of the Chinese republic. Informants did not agree that secret societies had been wiped out in Phnom-Penh, but all agreed that their power was insignificant after the 1920s.

2. LOCALITY ASSOCIATIONS

Associations whose members are recruited on the basis of locality of origin in China are commonly called *hui-guan* by the Chinese. Here the term will not be used to refer to locality associations recruiting on the basis of *xian* origin lest they be confused with the *hui-guan* uniting whole speech groups. *Xian* locality associations were present in Phnom-Penh only among the Cantonese, where there were between twelve and eighteen associations representing the major *xian* groupings.[2] The fact that they were not present among the Chinese of other speech groups probably results from the relatively small numbers of any but Cantonese in Indochina; in Thailand, where Teochiu predominate, it is only among

[1] That the secret societies operated within some of the *hui-guan* is also suggested by the fact that the popular word for *chef* was 'ang-bang' among the Min speech groups (Teochiu, Hokkien, Hainanese). According to Professor Chen Chi-lu (in conversation) this term is *hong-bang*, and relates to the *Hong-men Hui*, or the Triad Secret Societies.

[2] See W. Willmott 1967, Tables v–ix, pp. 18–24, for the *xian* origins of Chinese in Cambodia. See note 2 on p. 92 below for fifteen of them.

Teochiu that locality associations developed.[1] While the absolute number of Cantonese in Phnom-Penh was not much larger than that in Bangkok, Cantonese locality associations appeared in Phnom-Penh because of the stimulus of similar associations in Cholon, where the huge number of Cantonese allowed these associations to develop into large-scale concerns, even running their own schools.[2]

The Cantonese locality associations in Phnom-Penh apparently had few functions. They operated primarily as societies to provide funerals for those members whose progeny could not afford the expenses of burial. Furthermore, they cooperated with the *hui-guan* in arranging the shipment of bones to the various localities in Kwangtung Province every three years. Finally, they each had a reconciliation commission to deal with disputes arising between parties from the same locality.

It is altogether likely that the locality associations served functions beyond those of arranging funerals, shipping bones, and settling disputes. For instance, new immigrants from any area of Cantonese-speaking Kwangtung probably looked to the locality association on arrival in Phnom-Penh to solve problems of lodging, finance, and particularly employment. Furthermore, the nature of these associations suggests that they may have had functions related to the home-county in China, such as arranging correspondence, remittances, and travel to and from Cambodia. Locality associations had members all over Cambodia, so they probably also served as centres of communication for the Cantonese in the provincial towns; this would have been the case particularly for the *Dong-guan* locality association, for Chinese from *Dong-guan* form a large portion of Cantonese outside Phnom-Penh.

From the point of view of the political structure of the Chinese community it is important to note that the locality associations did not affect the power of the *hui-guan* or *chefs*. Limited to the

[1] From private correspondence with Professor Skinner; his book (Skinner 1958) implies the same thing.

[2] In 1909 there were, according to official figures, 38,000 Cantonese in Cholon ('Notice' 1909, 1071). The same source gives a total of 16,000 Chinese in Phnom-Penh, of whom about ten thousand would have been Cantonese. These absolute figures are gross underestimations, but they are useful for comparison, for there is probably a roughly equivalent factor of error in each. The actual number of Cantonese in Phnom-Penh at that time was probably about 30,000.

Cantonese, their membership did not cross-cut the various *hui-guan*, and within the Cantonese community they operated at a different level from the *hui-guan* that embraced all Cantonese. It is possible that the locality associations provided political parties in elections for Cantonese *bang-hui* and *chef*, but I have no information on this point. It is certain that the locality associations were not represented as such on the *bang-hui* (in marked contrast to Cantonese community associations in North America), and they possessed none of the sanctions available to the *hui-guan* for controlling the activities of their members. Therefore, we may assume that, while they entered into the organization of the Cantonese *hui-guan*, they did not represent significant groupings in relation to the power structure of the community in Phnom-Penh.

3. KIN GROUPS

I have argued elsewhere that lineages are seldom salient groupings among overseas Chinese because of the immigrant nature of at least the heart of the community (W. Willmott 1964a, 33; cf. Freedman 1957, 73; Amyot 1960, 163). The argument may be summarized briefly as follows: since most Chinese immigrants are unaccompanied adult males, and since many of them owe allegiance – at least at first – to a lineage in China, a system of lineages cannot be elaborated in the urban Chinese community abroad. (Indeed, the same may have been true of urban society in China as well.)

Exceptions to this general statement will be found in those overseas Chinese settlements that have a sufficiently long history to allow the development of some depth of local lineage organization but have not greatly modified their kinship system toward bilaterality or de-emphasis of the lineage. The Peranakan Chinese in Java and the less recent immigrants in Singapore have acculturated somewhat to Malay patterns so that their kinship system tends to bilaterality, de-emphasizing the lineage (D. Willmott 1960, 300 f.; Tan 1963, 120 ff., esp. 129 f.; Freedman 1960, 29). The Hainanese in Kampot Province may be an example of a settlement that has remained Chinese in its kinship system. One of my Hainanese informants belonged to a family that has lived in Kompong-Trach for five generations – by no means unusual in this area – but I was not able to determine the nature of lineage organization in this case. In Phnom-Penh, however, such depth would be indeed unusual, as it would be in any other part of Cambodia; for not only is the proportion of China-born higher elsewhere than in Kampot, but also many Chinese whose forebears have been in Cambodia for five generations have already assimilated into the Khmer population.

A contemporary example will illustrate how kinship ties may well have served to expand an enterprise and establish new lines or new areas of business. One wine company has retail outlets in several towns, each managed by a junior agnate of the founder, who has died. The sons of the Teochiu founder manage, respectively, the distillery, the Phnom-Penh outlet (headquarters for the company), and a rice mill acquired recently by the company; one of their sons manages an outlet in another town. No doubt such economic organization along kin lines existed throughout the French period.

But while this lineage may be held together by the nature of its economic enterprises, its effective depth is only three generations. Furthermore, there are few ritual aspects of lineage solidarity. The only ritual in which all lineage members participate, the annual 'family picnic' (as my friend called it) at Qing-Ming, takes place at the graves, not of agnates, but of female affines. Since the founder of the company returned to die in China, the ceremony takes place at the plot which includes the grave of his wife, the mother of the present partners in the wine company. This lady's parents are both buried in this plot, as are her three younger sisters, her mother's mother and her mother's mother's mother. The husbands of these women were all immigrants, whose kinsmen were in China, and one of them is buried in China. This is best illustrated by a genealogical chart (Fig. 1).

My informant, Ego in the chart, said that about seventy people go each Qing-Ming to this plot to carry out the rites of 'sweeping the graves'. Because sisters of the company founder's mother who are buried here also have living descendants, the consequent worshipping group does not approximate to the lineage involved in the wine company.

There is no reason to believe that this example would have been any less typical during the French period; if anything, lineage depth would have been shallower in times when the proportion of China-born was higher in Phnom-Penh than it is today.

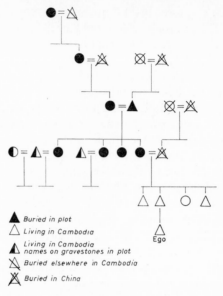

Buried in plot
Living in Cambodia
Living in Cambodia names on gravestones in plot
Buried elsewhere in Cambodia
Buried in China

Ego

FIGURE I

Like other overseas Chinese communities, that in Phnom-Penh did not exhibit a wealth of lineages with genealogical depth and segmentation. But in contrast to Chinese in almost every other part of the world, the Chinese in Cambodia did not organize associations based on clanship.[1] Clan associations are called *tong-xing hui* or *tong-xing qin-hui* because they include members of the same *xing*, surname. Every informant interviewed stated that *tong-xing hui* had not existed in Cambodia, and most expressed ignorance when asked specifically about some of the more common clan associations evident elsewhere.

The only clan association discovered in Phnom-Penh for the French period was a guild of drapers, all of whom had the surname *Guo* and came from the Teochiu district of *Chao-yang* in Kwangtung. A Mr Guo from *Chao-yang* established a successful drapery shop in Phnom-Penh about fifty years ago, and as it expanded he sent for clansmen from China to join him in the enterprise. For twenty years this process continued, until the

[1] Clanship in this context refers to the use of common surnames as a criterion of association. See Freedman 1957, 68; Amyot 1960, 163; W. Willmott 1964a, 33. An informant from Saigon-Cholon told me that clan associations were not present in that city among any of the speech groups.

shop was staffed by over a dozen Guo from *Chao-yang*. Although they did not come from the same village, nor belong to the same lineage, nevertheless there were traceable kin links between them. For instance, the wife of the original founder was an affinal relative of my informant's father. When the founder died, the various Guo working in the shop divided the profits and established themselves in separate shops, the son of the founder inheriting the original store; this happened about thirty years ago. They organized a guild among the drapers whose business was of a certain level.[1] This guild included most of the Guo from *Chao-yang* and controlled nearly half the drapery trade in Phnom-Penh during its existence. Its only trace today is seen in the large number of drapery shops which include the character *de* (virtue) in their names (e.g. *De-Hua*, *De-Fong*, *De-Xing*), each of which shops was founded by a member of the staff of the original store, *De-Long*.

Although all members of this guild came from *Chao-yang*, they formed only a small portion of the total Teochiu from that district, for one-quarter of the Teochiu in Phnom-Penh are from *Chao-yang*. On the other hand, my informant said that 80 per cent of the Teochiu Guo families in Phnom-Penh were in the guild. One is therefore justified in referring to this guild as a clan association rather than one based on locality.

I have no information on the functions of this clan association other than those related to commerce. One of its members was *chef* of the Teochiu *congrégation* from 1941 to 1953. This fact may suggest no more than that this man was quite wealthy and popular, but it might also suggest that the Guo guild took an active part in the politics of the *hui-guan*. To my knowledge, this guild is the only example of a clan association in Phnom-Penh during the period of French rule.

4. OTHER ASSOCIATIONS

Few associations other than those already described existed in Phnom-Penh during the period of *congrégations*. None of them had

---

[1] The drapery business is described by the Chinese as consisting of various levels between importer and rural retailer. The Chinese term used is *pan* (vessel), and the drapers in this guild were all *er-pan*, second level; that is, they bought directly from the importer. The term seems to refer more to scale than to level, for these shops did retail trade as well as selling to *san-pan* (third-level) drapers.

more than minimal significance for the political structure of the Chinese community.

Besides the five temples of the *hui-guan* and the one called the *Wu-bang hui-guan*, there were two Chinese temples that were independent of any *congrégation*. One of these is located on the small hill (the *phnom*) in what used to be the French quarter; it stands just below the terrace surrounding the Khmer temple and stupa that crown the hill. The other temple is on the main street of the business (Chinese) quarter of the city, Ang Eng (ex-Orhier) Street, where it moved in 1942 when the area in front of the Royal Palace was cleared to form a park.

Each of these temples consists of a single room, considerably smaller than most of the *hui-guan* temples. The principal deity is the same in both, *Ben-tou Gong*, who is described variously by different informants as the original ancestor of all the Chinese in Cambodia or as the god of the local area.[1] From the number of votive offerings – principally satin hangings – one may infer that these temples were frequented at least by those seeking super-natural aid. Like all non-Buddhist Chinese temples, these two include fortune blocks, sticks, and papers.[2] Each is run by a caretaker, one Hakka the other Teochiu, who lives from money offerings and the sale of ritual objects such as incense, paper money, and paper charms (*fu*). I was unable to determine the origins of these temples, but it was clear from interviews that there were no organized associations to either temple, and their rôle in the political structure of the Chinese community was therefore negligible.

Of the several private schools that existed prior to the Sino-Japanese war, only two have survived. (Others were established during the war, and many more after 1949; see chapter 7.) These

---

[1] Skinner (1957, 138 f.) describes *Ben-tou Gong* as originally associated with Teochiu and Hakka, in both Thailand and China. There are Hainanese temples to this god in Kompong-Trach and Tuk Méas, and the temple built at Siemréap in 1893 by Hokkien includes *Ben-tou Gong* as one of the two minor gods (the other is *Zhu-sheng Niang-niang*; the major god is *Jin-shui Xian-gong*, also known as *Xuan-tian Shang-di*).

[2] Fortune-telling paraphernalia in all the non-Buddhist Chinese temples visited comprised a pair of kidney-shaped blocks, a bunch of numbered sticks in a bamboo container, and an assortment of fortune papers numbered to correspond with the sticks. The only Khmer temple in which these items were found was the new temple at Phnom Kulen (Siemréap Province) that is perched on a giant boulder and houses the huge monolithic Buddha carved out of it.

two represent the diligent work of two individuals, who, according to brief histories available, made no attempt to involve other Chinese leaders in their ventures. Given the existence of the large public schools run by the *hui-guan*, it is unlikely that other private schools were different in this regard. These schools can therefore best be seen as special types of private enterprise, with little import for Chinese community structure.[1]

Finally, there were two Chinese theatre groups in Phnom-Penh, producing Teochiu and Cantonese opera respectively. At least one of these was professional, with full-time actors and its own theatre on Ang Eng (ex-Orhier). I did not determine the political rôle of these two associations, but I think it to have been minimal.

CONCLUSION

The most salient feature to emerge from this discussion of Chinese social organization in Phnom-Penh during the period of French rule is the paucity of associations with political functions. Compared with other cities in Southeast Asia, where Chinese developed a rich complex of associations with cross-cutting membership by using the criteria of locality, clanship, commerce, and sworn friendship, Phnom-Penh appears to have lacked that richness of associations that has been called 'the warp and woof' of overseas Chinese society (T'ien 1953, 10).

The reason for this dearth of associations is to be found in the presence of the *congrégation* system. Two complementary explanations can be presented to make the causal connection: the *congrégation* system provided a corporate group, the *hui-guan*, both with the ability to meet most of the extra-familial functions of the community and with the power to block any attempt at alternative organization.

Firth suggests that the 'criteria of what constitutes a corporate group have not...been clearly agreed' (Firth 1959, 215). He states further that 'the prime criterion for definition of a group as corporate is that its members collectively exercise a set of rights and may be subject collectively to a set of duties' (*ibid.*, 216). But

[1] The first law governing Chinese private schools in Cambodia was promulgated on 18 September 1924 (JOIF 1924, 1847–9). Other laws, making minor changes in the regulations and providing the conditions of qualification for teachers, can be found in the *Journal Officiel de l'Indochine Française* at the following places: 1929, p. 160; 1930, pp. 3593–4; 1933, pp. 971–3.

his subsequent discussion of the Tikopian *paito* includes, besides the question of collective rights, the following implied criterion of corporateness: 'These lineages acted also as major units of social action or social reference in many spheres, ranging from crisis of personal life to the provision of ritual offerings to ancestors and gods' (*ibid.*).

The justification of using the term corporate group in reference to the *hui-guan* in Phnom-Penh during the French period rests primarily on their multiple rôle in the organization of different aspects of social life; that is, it rests on the fact that they were 'major units of social action' in a variety of contexts. Second, their membership was distinct from that of other similar corporate groups. And, finally, they were corporate in the legal sense of owning property and defining collective rights and duties; although French law made them corporations only in 1935, traditional law within the Chinese community obviously recognized them as such from their inception.

Because the *congrégation* system comprised what for the Chinese was a natural grouping, the speech group, the *hui-guan* within the *congrégation* was a natural way to organize political, ritual, and to some extent economic activities. Furthermore, its finances were assured by the fact that it could collect its funds using sanctions applied to the taxes for the administration. Since no one could leave the country without permission from the *chef*, there was no possibility of escaping *hui-guan* responsibilities or any other obligations in the community. The *hui-guan* was therefore financially capable of undertaking the various functions of an over-all corporate group, and consequently there was little incentive to develop other groupings.

Alternatively, the *congrégation* system provided the *hui-guan* leaders, and notably the *chef* himself, with the power to stamp out any attempts at subversion of their and his authority. Elements suspected of opposition sentiments could be prevented from entering the country in the first place. In the case of opposition developing within the *congrégation*, the *chef* could simply arrange for the deportation of subversives. The fact that the sanctions for such actions lay completely outside the Chinese community, and were therefore not subject to Chinese political pressure, meant that the *chef* was practically secure in his power. The *hui-guan* also provided in its administrative positions the opportunity to wield limited power, thus satisfying some of those individuals who otherwise might have looked elsewhere for political position.

Put into the terms of individual behaviour, these two reasons can be expressed as follows: an individual aspiring to power was unable to seek it outside the *hui-guan* because the sanctions of the *congrégation* system gave the leaders the power to stop him, and these sanctions were beyond his power to affect. At the same time, few would be motivated to follow such an aspiring alternative leader because their needs were satisfied by the organization of activities in the *hui-guan*. In such a situation, alternative associations could expect neither leaders nor membership, and they did not therefore develop.

The specific test of this explanation lies in the examination of Chinese society in Phnom-Penh following the demise of the *congrégations*, and it is to this test that we now turn. The more general test will be sought in comparisons with other overseas Chinese communities in chapter 12.

6

The End of the *Congrégations*

For the sake of simplicity, the *congrégation* system imposed by the French has been described as if its life were congruent with the period of French hegemony in Cambodia, but in fact neither the beginning nor the end of the system coincided with the temporal boundaries of French rule. I have already pointed out that its formulation took place in 1892, eight years after the French began to take an active interest in Cambodian internal affairs. It did not dissolve at the time of French withdrawal, for the *congrégations* outlasted by several years effective French control over the Kingdom. An exact date for the end of the system is difficult to provide, however, for although the *chefs* were officially relieved of their duties in 1958, circumstances in Indochina following the end of the Sino-Japanese war never permitted the *congrégations* to re-establish the strong control they possessed *ante bellum*. Immigration was almost uncontrolled, France was fighting a war in neighbouring Vietnam, and conditions in Cambodia were generally unsettled prior to the granting of independence in 1953. Of the various factors eroding the system at that time, two are of prime importance: changes in immigration and the achievement of Cambodian independence. (The momentous effects of the end of the Chinese civil war in 1949, apart from their consequences on immigration, were not felt directly by the Chinese in Cambodia until after Chou En-lai's state visit in 1956.)

Paradoxically, the great increment in immigration before 1949 and its subsequent decrement both contributed to reducing the power of the *chefs* and *hui-guan* over the Chinese community in Phnom-Penh. I estimate that Cambodia received over a hundred thousand Chinese immigrants during the civil war in China – that is, between 1946 and 1949 – increasing the Chinese population of the country by one-third in four years (see Table, 1 p. 6). The effects of this increase on the demography of the Chinese community must have been drastic in the capital, where many of the immigrants, who were Teochiu in the main, worked on the docks or in construction. The Chinese quarter spilled over into neighbouring parts of the city, and new Chinese districts grew up in Chamcar Chen and Tuk La'ak. Much of this area was at first filled with extremely poor housing – overcrowded, insanitary, and subject to frequent fires in the dry season. Private initiative and government aid have since made it into a suburb of frame houses interspersed with an increasing number of ferro-concrete buildings. During the post-war chaos in Indochina, it was impossible for the *chefs de congrégation* to keep control over every immigrant in this great flood. Consequently, a *chef*'s power did not extend over his entire speech group, particularly among the Teochiu. By 1949, when the flood slowed to a trickle, the *chefs* were no longer in the position of total control they had enjoyed before the war, for the *hui-guan* were no longer the inclusive associations they once were. According to two ex-*chefs* whom I interviewed, about 22,000 Teochiu were registered in 1958 with the Immigration Service in Phnom-Penh, representing a population of perhaps twice that number, while the actual number of Teochiu in the city was about a hundred thousand.

Since 1951, Chinese immigration has been negligible, and this, too, had its effect on the *hui-guan*. With no new immigrants, the Chinese population became more settled, and a larger proportion of men acquired businesses. The *hui-guan* therefore lost some of their welfare and regulatory functions for new immigrants. Furthermore, with traffic cut off in the opposite direction as well, *hui-guan* receipts fell, and their functions in relation to mainland China (correspondence, shipping bones, travel arrangements) disappeared. All these factors affected the amount of support businessmen were willing to give to the *hui-guan* and their leaders.

Another kind of post-war immigration has had somewhat inverse effects on the Hainanese *hui-guan*. I refer to the migration into Phnom-Penh of thousands of Hainanese from the rural areas of Kampot Province following the decline of pepper cultivation during the Sino-Japanese and the First Indochinese wars. Between the end of the war and 1958, the Hainanese population of Phnom-Penh probably doubled, and it has doubled again since that time. Although Hainanese waiters worked in the restaurants and hotels of the capital before the war, the growth of the city has greatly increased the number of such jobs available. Furthermore, today many more are bringing their families to Phnom-Penh, and consequently the city has a large population of Hainanese immigrants. This has tended to strengthen the Hainanese *hui-guan* for precisely the inverse of the reasons that the end of immigration weakened the Teochiu *hui-guan*.

Cambodian independence in 1953 also had immediate consequences on the power of the *congrégations*. Under the French, Vietnamese had staffed the administration in Phnom-Penh, and the change to Cambodians following independence destroyed the particularistic relationships developed by the *chefs* with the personnel of the Immigration Service. The fact that Chinese now dealt with Khmer and Sino-Cambodians, with whom relations were cordial, rather than with Vietnamese, who were more antagonistic, meant that relations could be established with more ease by Chinese other than the *chefs*.

Besides changes in personnel, there were also changes in policy toward minorities, following independence. The new policy was to admit into the Cambodian community some of those classed as aliens by the French. A new citizenship act was promulgated in 1954 to implement this policy; it allowed many of those born in Cambodia to become citizens of the country merely by claiming that right (W. Willmott 1967, 79 f.). With these changes – and with the change from French to Cambodian political leaders in the country – the incentive to remain Chinese was greatly reduced, while both the incentives and the possibilities for Chinese to become Cambodian citizens were increased. Many chose to change their citizenship, which automatically took them out of the control of the *chefs*.

At the end of 1954, the government decided that the Chinese would henceforth pay their taxes directly to the treasury beginning with the fiscal year 1955, thus removing one of the two principal functions from the *congrégation*. Although the *chef*'s fiscal powers had not been great, nevertheless the responsibility of collecting taxes from his *congréganistes* reinforced his position of power over them, for it served to remind them that he could call on the might of the French colonial administration. The power to collect taxes also ensured the income of the *hui-guan*, which, once this power was withdrawn, must have had more difficulty in enforcing the payment of dues.

The immigration act of 1956 further limited the powers of the *chef* in several ways (JOC 1956, 789–98). The articles relating to newly arrived immigrants had little effect in the Chinese community, of course, for by that time Chinese immigration had ceased. Article 14, however, allowed free movement throughout the Kingdom to immigrants holding valid identity cards, and article 25 required that immigrants changing their place of business only make a declaration of intent to the local administration; these two provisions removed from the *chef* the power to restrict the movements of his *congréganistes* within the country. Furthermore, article 27, outlining the procedure for obtaining an exit visa, does not mention permission from the *chef*. Finally, article 32 mentions that the power to invoke the penalty of expulsion from the country 'belongs to the Minister of the Interior'. While previous laws had of course stipulated that deportation was the prerogative of the Administration, they had also laid down procedures whereby a *chef* could instigate deportation, apparently obliging the Administration to comply; this power was now taken away from the *chef*. In the light of these restrictions on the powers of the *chef*, the final paragraph of the law, stating that the *congrégations* would remain *en vigueur* until conventions were signed with the appropriate countries, perhaps suggests that the *congrégations* were thought to be useful as a means of communication but little else.

The process of whittling away the various functions of the *chef* left few real powers in his hands by the middle of 1956. Two years later, on 1 May 1958, the position of *chef de congrégation* was officially abolished in a circular from the President of the Council of Ministers (the Prime Minister). I was unable to find a copy of this circular, but an informant who had been a functionary of the Immigration Service in 1958 gave me the wording approximately as follows:

From the First of May, 1958, the *chefs* and *sous-chefs de congrégation* will cease their functions; henceforth Chinese will deal directly with the Immigration Bureau in Phnom-Penh and the Commissariat of the National Police in the provinces for their identity cards and all other matters.[1]

---

[1] My search for a copy of this circular was diligent but unfruitful. I was mistakenly advised that it was a circular from the Minister of the Interior, and a search by the personnel of that Ministry's records department, to whom I wish to

Given the fact that the *chefs* had minimal authority in any case, it may be useful to speculate on the reasons which provoked the circular at that particular time.

The ostensible reason for ending the *congrégations* in 1958 was that no independent nation could with self-respect endure the existence of what amounted to states within the state. Government officials explained to me that a situation where an important sector of the population was governed by their own leaders and under their own systems of political organization was repugnant to Khmer nationalists. This reason is entirely plausible in the light of our understanding of political motivations in newly independent countries. However, it does not explain the five-year lag between independence and the termination of the system, nor, indeed, does it explain adequately the change itself. Two additional explanations can be suggested.

One explanation for the move is that, like the new citizenship act, it reflects a change in official outlook toward treating the Chinese minority in Cambodia as an assimilable population. The French always considered the Chinese to be fundamentally different from the Khmer, participating in an immiscible cultural tradition which demanded different administrative methods and techniques from those used to govern the Khmer. The opinion of the present Cambodian government, on the other hand, appears to be that the Chinese can and should be assimilated into the Cambodian population.[1] The *congrégations* encouraged the maintenance of Chinese behaviour patterns and values by enforcing legal separation. Not only was the *congrégation* a separate state: it enabled a separate society to exist.

extend my thanks for kind cooperation, revealed no such document. None of the six ex-*chefs* I spoke to had preserved his copy. On a suggestion from one of them, I enquired at the offices of the Municipality of Phnom-Penh, but they were unable to produce a copy for me. The Immigration Service, to whom I also wish to express thanks for courteous and patient help in my research, were unable to find their copy because they had recently moved into a new building and did not have their files available at the time. It was only on the morning of my penultimate day in the country that I was directed to a man who had been a functionary in the Immigration Service for many years, and who told me that the circular had in fact come from the office of the President of the Council of Ministers and not from the Ministry of the Interior.

[1] During his tours of China, Sihanouk has made frequent statements about the close affinity of Khmer and Chinese. One of these, quoted to me by a Chinese friend, goes roughly as follows: 'There is not a single Khmer in whose veins does not flow some drops of Chinese blood.'

A more immediate explanation of the end of the *congrégations* lies in the development of friendly relations between Cambodia and mainland China. Immediately after the war the Kuomintang increased its activities in Phnom-Penh, basing its claim to the loyalty of overseas Chinese on its leadership of the anti-Japanese struggle over the previous years. A Chinese vice-consul was appointed to Phnom-Penh in 1946, and he became a full consul in 1951. During that time the Kuomintang succeeded in winning the active allegiance of three of the five *chefs* in Phnom-Penh. Four of the five *sous-chefs* were also openly pro-Nationalist, so the Kuomintang counted seven of the ten members of the council of *chefs*. Prominent among these were the *chefs* of the two main *congrégations*, the Teochiu and Cantonese. The Kuomintang therefore had effective access to the power structure of the Chinese community. This is not to say that many of the Chinese were pro-Nationalist, for most were carefully non-committal during the Chinese civil war. Some leaders, however, were publicly committed to the Kuomintang before 1949; and as late as 1956, when Chou En-lai first visited Cambodia, they remained in positions of leadership despite the fact that the vast majority of the Chinese community enthusiastically welcomed the representative of the new Chinese government.[1]

Chou's visit to Cambodia and the preceding visit by Prince Sihanouk to Peking were manifest signs of the ties of friendship and cooperation between the countries, ties that were formalized in a commercial and economic agreement signed in 1956 (*Cambodge* 1962, 73) and in the reciprocal establishment of embassies in 1958 and 1959 (*Cambodge* 1962, 74; JOC 1959, 449 f.). The negotiations leading to diplomatic representation probably included some discussion of the resident Chinese minority; but whether they did or not, it is obvious that the Cambodian government could not remain acquiescent to Kuomintang control over the Chinese in Phnom-Penh. The simplest way to get rid of Kuomintang power was to destroy the official sanctions supporting its leaders, and this was done by terminating the office of *chef de congrégation*.

[1] The enthusiasm of the Chinese community in welcoming Chou En-lai was attested by several informants. One young friend told me he had stayed all night on the pavement near the Royal Palace to hold a place from which to see Chou drive by. An Indian informant said he could not sleep for the noise the Chinese were making in the streets the night before Chou arrived. See also Burchett 1959, 24.

That this move was taken by a circular rather than by enactment, which would have been the constitutional way to change a previous law, suggests that it was intended to provoke a minimum of publicity. That it could be done at all suggests that the position of *chef* had already been stripped of almost all its duties and privileges. Thus the *congrégation* system, which had served to structure the government of the Chinese community in Cambodia for five decades, withered away.

It is interesting that the wording of the 1958 circular (as it was reported to me) makes no mention of the legal existence of the *congrégations* themselves. When questioned on this point, my informant insisted that the circular had referred only to the *chefs* and *sous-chefs*. The *congrégations* had been recognized in law as corporations in 1935, but the law had defined the rôle of the *chef* as crucial to their operation, for his was the only position recognized in law. The termination of the position of *chef* therefore placed the *congrégations* in a legally ambiguous situation of having an existence without function or structure. This ambiguity continues today: the *congrégations* remain the executors of such property as the schools, the temples, and other urban holdings despite the fact that they have no legal officers or structure.[1] Furthermore, the five *chefs*, although they have no legal status and never meet as a body, are collectively responsible for the property that once housed the Secretariat of the Five *Congrégations* and for the *Wu-bang hui-guan* temple.[2]

---

[1] Most of the cemeteries were ordered to move in 1959 because their locations interfered with plans for expanding Phnom-Penh. The land for the new cemeteries was acquired on long-term leases in the names of the present cemetery committees. The ex-*chef* of the Cantonese *congrégation* helped to negotiate the lease for the Cantonese cemetery in 1960, but he had nothing to do with the cemetery committee in 1962–63 (see note, p. 65)

[2] The Hokkien ex-*chef* had died before 1962, and his place had been taken by the ex-*sous-chef* in matters pertaining to the property owned jointly by all the *congrégations* in Phnom-Penh. The government appointed a M. Ben Kabo of the Immigration Police to wind up the affairs of the Secretariat of the Five *Congrégations* in 1958, but since any change might have disturbed some section of the Chinese community, the government has preferred to leave the situation in ambiguity, meanwhile borrowing the Secretariat building on a rent-free basis. For friction in Cholon over attempts to change the legal status of *congrégation* property, see 'South Vietnam's Chinese Problem' 1961, 147–8. The fact that the property of each *hui-guan* is owned in the name of the ex-*chef* has raised questions only among the Teochiu and Cantonese, where both ex-*chefs* are out of favour with other Chinese leaders because of their strong Kuomintang sympathies. In the three others, the legal fiction is easily maintained.

Although the *congrégations* remain, albeit ambiguously, as corporations, the *hui-guan* they contained have undergone considerable modification. The fundamental change from compulsory to voluntary associations has robbed them of much of their power over their respective speech groups: no longer need every Chinese belong to his *hui-guan*. The fact that none of their officers holds a position whose power is legitimized by laws outside the Chinese community means that control over members is limited to the informal sanctions that each officer can call upon within the *hui-guan* itself and in the Chinese community: no longer need any Chinese fear arrest or deportation if he refuses to follow the leaders of his *hui-guan*.

Today there is considerable variation between the *hui-guan* of the different speech groups. Among the Cantonese, at one extreme, the *hui-guan* had disappeared completely. The only trace I found of the Cantonese *hui-guan* in 1962–63 was a banner at the head of the cortège from the Cantonese temples in the 'procession of the gods' at *Yuan-Xiao* (see chapter 8), which read *Guang-Zhao-Hui Hui-guan*. Its urban corporate property is administered by the Cantonese school. The cemetery committee, now self-perpetuating, has assumed the cemetery property and carries out the functions originally assigned to it by the *hui-guan*, such as organizing funerals for indigents and making the arrangements at *Qing-Ming*. School board and cemetery committee are quite separate from each other.[1] Other political, ritual, and welfare activities of the *hui-guan* have disappeared.

The Teochiu *hui-guan* still exists, but in such modified form that it is only in historical terms that one is justified in considering it as a continuation of the previous *hui-guan*. There was little agreement among informants as to what functions the *hui-guan* served; several were ignorant of its existence, and one Teochiu even expressed disbelief in it until I had shown him a mention of it in the Chinese press. Today the '*hui-guan* committee', as it is

---

[1] There was antagonism between the Cantonese cemetery committee and the school head, which found expression in accusations of embezzlement in the Chinese press (*Mian-Hua Re-bao*, 30 March 1963; *Xin Bao*, 2–3 April 1963). The school head was the previous *chef* of the Cantonese *congrégation*; this man was considered to be a principal leader of the Kuomintang faction, and when I left Cambodia, he was in jail for alleged involvement in an attempt on the life of President Liu Shao-chi during a state visit to Cambodia in May 1963 (see chapter 10, p. 123 n. 1).

called by the Chinese themselves (*zhi-shi-hui*), consists of twenty-five businesses. The primary function of this committee is to supervise the Teochiu temple. It also organizes Teochiu participation in the celebration of *Yuan-Xiao*, at which time it collects tens of thousands of riels for its work. Another important function of the committee is that of enhancing the prestige of its members; it was described by several informants as a body that merely conferred honour on its members.

That the Teochiu *hui-guan* today has little political power is indicated by the ignorance of some Teochiu of its existence as well as by the statements of the better informed. It is also suggested by the fact that the committee is elected 'by the gods' rather than by the Teochiu businessmen of Phnom-Penh: the election takes place each year (during the week after *Yuan-Xiao*) in the Teochiu temple, where fortune blocks are thrown to determine which businesses will belong for the coming year. In 1963, not one of the committee chosen in this manner had served during the previous year. One friend of mine remarked that the gods are very clever at choosing not only the richest men, but from among them, those that are most likely to contribute money and effort to the work of the gods.

There exists a separate committee to supervise the Teochiu cemetery with no formal link to the *hui-guan* committee. The Teochiu school board, which runs the largest Chinese school in Cambodia, *Duan-Hua Zhong-Xue*, is also completely independent of the *hui-guan*, although some legal fiction must relate them, since the property is owned by the Teochiu *congrégation*, whose quasi-legal successor is the *hui-guan*. The *hui-guan* no longer undertakes welfare functions, nor does it mediate in disputes. In no way does it act as the centre of communications, either within the community or between it and the government.

The *hui-guan* of the three smaller speech groups in Phnom-Penh have been affected less than those of the Cantonese or Teochiu by the dissolution of the *congrégation* system. In the case of the Hokkien and Hakka, the reason may be the small size of the population (about four thousand each, see Table 2). Each of these *hui-guan* has a single committee to supervise both the temple and the cemetery. In neither case was I able to determine the relationship between this committee and the school, although in both cases the schools are on the same properties as the respective temples. Informants insisted that neither school was run by the *hui-guan* committee, both having boards independent of outside authority, but it is clear that there is a great deal of overlap between the *hui-guan* committee and the school board in each case. It is not unreasonable to assume that the *hui-guan* committee also serves as a mediating body for whatever disputes arise among members of the *hui-guan* and that it organizes welfare for indigents of its own speech group.

The Hainanese *hui-guan* was probably the least affected by the end of the *congrégation* system, and this for at least two reasons. Although catering to over twice as large a population as either Hokkien or Hakka, the Hainanese *hui-guan* nevertheless can maintain control over its constituents because so many of them are newly arrived in the city, without capital or security. Secondly, the Hainanese population is still largely confined to a narrow range of occupations, almost all owning or working in restaurants, hotels, and shirt stores. The result of this specialization is that the *hui-guan* can operate as a guild, claiming economic support from employers and, through them, from employees. For example, a Hainanese friend who worked in a restaurant contributed the equivalent of a week's salary toward refurbishing the Hainanese temple, despite the fact that he claims total disbelief in the form of religion it represents, simply because he did not dare refuse his employer's request. Several informants told me that the Hokkien still control the hardware trade in Cambodia, but because only a small proportion of Hokkien are involved in hardware, while the rest are engaged in many different kinds of trade and finance, the Hokkien *hui-guan* cannot operate as a guild.

The Hainanese *hui-guan* has very much the same structure as it had thirty years ago, probably more highly elaborated because of the twentyfold increase in the number of its members. The *hui-guan* owns one piece of urban property that includes a school and a small temple. There is an executive committee for the *hui-guan* directed by a head who also serves as chairman of the school board and of the cemetery committee. The executive committee is elected annually by the established Hainanese businessmen in the city; it appoints all other committees. Welfare is handled by a separate committee with its own chairman. The *hui-guan* may also include a reconciliation commission, but some informants stated that the executive committee itself mediates in disputes involving Hainanese. Money to run the activities of the *hui-guan* is collected in several fund-raising campaigns during the year, the largest at *Yuan-Xiao*. The school is not limited to Hainanese pupils, but only they receive financial aid.

Of the five *hui-guan* that controlled the Chinese community in Phnom-Penh during the period of *congrégations*, one has disappeared, one has become a body merely to organize ritual and provide prestige to its members, and two others have modified structures with diminished functions and power; only the Hainanese remains as an association with political functions equivalent to, if not quite as far-reaching as, those it enjoyed under the *congrégation* system.

The end of the status of *chef de congrégation* also spelled the doom of the *Zhong-Hua Hui-guan*, the Secretariat of the Five *Congrégations*; for without active *hui-guan* in the various speech groups, a federation of *hui-guan* was, of course, impossible. I have already stated that the previous *chefs* continue in name to administer the property of the Secretariat, but they never meet as a body, they have no functions as a category, and some of them are no longer leaders in the community.

The property of the council of *chefs* has been put to other uses today. The *Wu-bang hui-guan* temple houses a school, whose director was previously an administrative leader in the Secretariat of the Five *Congrégations*. The building on Ang Eng Street that housed the Secretariat is today used as a detention house, where prisoners, mostly prostitutes, are kept while they await trial. (A Chinese library that belonged to the Secretariat and was housed in the same building has disappeared.) This property is administered by the last general secretary, who must pay an annual *main-morte* tax amounting to 1.5 per cent of rentable value out of the rents he collects from the property surrounding the previous headquarters. He circulates notices to the five ex-*chefs* for their signatures.

Other associations have assumed the various functions of the council of *chefs*. The Chinese Hospital has been reorganized as an independent institution. *Yuan-Xiao* is supervised by a group of associations. Both these institutions will be discussed in later chapters. The over-all reconciliation commission has disappeared as a formal institution. In part its functions are superseded by the court system, to which many more Chinese are resorting than was the case under the French. An expert at the Ministry of Justice told me that even cases of debt between Chinese were heard in the municipal and higher courts in 1962–63. Of course, the fact that many more Chinese are today citizens of the country also contributes to an increasing number of them using the Cambodian court system.

7

The Rise of Voluntary
Associations

Elderly Chinese friends in Phnom-Penh were much more willing
to chat about how things were under the *congrégations* than they
were about the situation today. Partly, this preference reflects a
reticence to commit oneself on a subject that has inevitably
political implications. Partly also, it flows from a feeling that
what was once organized and simple has become chaotic, without
pattern, and difficult to comprehend. One Chinese friend, very
knowledgeable on the *congrégations*, when asked about contemporary Chinese society, remarked, 'It would be better if you
stopped your history when the *congrégations* ended in 1958. That
is the end. You say a man died; you do not have to describe how
he is buried: everyone assumes he is buried.'

Of course, Chinese society is not 'buried' simply because its
previous legal structure has disappeared. Compulsory and all-
embracing associations have been replaced by voluntary and
functionally more specific ones, and what were once formal lines
of communication and control have been replaced by informal
ones. In fact, a new social organization has evolved from the old,
and it is this contemporary social organization that forms the
subject matter of the next chapters.

In the previous chapter I have indicated that with the crumbling
of the *congrégation* system, the *hui-guan* were no longer able either
to fulfil all the organizational needs of the Chinese community or
efficiently to challenge those desiring to establish new associations.
A large number of voluntary associations have grown up during
the past decade because of these two facts. While their manifest
functions are more specific than were those of the *hui-guan*, they
nevertheless serve as political groupings offering leadership status
to a greater number of individuals and providing the units in the
political structure of the community.

Four kinds of new associations are present today: sports clubs, schools, clan associations, and mutual aid societies. In Phnom-Penh, the last category comprises only one major association: the *Lian-you Hu-zhu-she*; most other mutual aid associations fall within the *hui-guan* of the smaller speech groups. After examining these kinds of new associations, I shall reconsider the Chinese Hospital, the structure of which has undergone changes such that it, too, has become a voluntary association.

SPORTS CLUBS

When Chou En-lai, then Foreign Minister of China, visited Phnom-Penh in 1956, he exhorted the Chinese to be good citizens of Cambodia. His visit also awakened a great interest in developments in China, not the least important aspect of which was an admiration for the sports and cultural activities now encouraged among the youth.

In 1961, the Cambodian government launched a campaign to promote the development of sport in the Kingdom (*Cambodge* 1962, 289). From Prince Sihanouk down to the lowest village official, the administration not only encouraged, but participated personally in, sports activities. National tournaments have been held in athletics, boxing, cycling, football, volleyball, swimming, basketball, and table tennis.[1] The first four of these sports attract primarily Khmer, and swimming and volleyball are undertaken by several ethnic groups (the Vietnamese specialize in volleyball). Participation in basketball and table tennis, however, is overwhelmingly Chinese; it is around these two sports that most of the Chinese sports clubs have organized their activities.

The government campaign, following on Chou's visit, produced the impetus that caused scores of Chinese sports clubs, *ti-yu hui*, to spring up all over the Kingdom. There were thirty-one such clubs in Phnom-Penh in 1963, all but two of them established since 1956. Five of the biographies I collected refer to the presence of *ti-yu hui* before independence, stating that they were then very small, but none of my friends or informants corroborated their existence at that time. Perhaps the references are to small groupings

[1] Other sports with organized followings include tennis, weight-lifting, judo, and two types of boxing (English and Cambodian). Tennis is limited to the very wealthy, who can afford to belong to the only tennis club in the city. The other four sports attract primarily Khmer, notably members of the armed forces.

of elderly men interested in Chinese boxing. Besides the thirty-one clubs in Phnom-Penh in 1962–63, there were three more in the immediate suburbs at Kilometre 6, Pont Monivong, and across the Tonlé Bassac. From newspapers and interviews I collected the names of fifty-three other Chinese sports clubs in the Kingdom, but it is likely that the total number is not far short of the number of Chinese schools (two hundred), for every community large enough to provide a school can probably support a sports club as well.

The main Chinese newspapers sponsor clubs; groups of alumni from particular schools have organized clubs; and Chinese in various sections of the city have established clubs in their own localities. One sports club is sponsored by a locality association, that of *Zhong-shan*. The clubs range in size from thirty to over three hundred members. The largest, *Dong-fang*, was organized among graduates and students of the *Duan-Hua* School, although its membership is open to any Chinese who accepts its aims and rules. The clubs usually collect dues of thirty riels per month (about six shillings) from each member.

A prospective member of a sports club must find a sponsor within the club, he must complete an application form that is reviewed by the executive, and finally, he must go through a period of probation before being accepted as a full-fledged member. He is then eligible for elections to the executive (provided he is of Cambodian nationality).

Each sports club has a hall, the larger ones maintaining entire houses as clubrooms. The halls invariably contain a ping-pong table or two, which are in almost constant use. The walls are lined with photographs and lists of officers, trophies won by members, and myriad small satin banners presented by opposing teams whenever they compete. Those clubs that support basketball teams rent or borrow the courts of nearby schools during the evenings or on Sundays.

The members of sports clubs do not engage solely in sports, however. The second largest club, for instance, includes groups with the following activities: basketball, table tennis, Teochiu opera, Chinese orchestral music, Western orchestral music, girls' home-making, folk-dancing, and Chinese literature. Cultural and educational activities play some part in every sports club. The clubs also arrange parties for their members, notably at International New Year (1 January) and at certain of the Chinese festivals, such as Mid-Autumn and Double Fifth. (Western dancing does not take place at these parties, for it is considered 'yellow', but folk-dancing may be a major activity.)

Nor is club activity limited to education and recreation, for many of these sports clubs also undertake a programme of welfare for their members. An elderly Chinese, who was an adviser to a sports club, gave the following description of what his club undertook to do:

There are over a hundred members... According to my understanding, the main goal of the association is to gain more members, and we do not discriminate between kinds [speech groups?] of workers. There are three principles of organization: first, with regard to sport, to provide every young person the opportunity for physical exercise, such as playing basketball or ping-pong; second, with regard to literature and art, to provide every fellow worker the opportunity of learning to sing, learning to dance, and learning to read and write in the association during his leisure time; third, with regard to welfare, to provide fellow workers who are unemployed or in difficult family circumstances with a place to live and eat at the association, provided by the welfare aspects of the association until they have found work. This association must also be in fellowship with other associations in the overseas Chinese community and increase friendship with youth associations everywhere.

The last sentence of this statement indicates that the sports clubs have functions in the larger society. In the Chinese community, they produce most of the artistic events, such as opera at *Yuan-Xiao* and at Cambodian New Year. Their basketball and table tennis teams provide one of the main non-economic links between the capital and the Chinese communities in smaller towns. Sports clubs aid the cemetery committees at *Qing-Ming*, when thousands of Chinese crowd into the five cemeteries to perform rituals at the graves of their kinsmen (see chapter 8, pp. 91-3). Going beyond the Chinese community, the sports clubs help in such government-sponsored projects as collecting money for the new sports stadium and welcoming foreign delegations, besides providing the main participation in national basketball and table tennis tournaments.

The activities of one sports club are limited primarily to the rhythmic physical exercises known as Chinese, or shadow, boxing.

Many of this club's hundred members meet twice a week to participate in shadow-boxing classes. Unlike other sports clubs, this one holds little interest for youth; it recruits older men to whom this form of exercise appeals as a traditional Chinese art form.

Although all but one of the sports clubs comprise predominantly young people, none of them is limited solely to youth. The membership of the sports teams is certainly composed of young people, but the cultural groups often attract older men. Furthermore, every sports club has a director (*hui-zhang*) and a body of advisers (*gu-wen*) who come from among the richer businessmen in the city. The clubs rely on these advisers as their main source of finance, for the revenue from membership dues does not cover their expenses. Several informants, on both sides of the political fence, mentioned or hinted at Peking gold as another source of support for many sports clubs.

Built in the spirit of the new Chinese nationalism, the sports clubs follow a policy of recruiting members from all speech groups without discrimination. Some activities, however, such as opera troupes and directing traffic in the cemeteries at *Qing-Ming*, clearly place an emphasis upon a particular speech group within some sports clubs. Furthermore, the board of advisers of each club tends to come from a single speech group, for these men recruit each other and must work together to ensure that the club remains financially solvent. Most clubs therefore become associated with one or other speech group. Of those clubs not sponsored by newspapers (three), six are Cantonese, two Hainanese, and one Hokkien. Most of the other eighteen are Teochiu, but given the great preponderance of this language over all others, it is not possible to state with certainty that all of them are associated with that speech group. The *Lian-you* sports club, mentioned below, and at least one other club include advisers from various speech groups.

Together the Chinese sports clubs in Phnom-Penh included over four thousand members in 1963, and probably well over a hundred businessmen were involved as advisers.

CHINESE SCHOOLS

The many private schools in Phnom-Penh have sprung up mainly during and since the Sino-Japanese war, and especially since the official end of the *congrégations* in 1958, which coincides with the establishment of relations between Cambodia and China (Murray 1963, 20; *Mian-Hua Qiao-Jiao, passim*). There were about fifty Chinese schools in the capital and environs in 1963, of which three offered education beyond the sixth year. These schools were staffed with about 225 licensed teachers. There were also about twenty Chinese schools and training institutions providing evening courses in Chinese, French, English, Khmer, and various trades.[1] Of the day schools, six were 'public', in the sense that they were run by boards and for the benefit of the community. The rest were privately managed as profit-making enterprises – a form of organization that does not foster high standards in the face of the great demand for education by the Chinese community of Phnom-Penh. I have the biography of one man (he had been a bandit in China) who was unable to raise enough capital to start any other kind of business, so established a school, despite the fact that he had less than four years' schooling himself. The low standards of Chinese schools is the main reason Chinese give for not sending their children to a Chinese secondary school, and as a result a small number of children go to Hongkong or China for their secondary education.

The government figures on school attendance among Chinese refer to the enrolment that schools have been licensed to accept. In the province of Battambang, for instance, licences have been issued to schools to enrol a total of 988, but interviews indicated that the total enrolment in all Chinese schools in the province was from three to four times that figure. If we were to apply these proportions to the official figure for Phnom-Penh (8515), it would give a total of between 25,000 and 35,000. Even the lower of these figures is probably too high, for the number of schools and the enrolment given to me by informants for some of them indicates that the total school enrolment in the fifty Chinese schools in Phnom-Penh and its suburbs was about twenty thousand in 1962–63. The number of teachers licensed for these schools also suggests this is a maximum figure (compare Murray 1963, 21).

Since the number of Chinese children in Phnom-Penh between

---

[1] It is interesting that more Chinese were learning English than French in night schools in 1962–63, despite the fact that French is the second language of the country; this situation may have changed the following year.

the ages of five and fifteen, calculated from the 1961 census sample, was 38,000 we may conclude that a little over half the Chinese children of school age attended Chinese schools. Many of the remainder are in Cambodian state schools, for almost all Chinese children go to some school, no matter how great a sacrifice this may entail on the part of their parents. Often children attend three or six years of Chinese school, then switch to a Cambodian school to learn Khmer. A small number, about four hundred each year, complete their secondary education in Chinese.

Because of the great pressure for education among the Chinese, classes were crowded. Although the Ministry of National Education now does not permit over forty pupils per class, older licences still in force allowed sixty, and some schools were reported to have eighty pupils or more in each class. Fees averaged about 200 riels ($5.70) per month in primary schools, but some schools, for instance the *Lian-you* schools, charged less than half that much.

With these poor conditions and low fees, it was not possible for schools to pay salaries that were competitive with other occupational opportunities. Most teachers were therefore young, having just graduated from secondary school themselves. It was very difficult to get permission to bring teachers from abroad.

All the Chinese schools in Phnom-Penh teach in Mandarin, although the Cantonese school uses both Cantonese and Mandarin in the first grade. There were only three Chinese schools in the whole country that still taught in languages other than Mandarin beyond the first grade. One was a small, rural, Cantonese school in Battambang Province; the other two were in Rattanakiri Province and taught in Hakka with Mandarin as a minor subject

School books come primarily from Hongkong and Singapore, although some are imported from mainland China.

No federation of Chinese schools exists in Cambodia, although in 1963 there were informal groupings in Phnom-Penh of the main left-wing and right-wing schools. An association for teachers serves to publicize vacant positions and qualified applicants. Whatever supervision exists over the Chinese schools is exercised by the Ministry of National Education. One of the Ministry's eleven commissions concerns itself with private education, of which Chinese forms the major portion. This commission registers schools, authorizes textbooks, examines teachers, and carries out inspections to make sure that the schools remain within the laws governing foreign private schools (Kram no. 201-NS, JOC 1957, 2005-11; and Kram no. 129-NS). These laws stipulate that no Cambodian citizen may attend a foreign school, that each school must have a *répondant* (*xiao-zhu*) who is well known, and that each school must teach Khmer for a minimum of ten hours per week.[1]

Recent notice of more stringent government control over Chinese schools appears to be a reiteration of earlier regulations, with the clear inference of more consistent enforcement from now on. The Minister of National Education published a circular dated 13 June 1967, which requires Chinese schools to teach Khmer, to register the nationality of all pupils, to remain politically neutral, etc. – all points covered by already existing legislation. The circular indicates severe penalties for any infringement of these requirements ('Dragon').

Unlike some other governments in Southeast Asia, the Cambodian government does not require that teachers in Chinese schools be citizens of Cambodia, nor that they speak Khmer, only that they be qualified in their field. Furthermore, ministerial inspection, according to Chinese teachers, is primarily concerned with the numbers of pupils and classes, and there is therefore little dissatisfaction among Chinese concerning governmental interference in their schools. No issues have arisen between the Chinese community and the government on the matter of education.

It is apparent from what has been said that the schools themselves do not provide much scope for political leadership in the Chinese community. Certainly the status of teachers militates

---

[1] The law promulgated in 1957 regulating Chinese schools requires a minimum of ten hours per week at every level (JOC 1957, 2007). However, the Ministry of National Education, to whom I wish to express my thanks for cooperation in research, stated in 1962 that the minimum requirements were as follows:

Elementary schools (3 years):	15 hours
Primary schools (3 years):	12 hours
Secondary schools (3 years):	10 hours

To comply with these requirements, each Chinese school must hire at least one Cambodian teacher, who has the additional responsibility of reporting periodically to the Ministry on conditions in the school, thus providing an informal control not stipulated by law.

against their assuming leadership rôles beyond the schools: their poor salary reflects – and to some extent causes, of course – the low prestige of teachers, who are referred to by the wealth-conscious Chinese as 'wooden idols' (*mu pu-sa*) because they have no prospect of financial gain. The teachers' federation is therefore of little consequence in the political structure of the community.

School boards, on the other hand, provide both status and power for their members, particularly outside the capital, where they become the principal form of community association (see chapter 11). In Phnom-Penh, however, there are few boards, for most of the schools are run by private individuals. Of the six 'public' school boards, only two (the Hakka and Hainanese) are elected by any constituency beyond themselves, the others having become self-perpetuating since the end of the *congrégations*. Five of the six 'public' schools were previously administered by *hui-guan*; the other was established in 1945 by a Kuomintang-sponsored workers' association that has since disappeared. The largest school, *Duan-Hua*, previously owned by the Teochiu *hui-guan*, is run by a small committee of businessmen who are apparently self-appointed, not elected. Their position on the school board is therefore a reflection of political status achieved in other areas of society.

CLAN ASSOCIATIONS

In 1959 the Municipal government of Phnom-Penh ordered the Chinese to move four of their cemeteries further from the city. The Hakka cemetery was excepted because, lying north of the small market at Pochentang, it was too far away to interfere with urban development plans. The Teochiu cemetery had already moved two years previously, and there was some reluctance to undertake once again the great expense and trouble of exhuming the bodies, transporting the pots of bones, and reburying them in new graves. In order to save expense, the Teochiu cemetery committee decided to bury in a single mass grave all those bones unclaimed by descendants or other kinsmen. This move apparently aroused opposition among some Chinese, who felt that it was not an appropriate method to dispose of the remains of forefathers. Accordingly, groups of merchants with the same surname made collections to provide clan graves for the bones of clansmen without solvent descendants. The expenses involved no doubt deterred those with more unusual surnames from adopting this practice (a single grave site in the richer section of the Teochiu cemetery costs three thousand riels, £30; the price for a group grave was probably more), but members of the most familiar surnames were able to call on sufficiently wide support to make the project feasible. This support was than formalized into continuing clan associations called *tong-xing qin-hui*. These clan associations are not officially called *hui*, for in fact none of them are chartered associations. In their publicity they refer to themselves as the 'Zhang clan' or the 'Huang clan' (*Zhang-shi zong-zu, Huang-shi zong-qin tong-ren*). In conversation, however, the term *tong-xing qin-hui* is usually used.

In 1963, there were eight such clan associations in Phnom-Penh, representing the seven most frequent and the ninth most frequent surnames in the Chinese population.[1] These eight represent the following clans (in order of frequency of surname): *Chen, Lin, Huang, Li, Zhang, Wu, Wang,* and *Xie*. None of these clan associations existed prior to 1959. Before that, a common surname sometimes served as the criterion for recruiting to certain events – such as a Li banquet for a visiting movie star named Li – but no continuing and formal association existed that was based on clanship (with the exception of the Guo drapers' guild, which disappeared in the pre-war period; see above, pp. 51–3).

The clan associations are most evident at the time of *Qing-Ming*, for then each organizes a ritual at its respective clan grave and advertises the fact in the Chinese press. With a friend named Xie, I attended the ritual of the Xie clan association, which occurred four days after *Qing-Ming* and which was also the inauguration

---

[1] The frequency of different surnames in the Chinese community was obtained from a list published in the *Mian-Hua Re-bao* (24–27 December 1962) of individuals in Phnom-Penh who had correctly solved a puzzle in the paper. The list included 4637 names, representing 108 surnames, and was of course not limited to Teochiu; so far as I know, the most frequent surname that is disproportionately represented in another speech group is the twelfth, Lu, which is found predominantly among Cantonese. Telephone directories were not suitable for counting surnames because there are very few private telephones, most being listed under the name of the firm. According to the newspaper list, the fourteen most frequent names were the following (percentage of total in parentheses): *Chen* (15.2 per cent); *Lin* (7.5 per cent); *Huang* (5.7 per cent); *Li* (5.5 per cent); *Zhang* (3.4 per cent); *Wu* (2.9 per cent); *Wang* (2.8 per cent); *Guo* (2.8 per cent); *Xie* (2.4 per cent); *Yang* (2.3 per cent); *Lu* (2.1 per cent); *Zheng* (2.0 per cent); *Luo* (1.8 per cent); *Xu* (1.8 per cent).

of the newly completed grave. The Xie grave lies within the Teochiu cemetery; on its stone are some thirty names and the slogan, 'Honoured Grave of Former Sojourners Named Xie' (*Xie-shi Xian-Qiao Gong-mu*). My friend told me that the clan association had collected money from his family several times, but he did not belong to the association, nor did his father participate in its ritual. Less than a dozen people, mostly males, participated in the ritual we watched, which consisted of setting out a great display of food before the gravestone, repainting the stone itself, mass bowing before the sacrifice, and then the burning of paper money and cloth. After the ceremony, the men sat down to discuss the business of the association including finances and the date for the ceremony the following year. Two trucks and a Chinese orchestra had been hired for the occasion. I estimate that the entire ceremony, including publicity, transport, orchestra, and the sacrificial items, cost about eight thousand riels (£80).[1]

Other clan associations held ceremonies at their respective clan graves on various days just before or just after *Qing-Ming*. With the exception of the Wu association, none held their ceremony on the day itself, 5 April, because many people were involved in family ceremonies at private graves on that day. The Chen association held no ceremony while I was in the country, because their clan grave, a huge and elaborate monument in the Teochiu cemetery, was still under construction.

The fact that these clan associations developed because of dissatisfaction with the Teochiu cemetery committee does not in itself explain their limitation to that speech group, for the same problems of removal and reburial faced the other cemetery committees as well. Both historical and functional answers can be given to the question why clan associations did not develop among other speech groups. Historically, the Teochiu cemetery included a larger proportion of very old graves because the

[1] Three displays of food were set out: the largest before the gravestone, a much smaller one before the stone dedicated to the earth god (*tu-di zhi shen*), and a still smaller one at the back of the grave, which the men told us was also for the earth god. The main display included great trays of bread, sweets, biscuits, oranges and other fruits, cooked beef, chicken, ducks, crabs, and eggs, a cauldron of rice with thirty-six bowls and chopsticks, thirty-six cups of wine and an equal number of cups of tea, eight cases of soft drinks (sixteen dozen bottles), and a large barbecued pig, as well as such ritual items as incense, leaves and areca nuts, paper money and cloth.

Teochiu did not exhume bones (*zhi-gu*) for shipment to China. In 1959, therefore, there were probably more graves containing the remains of unremembered people in the Teochiu cemetery than in the Cantonese, for instance, despite the fact that the Cantonese cemetery may have contained a greater total number of graves at the time. In 1963 the graves in the Teochiu cemetery represented about three thousand individuals, not including the Chen clan grave and the large mass grave for unclaimed bones, the contents of which I was not able to determine. Graves in the Cantonese cemetery represented over six thousand individuals, but not all the pots had yet been reburied when I made the count in June 1963.

The functional explanation relates to the fact that associations already existed in the Cantonese speech group to fulfil the functions for which the clan associations developed among the Teochiu: the locality associations. In fact, the Cantonese locality associations organized the reburial of all unclaimed bones as well as those claimed by people too poor to pay for new graves. As a consequence, the Cantonese cemetery today has three classes of graves (the Teochiu has only two), the poorest class consisting of long concrete troughs provided by the locality associations and each marked according to locality. The pots of bones have been buried in these troughs, into the sides of which a small gravestone has been set opposite each pot. Unclaimed bones could be assigned easily to each locality because of the practice, common to all Chinese in Cambodia, of marking on the headstone the locality of origin of the deceased.

One may wonder why the Teochiu did not organize associations on the basis of locality rather than clanship when faced with the problem of disposing of the unclaimed bones. The answer may be that when confronted with the remains of previous generations, a Chinese thinks in categories defined by the practices of ancestor worship, and is therefore motivated to look after the bones of clansmen rather than those of people from the same locality. When the Cantonese locality associations were first organized, the problems were the logistic ones of transport and communication rather than the ritual ones of disposing of bones.

The similarity between Cantonese locality and Teochiu clan associations goes beyond their manifest functions, for both find support in the same section of the population: the elderly Chinese merchants who are most concerned about maintaining Chinese traditions, those who cannot fit into the more progressive atmosphere of the sports associations. Although clan associations are as yet too new to have broadened their functions beyond the tending of clan graves, it is altogether likely that they will develop into associations with all the same functions that locality associations serve among the Cantonese, and they may be expected to establish annual banquets, welfare programmes, and other activities for a formal membership as they evolve a more formal structure.

A MUTUAL AID SOCIETY

With the great increase in Chinese population immediately following the war, the suburb of Chamcar Chen, to the south-west of the main Chinese quarter, was soon filled with shacks and mat huts. The thousands of Teochiu immigrants living in this slum area were dockers, street pedlars, construction workers, or persons engaged in other kinds of manual labour, and they could not afford to build concrete houses like the ones inhabited by the majority of settled Chinese. Unlike many of the earlier immigrants, these immigrants had brought their families with them. The annual dry season, stretching from November to April, caused great misery in this community, for water was scarce, and fires were frequent. Then, in 1956, the new immigration law forbade eighteen occupations to aliens, and many of these men became unemployed. In response to their misery, the Teochiu workers established a mutual aid society, which they named the *Lian-you Hu-zhu-she*, the United Friends Mutual Aid Society. This association has since grown into the largest single grouping in the Chinese community, with various activities and sub-groups serving many functions.

The origin of the *Lian-you* Society at about the time of the new immigration law suggests that it was originally a grouping in opposition to the political structure based on the wealthier merchants, none of whom made any public protest about the new law. Although the *Lian-you* did not object publicly to the law, nevertheless the Society was organized among those Chinese who were most directly affected and who had little power in the Chinese community at large. In other words, it originated as a workers' association in conflict with the associations of merchants that controlled the Chinese community. The nature of the Society has changed somewhat since then, for today it has the support of businessmen from various speech groups, who help to finance it and take leading rôles in its committees. Its membership is still almost entirely Teochiu.

The *Lian-you* runs three schools, which provide the least expensive Chinese education available in Phnom-Penh. Fees at the *Lian-you* schools averaged about six hundred riels per session; at *Duan-Hua* School, the pupils paid two thousand riels (£20) per session. The three *Lian-you* schools were said to comprise more than a thousand pupils, making it the fourth largest Chinese school administration in Phnom-Penh.

The *Lian-you* Society has its own sports club, with basketball and table tennis teams. Under the general name of *Ren-de Shan Tang*, it sponsors various Chinese artistic groups, such as a folk-dance troupe, a traditional Chinese orchestra, and one of the two lion teams in the city. Besides these, it provides its members with benefits for unemployment, sickness, disaster, and death.

This association was described to me by a Kuomintang informant as a secret society, but I could find no evidence that it resembles Chinese secret societies in having sworn membership, secret ritual, or secret signs. It is certain that it presented strong opposition to the Kuomintang leaders of the Chinese community in 1956, and this tradition has continued since then. Now that the community is no longer led by men committed to the Kuomintang, the *Lian-you* has ceased to be a grouping in opposition to those in power; indeed, it now forms a major part of the Chinese polity (see chapter 10).

THE CHINESE HOSPITAL

With the end of the *congrégations* in 1958, the Chinese Hospital was faced with bankruptcy, for its entire income had come from the hospital levies collected by the various *hui-guan*. When these levies could be assured no longer, nine leading Chinese businessmen took the initiative to reorganize the hospital as a self-supporting institution (Chau Kon 1961, 19). One of these had been a *chef* (Hakka) when the *congrégation* system was dismantled; two others had been *chefs* of the Teochiu *congrégation* some years before the Sino-Japanese war.

Following a series of meetings, an association called the Chinese Hospital Committee to Aid Healing (*Zhong-Hua Yi-yuan Yi-liao Xie-zhu Hui*) was organized and chartered in 1961 to sustain the Chinese Hospital. This Hospital Committee, as I shall hereafter refer to it, consisted of about five hundred companies or business-men, each of whom pledged to donate a fixed amount every month to the hospital.[1] There were five categories of members; life members made a single donation of 20,000 riels (£200); the other four categories consisted of those who gave 500, 400, 300 and 200 riels per month (Chau Kon 1961, 41).

The constitution of this committee stipulated that it should meet every second year to elect a hospital board (*dong-shi hui*). Although the fifteen members of this board are elected by the entire committee, six of them must be Teochiu, three Cantonese, and two each Hokkien, Hakka, and Hainanese. Eight alternate members are also elected: three Teochiu, two Cantonese, and one each of the other three speech groups. The board then appoints each of its members to a specific office, there being a president, four vice-presidents, a treasurer and assistant, a secretary and assistant, and so on. A Teochiu, Mr Tan Soeun Hoa (*Chen Shun-he*), has been president of both the boards elected since the establishment of the new structure, and each of the other speech groups has provided one of the vice-presidents.

By 1962, the membership of the Hospital Committee had risen to 847 members, of whom 761 were in Phnom-Penh, representing between a quarter and a third of all the Chinese companies in the capital. This membership indicates that the Chinese Hospital Committee is the largest association of Chinese merchants in Phnom-Penh.

---

[1] Chau Kon states that the committee comprised 505 members, but the list he provides on pages 25–30 of the original members contains only 487 entries (Chau Kon 1961, 31 f.).

8

Religious Aspects of Chinese
Community Life

So far in this description of contemporary Chinese society, the discussion has been sociological to the exclusion of most cultural elements: I have discussed the associational structure of a minority without examining what sets it off from the majority.

An important aspect of culture, one that often clearly distinguishes one society from another and at the same time has political implications, is religion. Religious behaviour marks off a set of people both by exhibiting to others that they are different and by promoting solidarity within the set. Ritual observances that promote solidarity need not involve the congregation of members, for the repetition of rituals that are distinctly Chinese, even if they occur within the home, can reinforce solidarity by marking off the Chinese in their own minds from the non-Chinese; that is, ritual may be common without being joint.

Among the Chinese in Cambodia, most religious behaviour is individual or familial, involving the members of a family at most. Even at *Qing-Ming*, when large numbers of Chinese go to the cemeteries and several associations are involved in organizing the exodus from the city, the actual rituals are undertaken in most cases by individuals or families. The only major exception occurs at *Yuan-Xiao*, when a large part of the Chinese community is involved in the 'procession of the gods' through the city: a minor exception is the ritual in the Chinese Buddhist temples. These two subjects will be treated in separate sections later in this chapter.

The religious behaviour of Chinese families may be divided into three types: that which occurs at *crises de passage* in the lives of its members, that related to the yearly cycle of festivals, and the occasional ritual provoked by the contingencies of business, by illness, or by other misfortune. However, not all ritual is pertinent to a study of the political structure of the Chinese community. Once its importance as an identifying feature has been mentioned, the last category of occasional family ritual can be conveniently ignored, for it involves no associations or power relations beyond the family. In dealing with the other categories of ritual, I shall consider only the salient features, ignoring much detail that has nothing to do with my major subject.

'RITES DE PASSAGE'

The two main *crises de passage* marked by ritual are marriage and death. Birth ceremonies, such as the *man-yue* ('full-month') ceremony found among many overseas Chinese, are not practised in Phnom-Penh in any of the speech groups, with the exception of a small number of rich and tradition-oriented Cantonese; for them, *man-yue* usually involves a feast in a restaurant. Old-age ceremonies, known as *da-shou* (great longevity), are sometimes celebrated by rich and prominent men at their sixtieth or seventieth birthdays: friends present honorific scrolls and there is usually a feast as well. While I was in Phnom-Penh, a *Da-Shou* was celebrated by the elder statesman of the Chinese community, Mr Tan Soeun Hoa (*Chen Shun-he*) upon achieving his ninetieth year. A friend said that wealthy men sometimes celebrate *da-shou* at the age of fifty if they fear their health will not see them through another decade. Most of these events, however, are quite unimportant and elicit little public attention.

1. *Weddings*

Weddings among the Chinese in Phnom-Penh involve any or all of eight elements: (1) registration at the ward police station; (2) an announcement in the Chinese press; (3) a betrothal feast; (4) a ceremony at the groom's home; (5) a ceremony at the bride's home; (6) a feast given by the bride's family; (7) a feast given by the groom's family; and (8) a honeymoon. The rarest element is the first, for few Chinese in Phnom-Penh register their marriages with the administration. The critical aspect of marriage as far as the Chinese community is concerned is its publication; this is done either by inserting an advertisement in a Chinese newspaper or by giving a feast, and often by both.

Announcements in the press are made either at the time of

betrothal or of marriage. They are usually very simple, merely giving the names of the two spouses and indicating the fact that they are betrothed or married. Occasionally they take a more elaborate form in which the announcement includes the names of the spouses' fathers and states their agreement to the union; this is more common in betrothal announcements than in marriage announcements. During the five months October 1962 to February 1963, the main Chinese newspaper, *Mian-Hua Ri-bao*, included about ninety announcements, half of them for betrothals and half for marriages. Congratulatory advertisements during the same time related to almost four times that number of unions. These congratulations are usually placed by individuals, but occasionally by a sports club to which either groom or bride belongs.

Of the three kinds of feasts, the betrothal feast is by far the rarest. In fact, although several informants mentioned that they occasionally occurred, I knew of none during my sojourn in Phnom-Penh, during which time I was aware of scores of wedding feasts. The feast given by the bride's family is quite common, and that given by the groom is associated with almost every marriage.[1] Among 'modern' Chinese (progressive, *jin-bu*), this feast is often given by both bride and groom together; I was not able to determine who pays for such a feast.

The main marriage feast is usually held in a restaurant or public building. Occasionally a special pavilion is built over the pavement in front of the groom's family store to house the feasting guests. The pavilion, which is made of wood, canvas, and cloth decorations, usually extends across the fronts of neighbouring stores as well. At the start of the feast, the groom and three or four male attendants stand at the door of the pavilion or restaurant to greet the guests as they arrive. The guests proceed

[1] I attended the bridal feast of a restaurant cashier who was marrying a young photographer the following day. The feast was held at a prominent restaurant, where 180 people, mainly women and children, ate a seven-course meal that included sharks fins, washed down with soft drinks, beer, whisky, and mixtures of these. Each guest handed a 'red-packet' (*hong-bao*) to the bride's mother as they came into the room (her father was not present, probably because the parents are separated or divorced). During the meal, the bride, her mother, and three girl friends moved from table to table, drinking toasts with the guests. The bride wore a white dress with green and purple accessories; her attendants wore dresses in pastel colours. The feast lasted from 8.00 to 9.30 p.m. The groom was not present.

to a table by the door, where they present gifts of cash and are registered (with the amount of the gift) in the guest book. A Cantonese informant told me that the Cantonese usually give presents rather than money at weddings. Often there is a large piece of red silk upon which they sign their names. The guests then seat themselves, women at separate tables from men. During the feast, the groom goes from table to table, often accompanied by his bride, wishing the guests well and exchanging drinks with them. Grooms usually wear dark suits; brides wear white, pink, or pastel shades of blue or yellow; guests wear everyday dress. After the feast, the bride and groom are driven away in an automobile decorated with red ribbons and rosettes.

If there is a wedding ceremony, it occurs before the feast in the house of the groom, and involves the couple's paying respects to the parents of the groom, to his ancestors if there is an ancestral altar, and to the various gods represented in the house.[1] The ceremony at the bride's home precedes this ceremony. In the case of a friend of mine, the marriage was consummated after the ceremony and feast provided by the bride's family, and only the following day was there a ceremony and a feast at the home of the groom; this unusual order may be related to the fact that the marriage was to be uxorilocal. Neither ceremony involves a ritual practitioner, the older kinsmen deciding the forms of ritual and directing the principals through them.

An informant described to me the ceremony which took place in his home when his sister was married. The couple was directed by an elderly woman, a relative of the bride's mother, to bow four times to the earth god, to the kitchen god, to the Buddhist shrine (the father is a Buddhist), to *Tian-di Fu-Mu*, to the ancestral shrine (representing the bride's maternal grandparents), to the incense pot of the bride's newly deceased mother, to the god of wealth in the family store on the ground floor, and finally to the father of the bride. The couple then knelt before the father and

[1] The homes of Chinese businessmen usually include an ancestral altar if someone in the family has died in Cambodia. The altar carries an incense pot marked with the name of the deceased, and occasionally a photograph of the deceased. An altar to the god of wealth and the earth god is commonly found in all stores or homes; it consists of a plaque upon which is written *Wu-fang Wu-tu Long-shen, Qian-hou Di-zhu Cai-shen*, in front of which a few sticks of incense are usually burning in a pot. Other gods mentioned by informants as represented in their homes were *Tian-di Fu-Mu, Si-ming Zao-jun* (the kitchen god), *men-shen* (door gods), and *Da-sheng Fo-zu*.

offered him a cup of tea, for which he gave the groom a 'red-packet' (*hong-bao*). Throughout the ceremony a gramophone provided music entitled *Ba Xian Jia Xi*, which my informant said was 'very fortunate music'.

Some young people get married simply by going on a honeymoon at the same time as they insert an announcement of the fact in a newspaper. Such a marriage is called a 'travelling marriage' (*lu-xing jie-hun*) and is undertaken by couples who wish to avoid the expenses or obligations of a nuptial feast or whose parents are opposed to the marriage. When they return from their honeymoon, they may give a small party for intimate friends.

No mass marriage has taken place among the Chinese in Phnom-Penh. I was told that the Nationalist Chinese consulate attempted to organize one after the Sino-Japanese war, when such events occurred among Chinese in Singapore (Freedman 1957, 166 ff.), but the venture failed for lack of interested couples.

2. *Funerals*

In contrast to nuptial rites, which seem to involve no associations, funerals usually implicate whatever associations the dead person or his family belong to. It may also involve religious practitioners: some Chinese arrange for several Cambodian Buddhist monks to accompany the funeral cortège, and a few seek the Chinese Buddhist monks, but most hire the Chinese 'Taoist' practitioners.

A funeral begins with a parade through the streets of the city in the early morning, organized by one of the two Chinese undertaking firms in the city. A typical funeral cortège includes the following items, in order of march:

A tall, ornate paper sign giving the place of birth and name of the deceased in gold characters.

A number of *cyclos* (pedicabs), each carrying two large cotton banners, with appropriate slogans, donated by friends.

One or more Chinese orchestras, including drums, gong, cymbals, and sometimes an oboe or tin horn; if there are more than one orchestra they are interspersed with the *cyclos*; these orchestras are hired by friends.

Several tables, each carried by two Khmer workers, holding paper articles to be burned at the grave and food for the sacrifice by the grave, usually a paper house and a barbecued pig.

A table holding the photograph of the deceased.

The hearse, which consists of an ornate and colourful cart with a giant dragon head and tail, heavily draped with coloured cloths and painted hangings; it is pulled by a small truck, similarly decorated.

The mourners, wearing white or sackcloth.

The guests.

Several automobiles to carry the mourners and some guests to the cemetery.

The longest funeral cortège I saw included sixty *cyclos*, four orchestras, and six barbecued pigs. Others included folk-dance troupes, and Western brass bands. The chief mourners wear white clothing, other mourners wear white sashes or head-bands. Although there is considerable variation in the style of mourning dress, sons and daughters usually wear a sackcloth patch on their backs, while more distant descendants and affinal and collateral relatives wear a red patch. The chief mourner often carries a white wand, and occasionally he walks backwards beside the hearse.

At an agreed place, the parade disperses, and the mourners are placed in automobiles to accompany the coffin to the cemetery, several miles from the city. The coffin is placed in the grave at an auspicious hour determined by a geomancer, the food sacrifice is laid out before the grave, and the various paper articles are burned. The photograph of the deceased and one or two banners are then placed in the small mourning hall (*ai-si-ting*) at the cemetery, where they remain for several weeks.[1]

An announcement is occasionally placed in the newspapers following a funeral, usually in the form of 'tearful thanks' (*qi-xie qi-shi*) to those who participated in the funeral from the descendants of the deceased, all of whose names are mentioned. These

[1] At a Cantonese funeral, one of the chief mourners told me that the immediate family would visit the grave on the third, seventh, fourteenth, twenty-first, twenty-eighth, thirty-fifth, forty-second and forty-ninth days after the funeral, each time wearing mourning dress. On the third day, when I was at the cemetery, no ritual was carried out at the graveside, but the family retired to the *ai-si-ting* and remained there for some time.

Within the Teochiu and Hainanese cemeteries, geomancy is reduced to determining the correct time of burial, for the positioning and orientation of the graves is regimented. In the Cantonese, Hakka, and Hokkien cemeteries, the orientation of the richer graves may vary, but there is little scope for positioning because the plots are small, about fifty square metres. Geomancers have more scope when dealing with the wealthy Teochiu, for these men usually buy plots of land for private cemeteries.

announcements also publicize gifts made by the family of the deceased to various associations, such as a sports club, a school, or the Chinese Hospital. More rarely, an announcement appears before the funeral, giving the date and time of death and the funeral, and listing the kinsmen of the deceased in the various categories of relationship to him.

ANNUAL CYCLE OF FESTIVALS

With the exception of *Yuan-Xiao*, most of the yearly festivals involve only family ritual, many of them not even occasioning a visit to a temple. However, several elicit some activity from various associations, notably the celebration at *Qing-Ming* and the parallel celebrations by specific speech groups at *Chong-Yang* or *Dong-Jie*. I shall briefly describe each of the yearly festivals as they were celebrated by the Chinese in Phnom-Penh during the year I was there, ending with the celebration of the New Year, or Spring Festival, as it is now called in China.

Qing-Ming. The annual festival known in English as the Feast of the Tombs (D. Willmott 1960, 218) fell on 5 April in 1963.[1] On this day, those Chinese who have close relatives buried in Cambodia visited the graves to refurbish them and make ritual sacrifices. Since the vast majority of Chinese graves are in the cemeteries of the five speech groups, the concentration of thousands of Chinese in these cemeteries involved a considerable amount of organization, which was undertaken primarily by the cemetery committees.

The cemetery committees announced their plans in the Chinese press several days before *Qing-Ming*, and companies were asked to volunteer automobiles and lorries or to pay for buses to carry members of each speech group to their cemetery. Those in need of transport went to a place in Phnom-Penh designated in the announcement, whence they were taken to the cemetery between seven and ten in the morning. Between ten and one, transport returned them to the city. At the cemeteries of the larger speech

[1] *Qing-Ming* is regulated by the solar not the lunar cycle; it falls fifteen days after the vernal equinox and is therefore on a different day of the lunar month every year. Doolittle states that it is calculated from the winter solstice and falls on 5 or 6 April (Doolittle 1866, 44).

groups (Teochiu and Cantonese), the heavy stream of private
automobiles had to be controlled and parked. For this task, the
cemetery committees called upon sports clubs, whose member
acted as traffic wardens throughout the morning.

A public mourning ceremony (*gong-ji*) was carried out in the
public mourning hall (*gong-ji tang*) at the Hainanese and Hakka
cemeteries.[1] This ceremony was organized by the cemetery
committee and involved burning incense and paper articles, setting
out a ritual sacrifice, and a mass bowing (*bai*) of the members of
the committee and other prominent members of the speech
group.

Some of the locality associations carried out rituals at the
Cantonese cemetery, where there is a row of memorial stones to
the forebears from each of fifteen localities.[2] The graves in the
poorest section of the Cantonese cemetery, as already mentioned
are arranged according to district of origin, and this no doubt
contributes to a feeling of solidarity among those from one *xian*
as well as making it easier for locality associations to gain recruits
On the evening of *Qing-Ming* or the following day, each of these
associations held a banquet at one of the major restaurants in
Phnom-Penh, to which all Cantonese from the appropriate
locality were invited. The recent erection of clan graves has led
to the celebration of *Qing-Ming* by clan associations, an example
of which has been mentioned in chapter 7 (see pp. 79f.).

The celebration of *Qing-Ming* is repeated at *Chong-Yang* by the

---

[1] It is possible, but unlikely, that a similar ceremony was held at the new
Hokkien cemetery and at the old Teochiu *gong-ji-tang*; no such ceremony occurred
at the Cantonese cemetery, the new Teochiu cemetery, or the old Hokkien
cemetery.

[2] The following are the localities represented by stones; they are listed in the
order of the stones from east to west: *Nan-hai, Yao-Ming* (including both *Gao-yao*
and *Gao-ming xian*), *Bao-an, San-shui, Bo-lo, Hua-xian, Pan-yu, Si-yi, Zhong-shan,
Hao-shan, Zeng-cheng, Dong-guan, Qing-yuan, Si-hui, Shun-de*. A smaller stone
separate from the masonry that links these fifteen, stands at the eastern end of the
line, representing *Jiu-Jiang Xiang* of *Nan-hai Xian*. A ceremony was held before
this stone at *Qing-Ming*, involving a barbecued pig on a ritual tray marked *Nan-
hai Jiu-jiang*; there was also a separate banquet for people from this *xiang*, although
two of the four organizers were included among the five men who organized
the banquet for those from *Nan-hai Xian*. Only $14\frac{1}{2}$ per cent of the third-class
Nan-Hai graves are marked *Jiu-Jiang*, but eighteen of the forty-six first-class
Nan-Hai graves (39 per cent) are so marked, an indication that there may be a
concentration of rich men from this single *xiang* who might prefer an association
representing a smaller locality. No other *xiang* has such a large number of graves
in the first-class section of the Cantonese cemetery.

Cantonese and Hakka and at *Dong-Jie* by the Hainanese; these celebrations were less important than *Qing-Ming*, however, and attracted somewhat smaller crowds to the cemeteries.

Cambodian New Year comes just ten days after *Qing-Ming*, for both are fixed in relation to the solar cycle. The two days' statutory holidays (15–16 April) were observed by some of the Chinese businesses, and no animals were slaughtered in the abattoirs during that time. One of the sports clubs presented a concert on three successive nights. Twelve Chinese leaders called on the Royal Delegate to the Municipality of Phnom-Penh to present New Year's greetings from the Chinese residents of the city.

Double Fifth. The fifth day of the fifth month, celebrated in many parts of China (and Hongkong) as the Dragon Boat Festival, occasioned no celebration in Phnom-Penh other than the manufacture and consumption of *zong*, a steamed delicacy consisting of glutinous rice and various condiments wrapped in lotus leaves. These *zong* are eaten in the family and occasionally presented to friends. A few of my Chinese friends expressed a total ignorance of the origin and celebration of this festival, apart from the consumption of *zong* in their families.

An informant suggested that the Double Fifth does not occasion public celebrations in Phnom-Penh because of the similar Khmer Water Festival that occurs in the autumn. This explanation falls down, however, when one realizes that the festival is not observed with public ceremony by the Chinese in Saigon, Semarang (D. Willmott 1960, 218), Bangkok (Coughlin 1960, 110), Province Wellesley (Newell 1962, 120), or Singapore (Elliot 1955, 34); dragon boats are not popular anywhere in Southeast Asia. The only ritual observance I remarked on the Double Fifth in Phnom-Penh was a small sacrifice in the gutter before a Hakka bakery, consisting of some *zong*, fruit, and incense on a banana leaf.

Zhong-Yuan. On the fifteenth day of the seventh month some of the Chinese families in Phnom-Penh undertook rituals to pacify the unattended ghosts that might otherwise be malign. These rituals involved burning paper clothes and money and making libations to satisfy the needs of the ghosts. According to one friend, this festival used to be the occasion for a public sacrifice, but no such sacrifice took place in 1962 or 1963, nor had there been any for several years.

An article in the *Mei-Jiang Ri-bao* (8 August 1962) describes the *Zhong-Yuan* festival as follows:

Today is our country's traditional festival of the dead, which is one of the eight important festivals in the year. Since long ago, the overseas Chinese have preserved the old customs of their motherland. On this day, each family kills a chicken or a duck to make a sacrifice to the spirits. Everywhere there is a festive atmosphere. Some people visit their parents or friends on this occasion to congratulate the living and pray for the dead. Even if these customs are somewhat superstitious, that does not stop the overseas Chinese from continuing to celebrate this festival.

The article goes on to make a plea for more concern about the living rather than the dead.[1]

Zhong-Yuan was the occasion for a political demonstration in Phnom-Penh about a decade ago, when the Kuomintang organized a public sacrifice (*da-ji*) for the ghosts of the victims of communist persecution in China.

Zhong-Qiu. The Mid-Autumn Festival, on the fifteenth of the eighth month, is dedicated to the moon. For several weeks before the fifteenth, special pastries called 'moon-cakes' (*yue-bing*) were on sale in sweetshops, and by one week before the festival, stalls had been set up along the sidewalks, selling moon-cakes in a dozen different varieties. On the night of the full moon, many families prepared tables outside their doors, covered with displays of sweetmeats, fruit, candles, incense, and various decorations. The pavements were lined with these tables, and one saw them on nearly every balcony on the floors above. A great number of families sat near these altars, 'enjoying the moon' together (*shang-*

---

[1] I express my thanks to the Press Bureau of the Ministry of Information for translating this article into French.

Coughlin states that in Bangkok 'The Cantonese...go to the local cemeteries for simple memorial services...on this day' and that the festival is 'a memorial occasion when offerings are made to the ancestral spirits and the family graves are swept and put in order' (Coughlin 1960, 111). Coughlin has apparently confused *Zhong-Yuan* with *Chong-Yang* (the ninth day of the ninth month), for *Zhong-Yuan* is concerned with placating ghosts that are certainly not ancestors, while *Chong-Yang* (not mentioned by Coughlin) fits his description for the Cantonese.

yue). Many children pushed wheeled lanterns along the pavements, either home-made lanterns or more elaborate store-purchased ones in the shape of a lion or other animal. This festival was an occasion for young people to hold private dancing parties in their homes. Some tradition-minded women visited the two *Ben-tou-gong* temples, but the other temples were empty, although the caretakers, for whom the temples are homes, placed tables of food, candles, and incense outside the front doors.

October First, the National Day of mainland China, passed with little notice in Phnom-Penh. Some of the stores closed for the day, and the Chinese newspapers (with the exception of the pro-Kuomintang paper) appeared in red ink, but there was no public celebration or meeting. It is possible that in other years more stores close on October First, for in 1962 the day fell on a Monday after four days of holidays, including Sunday and three days for Prachum Ben, a Khmer religious festival honouring the spirits of the dead (Porée-Maspero 1964, 316 ff.). A reception was held at the Chinese Embassy on the Sunday, to which leaders of the Chinese community were invited; another on 1 October was attended by the diplomatic corps and Cambodian officials. Many of the schools also closed, and some of them held celebrations in the form of basketball tournaments. No animals were slaughtered or butchered on that day.

October Tenth, the Kuomintang National Day, was entirely ignored, although I was told by one informant that as recently as 1956 there was a great 'Double Tenth' feast that filled the three largest restaurants in the city.[1]

Chong-Yang, the ninth day of the ninth lunar month, is also known as *Chong-Jiu* (repeated nine) for that reason. This festival was merely an occasion for a special family meal for most Chinese in Phnom-Penh, but Cantonese and Hakka visited the cemeteries to attend to the graves in the same way that has been described for *Qing-Ming*. Some of the Cantonese locality associations held banquets. One Teochiu clan association chose this time to inaugurate the newly completed clan grave.

[1] Another festival that distinguishes the Kuomintang is Children's Day, which is celebrated on 4 April by the Nationalist schools, on 1 June by schools politically oriented toward mainland China.

Water Festival and Cambodian Independence Day. Two important Cambodian public festivals in Phnom-Penh occur in November, and each is the occasion for holidays. Independence Day on November 9 is celebrated with a military parade and fireworks. The Water Festival, which marks the change in direction of the Tonlé Sap River, involves three days of boat races and illuminated floats. All stores and businesses, as well as government departments, closed for both these festivals in 1962, but Chinese participation in them was limited to watching the parade and races. No organized activities took place in the Chinese community at any level.[1]

Christmas and January First, the latter a statutory holiday in Cambodia, were the occasions for private parties among some of the young Chinese in Phnom-Penh. Christmas is a holiday only for the small number of Chinese who are Christians.[2]

New Year or Spring Festival. The Chinese New Year, which is also celebrated by the Vietnamese as *Têt,* brought business in Phnom-Penh to a standstill for three days. Stores were closed, Chinese employees in businesses owned by members of other ethnic groups were given holidays, no animals were slaughtered,

[1] The Water Festival is not a religious festival for the Khmer population, for the ritual involves only the Baku of the Royal Palace, the Brahmins who have been ritual retainers to the crown since Angkorean times. It is a great spectacle, however, and holiday crowds line the shore for miles to watch the boat races. The boats are long, graceful, dugout canoes carrying from twenty to fifty paddlers or oarsmen and belonging to local Khmer temples or villages; they race in pairs, each boat competing eight times in the three days. On the final day, after the last race, all the boats descend the river *en masse,* and a Brahmin in the bow of the first canoe cuts a buffalo-hide cord stretched across a section of the river, thus symbolizing the royal blessing on the current now moving strongly toward the sea. The Khmer royalty and high officials, the diplomatic corps, and other invited guests (I was privileged to be included) watch the races from a floating palace and floating pavilions on the river before the Royal Palace. Each evening the ceremonies are concluded by a parade of illuminated floats, provided by government ministries and private companies.

[2] In Phnom-Penh there are a few Chinese Roman Catholics and a somewhat larger number of Protestants, perhaps three or four hundred, most of whom belong to a church administered by the Missionary Alliance. This mission board had missionaries stationed in Phnom-Penh, in Kompong-Speu, and in Battambang where a Chinese pastor from Hongkong led the congregation of about fifty. Other sects represented by missionaries in Cambodia include the Jehovah's Witnesses and the Seventh Day Adventists, but their congregations are very small.

and even the central market closed for three days, its only shut-down of the year (after remaining open day and night for five days to allow families to stock food). For a week before the event, extra stalls had been set up on the pavements to sell sweets and ritual articles. Calligraphers, working on the pavement, wrote black or gold characters on sheets of red paper, which were sold to be pasted over doors, down the sides of store-fronts, and in other conspicuous places to bring good fortune.

For most families, the New Year celebrations begin on *Dong-Jie*, the twenty-fifth day of the twelfth (or thirteenth) lunar month. On that day, the families of my Teochiu informants feasted on sweet dumplings called *tang-yuan*, after eating which each member of the family was considered to be one year older. Another feast was held on the eve of the New Year, and the next three days were spent visiting friends. For this visiting time, all the goods in the stores were covered with bright cloth, and flowering branches holding coloured lights were placed on the counters. Easy chairs were set around tables carrying sweets and tea (occasionally wine), and most of the shutters were closed across the front of the store, leaving a narrow doorway by which guests might enter.

During the first six days of the year a lion team called *Huang shao-shi* moved around the city with a great din, dancing in front of those stores and houses that had requested the dance and were willing to pay for it. (There are two such teams in Phnom-Penh, but only one was active during this week; it belongs to no sports club, but is an independent association that is called upon at special occasions such as New Year and the inauguration of a new building.[1])

Throughout the fortnight following New Year's Day, all the temples were crowded with women making sacrifices and throw-ing the fortune blocks. I saw a few men also in the temples at this time. An informant stated that many Chinese make a trip to visit the temple of *Bao-sheng Da Di* in the neighbouring town of

---

[1] The same lion team performed at the inauguration of the public ancestral hall (*gong-ci-tang*) at the Cantonese cemetery on 7 December 1962. It is possible that this team, like the other lion team, is sponsored by the *Lian-you* Mutual Aid Society, for the musical equipment it was using on both occasions was marked *Ren-de Shan Tang* (see chapter 7, p. 83). In the procession at *Yuan-Xiao*, however, this team formed part of the Cantonese cortège (see Appendix III); I did not remark what equipment it was using at that time.

Takhmau during this fortnight. This activity comes to a climax with *Yuan-Xiao*, on the fourteenth and fifteenth days of the first lunar month.

Yuan-Xiao

The celebration of *Yuan-Xiao* makes it the only festival of the year that publicly marks off the Chinese community from the rest of the population in the capital. At *Qing-Ming* all the activity occurs in the cemeteries, which are several miles from Phnom-Penh, but the 'procession of the gods' (*you-shen*) at *Yuan-Xiao* goes along all the main streets of the city, where great crowds of people observe its progress. The amount of organization necessitated by the celebration of *Yuan-Xiao* brings many Chinese associations into activity at this time. Temples, sports clubs, *hui-guan*, the *Lian-you* Society, lion and dragon teams, and musical clubs all participate in the procession and other activities at *Yuan-Xiao*.

In China, *Yuan-Xiao* was celebrated by the Hokkien and Teochiu, but it was not important to the Cantonese. De Groot gives an account of the celebration at Amoy that has many interesting features similar to the celebration in Phnom-Penh today, including spirit-possession and self-torture, but the massed procession of idols and mediums did not occur at Amoy (De Groot 1886, 124–45).

The celebrations I observed began on the evening of the thirteenth, when opera was presented before three of the temples: Teochiu, Cantonese, and Hokkien. Professional opera companies and the opera groups of sports clubs presented Teochiu, Cantonese Hokkien, and Peking opera for five or six nights on temporary stages constructed in the temple courtyards; the Teochiu had constructed their stage in a large vacant field near the temple because the courtyard itself is too small to hold the great crowds attracted by the opera.[1] The whole Chinese section of the city

[1] Because the opera at *Yuan-Xiao* is 'played for the gods', the Teochiu had constructed a temporary temple facing the stage, in which were placed the smaller idols from the temple. A similar construction was made in July 1963, when the Teochiu temple celebrated the completion of refurbishing, at which time two companies presented opera simultaneously on separate stages in the same field, and the temporary temple held no idols, only ornate paper gowns that were burned on the third day of the celebrations. This was a rare event that had not occurred for over a decade.

was crowded with people, visiting the cinemas, eating in the restaurants, or milling in the streets between temporary booths selling refreshments, sweets, fruit, and small manufactured articles.

The 'procession of the gods' takes place on both the fourteenth and fifteenth of the month. On the fourteenth at about noon the procession began to assemble on the street along the river (Quai Sisowath), beginning at the *Wu-bang hui-guan* Temple. Small cortèges from the various temples in the vicinity of Phnom-Penh came from all directions, many of them from Vietnamese areas. Each cortège included a sedan chair or a cart which carried an incense pot and frequently an idol under a wooden canopy; behind this canopy was a small wooden platform on which usually stood a medium, dressed in satin costume or in the bib, or 'stomacher', that Elliot describes as the costume of possessed mediums in Singapore (Elliot 1955, 51). Some mediums sat in chairs of nails or knife-blades, and one lay on a bed of nails; all had instruments of self-torture, such as swords, spiked balls on lengths of chain, or skewers through their cheeks (cf. *ibid.*, 51–6).

The mediums became possessed between noon and two o'clock, during which time many of them entered the *Wu-bang hui-guan* temple, where they were 'tested' by a master of ceremonies standing at the altar tables. Each medium who passed the 'test', which consisted of questioning and cracking a whip, was then led to the table, where he cut his tongue on a sword and licked blood onto charm papers (*fu*) for the spectators, who crowded every available space in the temple (cf. *ibid.*, 56 f.). By two o'clock, all the mediums (51) were in a state of possession, and the procession moved off. Exactly the same procedure was followed the next day, with many more mediums involved (82). The make-up of the procession is listed in Appendix III.

The procession followed the same route on both days. From the *Wu-bang hui-guan* temple, it went down the Quai Sisowath to the Royal Palace, where each medium got down from his chair or platform, cut his tongue at an altar before the main gate, and danced among exploding firecrackers, while policemen tried to hold back the crowds that pushed close to have a better view. From the Palace, the cortèges moved to the centre of the city, where they went up and down every street, twice circling the central market in the process. Although they were expected to follow a prescribed route, the procession cut across itself so often that the cortèges moved almost at random through the streets. The Hainanese cortège went its own way in order to visit each of the major restaurants and shirt stores, where the medium cut her tongue before an altar and danced among exploding fire-crackers. At ten-thirty, the last cortèges were still circling the market, and the streets were not quiet until midnight.

According to Vietnamese and Chinese friends, many of the cortèges were Vietnamese. A Chinese who helped to organize the procession each year stated that about seventy per cent of the mediums were Vietnamese, including several of the mediums representing Chinese temples. Despite this fact, however, the procession is recognized as a Chinese event in the city, for until several years ago, when Vietnamese spirit mediums began to join, it was only the Chinese who participated. Even today there is no Vietnamese representation among the groups that head the procession, nor do Vietnamese leaders participate in organizing the event. Clearly, their presence in the persons of mediums and their retinues represents an attempt by small groups of Viet-namese to take advantage of what is essentially a Chinese ritual.[1]

The procession serves not only to reinforce traditional Chinese cultural identity in the city; it also elicits activity from a great number of Chinese associations. Besides the eight non-Buddhist Chinese temples, four of which represent *hui-guan*, there were ten performing groups (music, dance, opera, lion, and dragon), the *Lian-you* Society, and about sixty-five companies represented in the procession.

The procession also necessitates coordination by a body standing over these associations. Several informants stated that there was an over-all organizing committee, and its existence was evidenced by at least two important features of the procession itself. The first is the presence of a few items – lanterns and banner at the beginning and fifty banners carried by identically uniformed girls – which represent the Chinese community as a whole rather than any sub-group of it. Second, the order of cortèges is far from haphazard. At the head was the Teochiu temple cortège, followed by a series of artistic groups and then the cortèges of four more

[1] Spirit-medium cults have existed in Annam for centuries. As early as 1631 European travellers mention them in Cochinchina (Durand 1959, 22). But informants agreed that Vietnamese mediums have been evident in the *Yuan-Xiao* procession at Phnom-Penh only during the last few years.

Chinese temples, interspersed with only four other cortèges. Then came thirty-three cortèges with male mediums (the last of which was the only Khmer-loeu in the procession) followed by all the cortèges of female mediums with the exception of the Hainanese. At the tail of the procession came the Hokkien and *Wu-bang hui-guan* cortèges. According to one of the organizers, the order is decided by lot, but it is clear that lot operates within categories rather than among all the participating groups. (The presence of a small number of other cortèges among those of the Chinese temples may be the result of queue-jumping, for I saw some astute jockeying for position before the procession started.) The Hokkien were in the penultimate position because of a dispute that almost caused them to withdraw entirely: by agreement between the organizers, the Hokkien were to have gone first this year, but the Teochiu usurped that position, claiming far greater numbers, and the Hokkien therefore decided to go at the end of the procession to distinguish themselves from the other Chinese temples.[1] It was traditional for the *Wu-bang hui-guan* Temple, with the 'most powerful' medium, to go last.

The fact that the municipal administration tolerates the event suggests that some form of representation has been made from the Chinese community, for the procession causes a great deal of noise and disrupts traffic throughout the business quarter of the city for two days. I was told that the Chinese pay what they call 'music tax' (*yue-shui*) before this event: a large sum of money to ensure government acquiescence. The amassing of this money must involve considerable organization.[2]

[1] An informant said that the Teochiu had 'bought' their place at the head of the procession, which makes one wonder who was in a position to sell it. When the Teochiu rationalized their claim to go first on the basis of greater numbers, the Hokkien retorted (inaccurately) that they represented an entire province of China, while the Teochiu were only from a single *xiang* [*sic*].

Another informant stated that the reason the Hokkien went last was that they finally agreed to participate too late to enter anywhere but at the end of the procession. This does not explain why they took the penultimate position on the second day as well, and I therefore prefer the explanation I present in the text. A friend told me that the Hokkien had always been in more favour with the Cambodian king, only the Hokkien medium being permitted to enter the actual palace precincts at *Yuan-Xiao*; in 1963 no medium entered the palace grounds.

[2] There is some evidence that the administration does more than acquiesce in the holding of the 'procession of the gods'. Several informants told me independently that high civil servants had approached the Chinese community several years ago when the Chinese had decided to discontinue the procession. While the more cynical hinted that this was because some officials were reluctant

Informants did not agree as to the composition of the organizing committee for the 'procession of the gods'. In answer to my queries as to who undertook the over-all organizational responsibilities, the following answers were given: (1) 'a committee of Teochiu billionaires'; (2) the Teochiu *hui-guan*; (3) the *Lian-you* Mutual Aid Society. Of these, the first seems the most probable, for either of the other associations would have great difficulty amassing the necessary money. Furthermore, the procession involves some consultation between the leaders of the five speech groups, and this suggests that some of the responsibility lies beyond the Teochiu community in a body of over-all leaders, which could be mustered by neither the Teochiu *hui-guan* nor the *Lian-you* Society.

A Chinese friend in Cambodia wrote me that the procession at *Yuan-Xiao* the following year (1964) was organized by a committee representing the entire Chinese community. However, the procession was not as elaborate as in 1963, when all my informants agreed they had never seen as great a celebration. My friend implied that the new economic measures (the nationalization of banking and foreign trade announced in December 1963) had dampened Chinese enthusiasm for the celebration.

CHINESE BUDDHIST TEMPLES

Non-Buddhist temples use the character *miao*, while Buddhist temples are called *si* or *tang*. Of the eight Chinese Buddhist temples in Phnom-Penh, two have resident monks, four have nuns, and the other two have only lay caretakers. All the temples represent Mahayana Buddhism. With the exception of one, all the temples have been built since 1947. The exception is a temple established twenty-five years ago and run by an elderly woman who earns her living by foretelling the future; although the woman claims to be a Buddhist and the iconography in the temple is clearly Buddhist, the monks and nuns in the other Chinese Buddhist temples are reluctant to recognize this temple as one of their number.

to forgo a rich source of gain, others suggested that the administration was concerned because of the danger of calamities, such as sickness and flooding, if it were not held. The fact that the main gate of the Royal Palace is an important point for ritual on the route of the procession indicates that the administration takes some interest in these rituals.

According to the monks in the most prosperous of these temples, there are not more than ten thousand Chinese Buddhists in Cambodia. They are to be found in every speech group, but are predominantly Teochiu; of the three monks and two nuns I met, both nuns and one monk are Teochiu, although all of them came to Cambodia from a monastery in Canton (as did the other two monks, who are from Kiangsi). All the temples are located in Chamcar Chen, that area of Phnom-Penh where the post-war Chinese immigrants (mostly Teochiu) built a new Chinese quarter.

The two temples attended by monks are both modern ferro-concrete buildings with elaborate images of the Buddha. In one, called the *Zhong-hua Zheng-jue Si*, the wooden image and gilded canopy were bought in Hongkong for over £500. A four-metre painted cement image of the Buddha stands in the centre of the other, the *Xi-fang Nian-fo She* Temple, the walls of which display the names of Chinese donors in painted plaster characters. It is obvious from these riches that the monks are able to collect substantial sums of money. But they hold no place among the secular leaders of the community, and the nuns, all of whom live in rather shoddy wooden temples, also have no status except in relation to their few adherents.

These Chinese Buddhist temples hold regular services on the first, eighth, fifteenth, and twenty-second days of the lunar month. No association unites the temples, nor indeed have the lay adherents of any of them formed an association. In short, the Chinese Buddhist temples appear to be isolates, standing apart from the mainstream of power relations in the community, and with little influence upon it.

As well as the Buddhist temples in Phnom-Penh, there is also a Chinese Buddhist temple in Takhmau, about twelve kilometres to the south. In Phnom-Penh itself, incense pots representing deceased Chinese are also found in a Vietnamese Buddhist temple, staffed by three priests, which stands on the property belonging to the Secretariat of the Five *Congrégations* on Ang Eng Street. It was endowed by a rich Chinese lady, Madam *Chen Guang-yu*, who was married to a Vietnamese, was widowed at an early age, and then proceeded to amass a fortune on the basis of her husband's modest capital. Before she died, at the round age of 100, she gave her property to the Chinese community on condition that it maintain the Vietnamese temple built by her husband. This

remarkable woman is memorialized by a plaque and a bust in the
building now serving as a detention house for prostitutes awaiting
trial.

According to several Chinese Buddhist priests and nuns, there
are two women's vegetarian halls in Phnom-Penh and a man's
hall in Kep that adhere to the Great Way of Former Heaven
(*Xian-tian Da Dao*). This religious sect has been described in
Singapore and China by Dr Marjorie Topley (Topley 1961 and
1963; Freedman and Topley 1961, 10 ff.). Unfortunately, I
became aware of the existence of these halls in Cambodia only
shortly before leaving and was therefore unable to investigate
them.

9

Economic Aspects of Chinese Community Life

When an anthropologist undertakes fieldwork in a developing country, he discovers that certain areas of social life are more difficult than others to investigate. When his subject is an ethnic minority like the Chinese, which holds an important position in the economy of the country yet includes many aliens, the examination of its economic aspects is extremely difficult, for neither government official nor Chinese merchant is willing to discuss the workings of a Chinese company, Chinese domination of a trade or sector, or the economic organization of the Chinese community as a whole. The analysis of economic problems cannot be undertaken solely on the basis of data provided by observation, for the quantities involved (particularly money) are seldom observable. In consequence, the data I have collected on the economic aspects of the Chinese community are far from full, and I therefore present them with some misgivings. What material I have points to one or two conclusions that are important to my main thesis, however, and for this reason it is worthwhile including a section on the economic organization of the community. The rôle of the Chinese in the Cambodian economy has been discussed elsewhere (W. Willmott 1967, 44–64).

The unit of the Chinese economy in Cambodia is the private company, usually owned by an individual family and passed from father to son. Each company owns or rents a store-front, in the main room of which business is transacted; in the back rooms and on the floors above live the family and employees. Often one company is engaged in several lines of business, such as manufacture, import-export, and wholesale; but almost every company retails as well: the store is the typical form of company among the Chinese in Phnom-Penh.

Under the *congrégations* the company was the unit of overseas

Chinese society in general. A new immigrant was usually attached
to a company until he was able to start on his own. It was companies that were represented on the committees of the *hui-guan*.
Indeed, the company took on such importance in establishing the
status of individuals that a man was often called by the name of
his company. For instance, the most famous Cantonese in recent
Cambodian history was Mr *Ye Pei-chen*, who was *chef de congrégation* from 1905 to 1929 and recognized spokesman for the whole
Chinese community, receiving many decorations from the King
during that time; both in conversation and in print, he was
called *Bao Xing* or *Ye Bao-xing* after the name of his company.
Today, traditionist (see below, pp. 115 f.) associations usually use
company names in lists of officers and members, while modernist
associations tend toward the use of personal names.

The personnel of the Chinese company in Phnom-Penh is
provided largely by the owning family itself. Children work in
the store when they are not in school or preparing lessons; a son
usually remains in the store until he becomes its owner, although
some leave to form their own or subsidiary companies. Occasionally a man will join the store of his wife's father.[1] If the family
is too small to staff the store, additional personnel may come from
among kinsmen. Some stores also hire two or three additional staff
as salesmen or accountants; these men live in the store and eat
with the family. Of the 208 Chinese stores in the sample of
households from the 1961 census in Phnom-Penh, thirty-nine
included hired personnel that were not kinsmen, while sixty-two
included kinsmen, who probably helped in the store, but no
non-kinsmen; the remaining 107 consisted of stem or nuclear
families. Shortly after the Sino-Japanese war, B. P. Groslier found
that Chinese households in Saigon included more non-kin than

[1] I was told by two Cantonese informants that it is common for a Teochiu to
live with his wife's family. Perhaps the practice so shocks Cantonese that they
overemphasize what may be a rare occurrence but one which to them would be
unthinkable except through some type of son-in-law adoption. I knew of one
case, that of a Teochiu lad from another city who had come to Phnom-Penh to
study. After his marriage to the daughter of his landlord – hastened by un-
avoidable circumstances related to his studies – he remained in Phnom-Penh to
complete his course of studies, and therefore the couple lived with the bride's
family. Eight of the thirty-five biographies of Teochiu businessmen in Phnom-
Penh refer to capital being supplied by the wife's family, and in several there is
the implication or statement that the man inherited the business of his wife's
father.

did Vietnamese, which suggested to him that the Chinese in Saigon had a more urban mentality than the Vietnamese (Groslier 1954, 10). In Phnom-Penh, non-relatives are often young men from the provinces who are making a start in the capital, and they find places through business relationships between their father's companies and firms in Phnom-Penh.

Within one store it is unusual to find persons from different speech groups. Even when hiring persons who are not kinsmen, a businessman is likely to seek individuals from his own speech group, even from his own district. One therefore finds that the entire personnel of a company usually speaks one Chinese language. The major exception to this pattern is found in the restaurants in Phnom-Penh, where a division of labour along ethnic lines apparently exists. Almost without exception, the restaurants are owned and managed by Hainanese, and the male personnel are also Hainanese: kitchen staff, waiters, accountants, and buyers. The female staff, however – waitresses and cashiers – are almost all Cantonese, and the cleaning staff, both men and women, are usually Khmer. In the three large restaurants owned by Cantonese, the entire staff is Cantonese with the exception of the Khmer cleaners.

Occupational specialization by speech groups is not as apparent as it is reported by informants to have once been. Only among the Hainanese, as I have already mentioned, does one find the entire speech group in a narrow range of occupations: restaurants and hotels, shirt manufactories and stores. The great preponderance of Teochiu among the Chinese population means that they predominate in almost every sphere of economic endeavour, with the following few exceptions: bakeries, which are all owned and staffed by Hakka; hardware, controlled by Hokkien; and those occupations monopolized by the Hainanese. I have the impression that Cantonese are still found in a disproportionate number in carpentry and mechanics, Hakka in dentistry and traditional pharmaceutics, but there are also many Teochiu in these occupations.

Most of the capital in Chinese businesses has come from the savings of the owner himself. In twenty-five of the fifty-one biographies collected from Chinese businessmen in Phnom-Penh, it is stated that initial capital came entirely from individual savings, many of the men working up to fifteen years as employees to save their investment. Capital may also come from kinsmen, either from a family member who has previously established his own business (ten cases) or from the parents of one's wife (nine cases).

Another method of raising capital is through the tontine, but the nature of tontine suggests that it is used to raise capital for speculation rather than for starting a man's first company. A businessman who urgently needs a large sum of money calls together nine or eleven others (tontines usually have ten or twelve members) who are willing to form a tontine with him. Each contributes an agreed amount at the first meeting, all of which goes to the organizer. The tontine then meets each month, at which time each member contributes the same amount, the total going to one of their number according to a predetermined formula.[1] By the end of the year, each member will have had at his disposal a large sum of money approximately equivalent to the total he paid in monthly instalments through the year. Although it is not possible to get an estimate of the amounts of capital raised by tontine in Phnom-Penh each year, informants asserted that the practice was common at all levels of Chinese society, with instalments ranging from ten to as high as 100,000 riels (two shillings to £1000).

In recent years, Chinese companies have looked abroad for capital, particularly to Hongkong and Singapore. Some have signed contracts to act as Cambodian agents for larger firms in one of these cities, and among import-export companies this has become a common way of financing business. This form of capitalization may depend on more universalistic relationships, for some businessmen may be dealing with large firms with which

---

[1] In Phnom-Penh several methods are used in tontines to choose the winner each time. It may be done simply by lot among those who have not yet won. More common in business tontines that involve large sums of money is a method of bidding whereby every member who has not yet won submits a closed bid stating the amount he would be willing to return to each member, the highest bidder receiving the sum. If a man needs money at that moment, he will enter a high bid; if he prefers to wait until later in the course of the tontine, he will enter a low bid. The amount bid may be returned to all members of the tontine or only to those who have not yet won, depending on what was decided at the start of the tontine. Large tontines are settled monthly at a feast, usually one that includes barbecued suckling pig as the main dish. The feast is provided by that evening's winner. The tontine is often called a 'cooperative loan society' in the literature on China. Different types of tontine in China are described by L. S. Yang 1952, 77 f., Simon 1868, and Doolittle 1866, 147-50.

they have no other connection. However, the question of economic ties between overseas Chinese in various parts of Southeast Asia has not yet been examined by anyone, so far as I know, and it is altogether possible that the economic relationships between Chinese in different countries are as particularistic as those upon which trust is based in any one country.[1]

Phnom-Penh has few Chinese trade unions or guilds. The only one for which I have positive evidence is the Association of Dental Technicians, who participated in the *Yuan-Xiao* procession with a dragon team and one of whose members was an organizer of the procession as a whole. I was told of the existence of a butchers' guild, strong evidence for which is provided by the announcements in the Chinese press that no meat would be butchered on October First, which is not a Cambodian holiday. A special event such as the visit of a Chinese dignitary may evoke *ad hoc* committees in various trades to assure an organized demonstration, but these committees disappear after the event. For instance, when President Liu Shao-chi of China visited Phnom-Penh, a committee, appointed by the over-all Chinese welcoming committee (see chapter 10, pp. 120 f.), organized the drapers to stand together with a banner of welcome; but there exists no continuing association of drapers. Informants mentioned guilds of motorcycle repairmen, teashop owners, restaurateurs, and goldsmiths, but I was not able to discover officers, offices, or press notices of any of these, and several informants denied that any of them existed.[2] No government licences have been issued for any such organizations. It appears, therefore, that the Chinese companies in Phnom-Penh are able to operate with a large amount of autonomy.

Whatever formal control exists over commercial affairs in Phnom-Penh is exercised by the government. A commercial code was promulgated in 1950 (Clairon 1962), which replaced the French code in force until that date. This code describes in detail

[1] Uchida (1956) does not discuss this question. It would be a difficult problem indeed to investigate, but one worth tackling by an economic anthropologist or an economist with some anthropological training.
[2] I do not consider the denial of the existence of guilds as strong negative evidence by itself, for the existence of various associations, the *hui-guan* for instance, was repeatedly denied to me by some informants.

It is possible that the *Lian-you* Mutual Aid Society began as a union of stevedores, for many of its original members were thus occupied; an association of stevedores now existing in Phnom-Penh is made up entirely of Khmer. References to guilds of restaurateurs and tea-shop owners may refer to the Hainanese *hui-guan*.

the requirements and procedures for business licences, for contracts, for bankruptcy, and for dealing with fraud. The Chamber
of Commerce of Cambodia, to which every business firm must
belong, acts as a quasi-governmental agency, undertaking many
administrative aspects of control, such as issuing permits and
assuring standards. A more direct control is maintained through
government agencies, the most important of which is the import-
export agency established following the nationalization of foreign
trade on 1 January 1964. Prior to that, the government was able
to control imports to some extent through the *Office National
des Changes* of the National Bank. Because the open market rate
for the riel was considerably lower than the rate fixed by law,
there was a strict control over the amount of exchange any
enterprise was permitted, and the categories of goods imported
with available dollars, francs, or other currencies, was determined
by the Ministry of Commerce.[1]

Two points emerge from this brief discussion of economic
organization. First, Chinese business operates primarily along
particularistic lines in Phnom-Penh; that is, economic relationships
are congruent with other social relationships that reinforce and
guarantee the economic transactions involved. But while this is
true within and between companies, it does not provide an
economic structure to the community, for the second conclusion
that emerges is the lack of over-arching economic associations or
formal mechanisms of control within the Chinese community.
There is a situation of relatively free competition that is controlled and regulated by the government. To what extent this
regulation lies outside the Chinese community will be discussed
in chapter 10.

[1] While the *déblocages* of official exchange were restricted to the purchase of
goods indicated by the Ministry of Commerce, the National Bureau of Exchange
(*Office National des Changes*) permitted exporters to retain a fraction of the
foreign currency earned through exports for their own use. These *EFac* funds,
as they were called (short for *Exportation – Frais-Accessoires*), could either be used
by the exporter himself or sold to importers to purchase luxury goods not permitted
in the allocations of official exchange: passenger automobiles, foreign foods,
cosmetics, etc. (see Chau Kon 1963, 92). This practice has been discontinued
since the end of 1963, a government agency now handling all legal imports.

10

Leadership in the Chinese Community in Phnom-Penh

The brief examination of contemporary Chinese social life presented in the last three chapters bears out what was said earlier: the Chinese community today is more open, both culturally and politically, than it was under the *congrégations*. Community boundaries are not so clearly drawn, and not as many aspects of community life are under the control of its leaders. In this situation, Chinese voluntary associations take on a definitive rôle, for participation in them becomes the main criterion of being Chinese. The associations also become the principal units in the political structure.

While leadership must be less formal today than it was in the *congrégations*, there are still areas of Chinese society in which leadership is necessary or can operate. Certainly, Chinese control over recruitment to the community has disappeared, for immigration is no longer a factor. It is also true that economic organization is more diffuse today and lies outside the control of the Chinese associations, if not beyond the influence of some Chinese leaders. However, the main ritual events demand as much coordination as they did before, if not more. Education, still predominantly a speech-group matter so far as the 'public' schools are concerned, involves the maintenance and expansion of school organization, although matters of standards and supervision have been taken over largely by government. Finally, the associational structure itself generates problems that demand leadership.

One important area of power that appears to have diminished considerably for community leaders is the mediation of disputes. Disputes arising between members of the same association are no doubt dealt with in some way by that association. But when there are many functionally specific associations, the nature of disputes that they can handle is probably not of importance to the community. Two members of a sports club might take a dispute about rights over the club chess set to the executive committee, but it would seldom happen that two businessmen disputing over access to a specific market, or two men disputing over a woman, would belong to the same sports club. The major exceptions are the continuing Hainanese and possibly Hakka and Hokkien *hui-guan*, since each of these associations comprises most of the businessmen of its speech group. The *Lian-you* Mutual Aid Society might be another exception, although it should be noted that the absence of many businessmen from this association would limit the disputes it could handle to those arising between individual workers. Major disputes with implications for community organization apparently can no longer be handled within the Chinese community. I say 'apparently' because it is possible that the leadership structure discussed in this chapter is able to deal with some kinds of disputes, but I have no evidence on this point. Even if this is so, it must be borne in mind that a Chinese is no longer forced to abide by the decisions of these leaders, for he can go to court without endangering his status in the country.

Many disputes today may go unsolved, causing added strain within the Chinese community. During my stay in Phnom-Penh, a dispute arose that might have been settled by the over-all reconciliation commission had the conflict arisen under the *congrégation* system. A group of Chinese attempted to displace the Chinese lessee of a petrol station by suggesting to the British petrol company that he had broken his contract in selling Russian-built automobiles at the station. The lessee claimed to be within his rights because the contract made no mention of selling automobiles, but he could appeal to no body for mediation. He therefore had to resort to self-help to secure his position, and published an advertisement in one of the French language newspapers extolling the virtues of the director of the petrol company. This move was not thought to have guaranteed a renewal of his contract, however, which was to expire in 1964. No settlement to this dispute was possible in the contemporary situation, for it involved no action that could be taken to courts and no other medium was available.

METHOD OF ANALYSIS

No one undertaking a study of community leadership can ignore Professor Skinner's analysis of the political structure of the Chinese community in Thailand (Skinner 1958). Through painstaking research and sophisticated analysis, Skinner has shown how the various business and non-profit associations are woven together by interlocking boards of directors to produce a network of associations through which the various blocs of leaders are able to control much of Chinese community life in Thailand.

Except in the matter of scale, the community under discussion here resembles in most respects that studied by Skinner. One is safe in assuming, therefore, that the patterns of leadership are also similar. No attempt will be made here to parallel Skinner's work, for the data I have gathered on leaders are inadequate for such an intensive analysis. I was not able to undertake extensive interviewing, both because of insufficient time and because of the unwillingness of Chinese leaders to meet me. Those leaders to whom I spoke confined the discussion to situations past and were reluctant to discuss contemporary questions. The data therefore come primarily from newspaper articles and advertisements in the Chinese press, from lists of officers, and from numerous chats with informants who were not themselves leaders in the community. I have lists or partial lists of officers for the following Chinese associations in Phnom-Penh: the Chinese Hospital Committee, all four *hui-guan* (Teochiu, Hokkien, Hainanese, and Hakka), nine sports clubs, the *Lian-you* Mutual Aid Society, seven clan associations, six locality associations, all five cemetery committees, five 'public' schools, and three private schools. I also have lists of previous boards of the hospital and several 'public' schools. Some difficulty in identifying leaders resulted from the fact that some associations listed companies while others listed individuals, but many of these were matched through the Hospital Committee lists and various directories, as well as through informants. The most serious gap is lack of information on the economic power structure.

Because of these considerations, this chapter focuses primarily upon what Skinner calls the 'organizational structure' of the Chinese community (Skinner 1958, 200), but which I prefer to call the associational structure:[1] that is, the relationships between

---

[1] The term 'organizational structure' is an anomaly to any student of Professor Firth (e.g. Firth 1951, 35–6; Firth 1955)! It is clear from its context that the term used by Skinner refers to the structure of associations in Thailand (Skinner 1958, 200–8).

the various associations within the community, in this case ignoring companies. This will provide the basis for a description of the structure of leadership and power.

If the discussion were limited to the political structure of the Chinese community in isolation, the lack of information on economic associations would be somewhat less important than one might suppose, for economic power lies primarily outside the Chinese political structure. Nevertheless, the thorough analysis of the associational structure would certainly entail more knowledge than I possess of the Chinese financial and trade groups. For this reason, the reader should be aware that Skinner's terms are used here without the operational rigour of definition they were given in his study; they are used to suggest the presence of a pattern, albeit based on impressionistic material.

An opportunity to examine the organization of leadership in the Chinese community was provided by the visit of President Liu Shao-chi to Cambodia in May 1963. In order to ensure an orderly and enthusiastic reception for the President of the People's Republic of China, the leaders of the Chinese community set up at a moment's notice an elaborate structure of committees that involved a total of almost eighty people from every speech group and many associations (these committees will be discussed in more detail in a later section). Altogether, information was collected from various sources on more than two hundred leaders.

The over-all pattern that emerges from these data is of a closely-knit network of associations, with interlocking leaders forming the links between them and arranging them into a rough hierarchy of power. This hierarchy of associations in a limited sense replaces the hierarchy of types of leaders within the *hui-guan* under the *congrégation* system.

It should be noted that the distinction between political and administrative leaders can no longer be made (except in analysing aspects of the leadership rôle), for today every Chinese leadership position has aspects of both administrative duties and policy-making. Because the Chinese come under the jurisdiction of Cambodian law, there are today no Chinese leaders with the power to impose their policies on unquestioning followers. To put it another way, the sanctions of power of Chinese leaders today lie within the Chinese community; every leader must win his following in competition with other aspiring leaders, for no Chinese is obliged by law to follow a particular leader or to participate in a particular association. Conversely, in no association is power so concentrated as to produce a category of administrative leaders who cannot themselves influence policy. Today the leaders of any Chinese association are able to initiate policy, even to establish new associations, if they can muster sufficient followers.

In this situation, the power of a particular leader depends on three structural variables: the number of associations in which he holds office, their size, and their nature. This last variable, types of associations, needs some exposition.

TYPOLOGY OF ASSOCIATIONS

From the description of associations and their activities presented in the last chapters, it is possible to abstract a typology that clearly differentiates, at least among the Teochiu majority, two kinds of association. The criterion of this typology is the orientation of associational activity, which in turn relates to the constituency of recruitment. On this basis, I shall distinguish between traditionist and modernist associations and then present an intermediate category. The term 'traditionist' is preferred to 'traditional' because these associations are not necessarily traditional in the sense of being associations found in pre-contemporary China. It is their orientation rather than their existence that is traditional.

1. *Traditionist Associations*

The traditionist associations in the Chinese community in Phnom-Penh are those oriented toward traditional Chinese values. They appeal to loyalties that were salient in China thirty years ago, when most of Cambodia's present Chinese immigrants still lived there. This category includes the clan and locality associations, the cemetery committees of each speech group, the Teochiu *hui-guan*, the opera societies and other performing groups.

The membership of these associations consists primarily of older Chinese who were born in China: they are moral sojourners in that their values are oriented more toward China than toward Cambodia. Few of the youth are interested in activities sponsored by these associations, for the criteria of recruitment do not inspire their loyalty. The older generation of Cambodia-born also have less concern than do the immigrants for this kind of association.

The leaders of traditionist associations also come from among the immigrants. In the main, they are businessmen who are not very wealthy but who have succeeded at least in establishing their own companies and therefore have some standing in the Chinese community. For them, being Chinese involves carrying out the necessary rituals for the deceased and the gods, and this (as well as desire for power) forms their motivation for leading these associations. Their power is, in any case, limited, for these associations appeal only to a small minority, and many of them are active only at *Qing-Ming* and equivalent festivals.

2. *Modernist Associations*

The modernist associations are those whose activities are oriented toward more universalistic values. They include the Chinese Hospital, the sports associations, and the schools. In none of these associations is there a manifest appeal to loyalties narrower than the Chinese community as a whole. Their functions are specific but relate more to life than to ritual – and to life in Cambodia rather than in traditional China. They therefore attract youth and Chinese born in Cambodia, although many immigrants also belong to these associations.

Leadership for the modernist associations is by no means limited to Chinese born in Cambodia; quite the contrary, many of them are immigrants.[1] In general, they are wealthier than leaders of traditionist associations. Motivation for accepting positions as advisers in sports clubs has to do primarily with a desire for power, for many of the manifest activities of these clubs do not appeal to older men. They do, however, organize cultural events that serve as a form of ritual to mark off the Chinese community as a whole. Chinese schools also help, of course, to perpetuate distinctions between Chinese and Cambodian populations.

Of the fifty-five officers of Teochiu traditionist associations on whom I have information, only thirty-three belonged to the

---

[1] The leaders of the sports clubs referred to in this and subsequent paragraphs are the advisers rather than the elected executives. The latter bodies are made up of young people whose influence is limited to the clubs themselves and who do not usually hold positions in other associations in the structure.

Hospital Committee, while all officers of modernist associations belonged to this body. I know of only three officers of Teochiu traditionist associations who were also officers of modernist associations; only five others participated in the *ad hoc* committees to prepare for the visit of President Liu Shao-chi. A separation between traditionist and modernist leaders in the Teochiu community is therefore suggested by the data, although it is possible that better information would indicate more overlap.

Among the Cantonese, the data show more overlap between the leaders of the two categories of associations. Of the fifty-seven leaders of Cantonese traditionist associations for whom I have information, forty-two are members of the Hospital Committee, and twelve of these are officers in modernist associations, including the *ad hoc* committees. This greater overlap may result both from the smaller scale of organization among the Cantonese and from the density of leadership, if one may thus characterize the relatively larger number of Cantonese associations and hence leaders.

In the three smaller speech groups, the distinction between traditionist and modernist associations can be made only at the bottom of the associational hierarchy, between cemetery committees on the one hand and sports clubs and schools on the other. All these associations are politically subordinate to the three *hui-guan*, which fall into an intermediate category.

3. *Traditionist-Modernist Associations*

Besides the Hokkien, Hainanese, and Hakka *hui-guan*, the *Lian-you* Mutual Aid Society can also be described as an association with both traditionist and modernist orientations, as can the one sports club that focuses on Chinese boxing. With the exception of the sports club, all these associations originally appealed to narrow, traditional loyalties, and only in the case of the *Lian-you* Society has the appeal later broadened. On the other hand, all these associations participate in the political life of the community at a higher level than do the Teochiu and Cantonese traditionist associations. Furthermore, four of these associations contain both traditionist and modernist associations as subsidiary bodies. And finally, the membership of these associations includes both immigrant and local-born, both China-oriented and Cambodia-oriented, both young and old, both rich and poor. In short, these associations fall between the two categories I have defined.

ASSOCIATIONAL STRUCTURE

Although the three categories of associations described above cannot be ranked into a neat hierarchy, nevertheless there are some hierarchical characteristics associated with the typology. Traditionist associations, as one would expect from the description, are to be found only at the bottom of the associational structure, few of them exercising power over other associations and those few only over other traditionist associations. The traditionist-modernist associations occupy the middle reaches of the structure together with a large number of modernist associations. Modernist associations are found at every level of the hierarchy.

The apex of the Chinese associational structure in Phnom-Penh consists of the managing board of the Chinese Hospital, whose fifteen members are elected by the Hospital Committee every second year. These men are the most powerful in each speech group, and between them they participate in the leadership of at least twenty other associations, probably twice that number, including all the *hui-guan*, the *Lian-you* Society, the largest school, and the three largest sports clubs. That they are the recognized leaders of the Chinese community is evidenced by the fact that eleven of the fifteen, with the addition of only one other leader, 'represented the Chinese community' in presenting good wishes to the Royal Delegate to Phnom-Penh at Cambodian New Year (*Mian-Hua Ri-bao*, 16 April 1963, p. 1).

The elections for the Hospital Board also suggest that this body comprises the recognized leaders of the community. Thirty-six candidates were nominated for the Board, of whom thirteen were Teochiu, eight Cantonese and five from each of the other three speech groups. The average vote of the fifteen successful candidates was 459, with a spread from 356 to 545, while the average vote of the other twenty-one candidates was 33, with a spread from 6 to 151.[1] Furthermore, there was complete continuity from the previous Board elected two years before, and only three of the eight alternates changed in the same period.

The head of the Hospital Board was a revered gentleman of ninety-one, Mr Tan Soeun Hoa (*Chen Shun-he*), who was once

[1] The average vote of the eight alternates was 65, with a spread from 16 to 151; the average vote of the thirteen unsuccessful candidates was 14 with a spread from 6 to 34.

chef of the Teochiu *congrégation* and served in 1963 as the elder statesman and spokesman for the Chinese community as a whole. (Mr Tan, however, was not part of the New Year delegation to the Royal Delegate, and he received only the second highest vote in the Board elections of 1963.)

A diagram of the structure of voluntary associations in the Chinese community is presented in Figure 2. The heavy lines

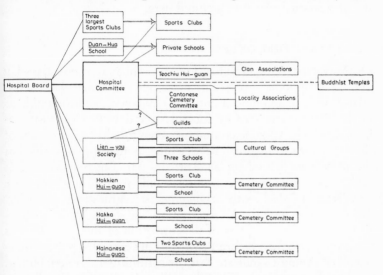

FIGURE 2

represent relationships of formal subordination, such as that between a *hui-guan* and its cemetery committee, while the light lines represent relationships through interlocking leaders. An impression of relative power is suggested by the positioning of associations or categories of associations, those at the right being less powerful than those at the left. (The lines are not as rigorously defined as those in any of Skinner's diagrams of the associational structure of Thailand's Chinese community; Skinner 1958, 202–5.) The arrows indicate lines of influence without interlocking leaders.

Special mention should be made of two isolates, only one of which appears in Figure 2. The Chinese Buddhist temples are linked in the diagram by a dotted line with the Hospital Committee to indicate that some of the principal donors to these temples are also members of the Hospital Committee. The affairs of the temples, however, are run by the resident nuns, monks, or caretakers, who have little to do with the political structure of the Chinese community, as already indicated in chapter 8. The other isolate is the system of associations whose leaders are sympathetic to the Kuomintang, which will be discussed in a later section. It does not appear in Figure 2 because there was almost no overlap between its leaders and those operating within the associational structure pictured here.

THE STRUCTURE OF LEADERSHIP

On May First 1963, President Liu Shao-chi arrived on a five-day visit to Cambodia. For security reasons the actual date of his arrival was not announced until the day before, and the residents of the city had been aware for only five days that the visit was imminent. The Chinese community therefore had a minimum of time in which to organize its welcome. A meeting was called at the *Duan-Hua* School on 28 April by Mr Tan Soeun Hoa, at which an organizing committee and sub-committees were established to deal with arrangements, registration, publicity, finance, liaison with the Administration, and so on. The announcement in the Chinese press of the formation of these committees came only two days before President Liu's arrival. I present these details of timing to indicate that the committees were established to provide maximum efficiency, and were therefore in all probability composed of the leaders with real power in the community.

The president of the welcoming committee was Mr Tan, head of the Hospital Board. Of the five vice-presidents – one representing each speech group – four were vice-presidents of the Hospital Board; the fifth was an unsuccessful candidate at the Board elections but had led the New Year delegation to the Royal Delegate. Of the twenty-two officers of the committee, forming the organizing committee and the heads and assistant heads of the sub-committees, five were members of the Hospital Board, and ten more were alternates, candidates, or scrutineers at the Board elections. Only one member of the Hospital Board did not participate in the welcoming committee in any way. These facts are summarized in Table 4.

It is evident that the leaders who took charge in this emergency

TABLE 4. Congruency in Leadership of Chinese Hospital
and Welcoming Committee

| Hospital Officers | President Vice-Pres. | Welcoming Committee Officers | | | |
		Committee Officers	Committee Members	Total Participating	Not Participating
Hospital board (15)	5	5	4	14	1
Alternates (8)		3	4	7	1
Candidates and election scrutineers (20)	1	7	5	13	7
No position in hospital		7	37	44	
Totals	6	22	50	78	

affecting the entire Chinese community were to be found primarily in the Hospital Board. Among these fifteen men, it is not possible for me to determine an apex leader. Mr Tan was too old to be an effectively powerful force. Although some idea of differential influence might be gained from analysing the total votes for each member in the elections to the Board, there is little correlation between these votes and the relative position of each man in the welcoming committee for President Liu. Furthermore, the fact that the constitution of the hospital requires a certain number of board members from each speech group militates against votes being a useful indicator of power, except in differentiating between members of the same speech group. The number and size of the other associations in which these men hold leading positions would be a more accurate indication of relative power, but my data are incomplete on this point.

The important conclusion emerging from this section is the close congruency between emergency and associational leadership in the Chinese community. Not only is the same body of leaders involved in both the on-going and the emergency associations, but their relative positions are somewhat similar in both situations.

It must be pointed out that the nature of the emergency demanded the participation of those leaders who had contact with the network of associations forming the political structure of the community: it did not demand leaders in the economic sphere, for no economic policy was involved. The congruent leadership

and associational structures that emerge from this analysis therefore take no account of the economic leaders in the city, who are
Sino-Cambodian rather than Chinese.[1]

THE PRO-KUOMINTANG ASSOCIATIONS

Before Cambodian independence, the Kuomintang took an active
part in the leadership of the Chinese community in Phnom-Penh,
not only through the *hui-guan*, but also through various other
associations that they directly sponsored, such as trade unions and
reading clubs, which have since disappeared. With the end of
the *congrégations* and the recognition of mainland China by the
Cambodian government, Kuomintang influence shrank. Rather
than participating as a minority clique within the main associational structure of the Chinese community, those leaders who
remained sympathizers to the Kuomintang developed a separate
structure of associations. In 1962–63, this structure included two
or three sports associations, several schools, and one daily newspaper, the *Xin Bao*. The newspaper has since ceased publication.
The right-wing private schools looked to the Cantonese school
for leadership in matters of curriculum and policy. Both schools
and sports clubs recruited their advisers from among right-wing
businessmen.

The associational structure comprising these associations sympathetic to the Kuomintang is diagrammed in Figure 3. Because no
Nationalist Party exists as a legal entity, the rectangle formed of
dotted lines at the centre of the diagram represents the group of
businessmen who used to be prominent members of the Kuomin-

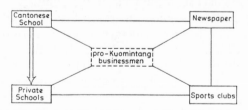

FIGURE 3. Relationships between pro-Kuomintang associations
in Phnom-Penh, 1963

[1] For a discussion of the Sino-Cambodian élite and its influence on economic
policy in Cambodia, see the final chapter of my book, *The Chinese in Cambodia*
(W. Willmott 1967, 98–101).

tang. The diagram is drawn to indicate no hierarchy of associations but merely the presence of associational links. Very few leaders and associations are involved, and relationships other than interlocking officers are therefore more crucial to this structure than they were in the structure pictured in Figure 2. Indeed, one might avoid the word 'structure' in this case, for we are dealing here with a form of social organization that has little formal reality and may have very little permanence.

For obvious reasons, pro-Kuomintang leaders did not participate in the committees established to organize the welcome for President Liu Shao-chi. An emergency of much smaller dimensions but affecting these leaders occurred on 19 February 1963, when the editor of the *Xin Bao* was assaulted by unknown assailants (*Xin Bao*, 20 February 1963, p. 1). This event occasioned no meetings to my knowledge other than dyadic consultations between some of the leaders.[1] No structure of leadership was apparent within the group of pro-Kuomintang associations, except that the two apex leaders – the ex-*chefs* of the Cantonese and Teochiu *congrégations* – can be identified.

It is interesting that the Kuomintang associations do not include any of the traditionist associations. It may appear paradoxical that associations which are conservative in tradition are not right-wing in their political orientation. Traditionist leaders are oriented toward China, and that it is now under communist control does not deter them, for their loyalty is essentially a-political, based upon ties to the motherland rather than on political convictions.

To state that there were no links whatsoever between this small group of associations and the main associational structure of the Chinese community would be distorting the facts. There

[1] Those Chinese sympathetic to the Kuomintang were in opposition to the main lines of Cambodian foreign policy at the time, and therefore they were under constant police surveillance; they did not hold large meetings for fear of being accused of plotting against the government. The fact that the assault on the editor of the *Xin Bao* passed entirely unnoticed by either the police or the press (with the exception of the *Xin Bao* itself) indicates the isolated position of Kuomintang sympathizers in Cambodia at that time.

According to several well-informed sources, an attempt had been planned on the life of President Lui Shao-chi and Prince Sihanouk as they drove from the airport on 1 May 1963; several local Kuomintang leaders were implicated in the plot and subsequently arrested (AKP, no. 4435, 10 May 1963; *Réalités Cambodgiennes*, no. 355, 10 May 1963, p. 4).

appeared to be no overlap of leaders between the two, for I know of no officer of a pro-Kuomintang association who is also an officer of an association in the main structure. There were pro-Kuomintang businessmen in the Hospital Committee, however, and several of them were in positions of economic prominence that gave them some purchase on other businessmen who did not share their political convictions. Nevertheless, the striking fact is the great separation between pro-Kuomintang and other leaders in the Chinese community, a separation that is enabled by two contingencies of the Cambodian situation. One is the situation of relatively cordial relations with the majority population, which allows political splits to persist within the Chinese community by providing no threat against which all Chinese need unite. The second fact is that Chinese associations lack economic power in the nation, and political divisions between them therefore have little effect on the opportunities of their leaders to amass wealth.

THE STRUCTURE OF POWER

The political structure discussed in this chapter represents the organization of power in a field that excludes at least two important areas of political activity: economic decisions lie primarily outside it, and many disputes are no longer settled by it. Except at a very low level, economic policy is generated, applied, and amended by the government and by the Sino-Cambodian upper class, and the less wealthy Chinese merchants have slight influence upon these groups. Disputes the parties to which are not members of the same association are settled in court. The issues dealt with by the Chinese political structure are those aspects of the polity that have to do with the organization of activities within the Chinese community, with its attempts to maintain its identity, and those that are generated by the associational structure itself. In short, they have to do primarily with the organization of ritual and with the maintenance and establishment of relative status within the Chinese voluntary associations.

Around these issues has grown up a structure of leadership based on the web of interlocking officers that unites all the associations (with the exception of the pro-Kuomintang associations and the Buddhist temples) into one network. This network can be described as a hierarchy of associations because of the fact that those leaders with the most power are concentrated in a small number of associations, at the head of which stands the Board of the Chinese Hospital.

The question that must now be dealt with is the structure of power within the Chinese community: that is, the presence of blocs among leaders, groupings of subordinates around key leaders who integrate them into the larger network of power. I have already disclaimed the ability to distinguish relative power among the fifteen members of the Hospital Board, but it is clear that this body unites the key leaders of several power blocs.

The leaders of each of the three smaller speech groups form blocs: the Hainanese, the Hokkien, and the Hakka; in each case the key leader, who links his bloc to the Hospital Board, is the chairman of his *hui-guan*. Among the Hainanese, the second member of the Board is not an important leader; among both Hakka and Hokkien, the second members have important links beyond the Chinese community, but are not prominent in the associations of their speech groups.

A fourth bloc includes men from various speech groups who lead the *Lian-you* Society and some of the major sports associations. Under the control of this bloc is a large number of lesser Teochiu leaders who do not themselves form a bloc. Neither do the leaders of the Teochiu traditionist associations form a bloc, but appear relatively isolated from each other.

There seems to be no bloc of Cantonese leaders, although some Cantonese belong to the fourth block described above. No bloc emerged from the Cantonese *hui-guan*, for it disintegrated more thoroughly than did any other because of the split between pro-Kuomintang elements (including the *chef*) and the others. Furthermore, the Cantonese do not count any of the richest Chinese in Cambodia among them, probably because Cantonese wealth was concentrated in Saigon rather than Phnom-Penh (see W. Willmott 1967, 47 and 60).

The relations between these blocs and the bloc of powerful Sino-Cambodian élite does not proceed through the Hospital Board, but directly from each bloc. This is a further indication that the Hospital Board brings together leaders from each bloc only for aspects of polity that are not related to economic issues, and that the political structure I have described relates to aspects of power that are therefore tangential to the most important questions affecting the Chinese.

What, then, remains of the *congrégation* system in the political structure of the Chinese community in Phnom-Penh today? Virtually nothing. Most of the previous *chefs* have been deposed as leaders (except in the relatively unimportant Kuomintang associational structure). The status of *chef* has itself disappeared, and with it the definition of the speech groups into separate power blocs. Although three of the five power blocs described here are contained within the three smaller speech groups, this cannot be considered a legacy of the *congrégations*, for there is a similar situation in Bangkok, where minority speech groups also provide power blocs (Skinner 1958, 211).

In place of a political structure composed of blocs representing discrete speech groups and integrated only through the topmost leaders of each, there is today a far more complicated structure, with power relationships developing between speech groups at various levels and through a multiplicity of associations. Most important of all, there is today a bloc composed of men who are at the same time both Chinese *and* Cambodian, and who are in positions of power over important aspects of Chinese community life without themselves participating in the leadership of the associational structure. Today's most powerful leaders not only transcend the *congrégations*: they transcend the Chinese community itself.

Chinese Social Organization in Smaller Towns

The discussion thus far has dealt almost exclusively with the Chinese community in Phnom-Penh. When asked about Chinese communities in places other than the capital, several of my informants replied that the *hui-guan* organization existing within the *congrégation* system was still functioning in many towns. An assistant who visited most of the provincial cities and towns on my behalf reported that in these towns the Chinese still spoke of the principal leader as *bang-zhang*, the Chinese word for *chef de congrégation*. In order to examine Chinese social organization in a small town, I spent a month in Siemréap, as well as undertaking some research into its history and demography. Although it is in some respects atypical, a discussion of the Chinese community in Siemréap, both during the French period and today, can serve as a useful indication of how Chinese society is structured elsewhere in Cambodia. In the final section of this chapter, I shall indicate how some other communities differ from that in Siemréap today.

THE FRENCH PERIOD

Siemréap was one of those regions where all the Chinese were grouped into a single *congrégation* regardless of speech groups, and the *hui-guan* therefore took on a somewhat different form from those in Phnom-Penh. It was known as the *wu-bang gong-so* (association of five *bang*), although, so far as I could determine, it was not internally segmented into associations based on speech groups.

Prior to the Sino-Japanese war, the Chinese population of Siemréap numbered only several hundreds, for there was little trade in the area before the ruins of the Angkorean cities became a major tourist attraction. The first Chinese settlers were Hokkien, but throughout the French period Cantonese and later Teochiu moved to Siemréap, many coming via Bangkok. According to the gravestones in the Chinese cemetery, about half the Teochiu were from *Jie-yang*, while two-thirds of the Cantonese came from *Dong-guan*. All were engaged in trade and handicrafts in and around the market, buying fish from Vietnamese fishermen and rice from Khmer peasants and retailing various goods in exchange.

A temple had been built in 1893 by the early Hokkien settlers, but it ceased to be the headquarters of the *hui-guan* after the new market with its surrounding brick stores was built some time before 1920.[1] From then on, the store of the *chef* became the *hui-guan* office. The *chef* seldom changed, the rule of four *chefs* spanning the entire period from 1907 (when Cambodia regained Siemréap from Siam) to 1958.

No *bang-hui* was elected in Siemréap, the number of merchants being small enough so that general meetings could conduct the business of the *hui-guan*. Elections for the *chef* were advertised to all members of the *congrégation* (i.e. all Chinese in Siemréap) as the law demanded, but in fact the electors were limited to those Chinese with business houses. Those operating market stalls as well as workers, employees, and pedlars did not vote. Rich and poor informants alike explained to me that this limitation was justified because the *hui-guan* was concerned with spending money donated only by the merchants, for unlike those in Phnom-Penh the *hui-guan* was not supported by a universal levy.

The *chef* served as general secretary of the *hui-guan*, and in fact his duties were much broader than those of his counterparts in Phnom-Penh. No committees were appointed, but the *chef* himself supervised the cemetery, looked after welfare matters, and ran the school. He had close relations with the residency, for the administrative community of Siemréap was small enough that he could be consulted on many matters of government in the district. He also attended social events on festive occasions and receptions organized by the *Résident* for visiting dignitaries.

From his connections with the administration as well as from his individual supervision of the *hui-guan*, the *chef* was able to wield more personal power than did the *chefs* in Phnom-Penh, who relied on their fellow merchants to a much greater extent.

[1] The market and its surrounding stores is mentioned by Beersky, who visited Siemréap in 1920–22 (Beersky 1923, 30).

Usually the *chef* was the wealthiest Chinese in town, and probably had some power in controlling trade. Furthermore, there was no reconciliation commission, the *chef* himself acting as arbiter for disputes within the community.

Although there are some differences in particular points, the picture presented here of the Chinese community in Siemréap applied generally to most smaller towns in Cambodia. Interviews indicated that in most towns of one *congrégation* the *chef* had great personal power, was usually the wealthiest man in the community, and had frequent interaction with the local *Résident*. Most of these men spoke French or learned it in office.

An important exception to this general picture of rural organization was to be found in Kampot Province, for here the specialization of the Hainanese in the production of pepper meant that the *hui-guan* operated as a guild of pepper planters besides providing the functions of welfare, education, public ritual, and political organization. In these circumstances, the *hui-guan* took on much more significance in relation to the *chef*, who acted, much like the *chefs* in Phnom-Penh, as a leader of a committee rather than as a personal ruler of the Chinese community. In Kompong-Trach, the centre of the pepper-planting area at that time, the Hainanese *hui-guan* (there was a second *congrégation*, composed almost entirely of Teochiu but also including Cantonese, Hokkien, and Hakka) developed the type of committee structure that was found in Phnom-Penh, with administrative positions of various kinds; the *sous-chef* (my informant) acted for many years as the French-speaking agent of the *hui-guan*, with considerable administrative power despite the fact that he was not a wealthy man. Although it might be argued that the comparative complexity of the Hainanese *hui-guan* in Kompong-Trach resulted merely from the difference in scale (there were about two thousand Hainanese under its jurisdiction in 1930), *hui-guan* of comparable sizes in Pursat, Mongkol-borei, and Maung were closer to the pattern described above for Siemréap than to that of Kompong-Trach. Unfortunately I have no information on the Teochiu *hui-guan* in Kompong-Trach, which included no pepper planters and would therefore test the suggestion that its economic functions determined the complex structure of the Hainanese *hui-guan* in the same town.

In neither Siemréap nor Kompong-Trach, nor in any other

community organized into a single *congrégation*, were there alternative associations to the *hui-guan* during the French period. As in Phnom-Penh, so in the smaller centres the *hui-guan* monopolized all political power and served adequately the various functions of community organization. In Siemréap and similar centres, this meant that in effect one man organized and controlled the whole community; such men were not unlike the Chinese 'rajas' that ruled the smaller communities of Java. Although the *chefs* in Phnom-Penh were certainly powerful men, their authority was limited by the necessity of relying on the other wealthy merchants in their speech groups. Where there was a ruler in the smaller Chinese communities during the French period, there was a ruling class in the Chinese community of Phnom-Penh.

CONTEMPORARY CHINESE SOCIAL ORGANIZATION IN SIEMRÉAP

In 1963, the town of Siemréap had a population of about eleven thousand, of whom about thirteen hundred were Chinese.[1] Of these, about half were Teochiu, another quarter Cantonese, and the remainder primarily Hokkien, with very few Hakka or Hainanese.[2]

Several factors contributed to the rapid growth of the town after the end of the war, not the least of which was the great increase in the number of tourists visiting the nearby ruins of Angkorean cities. The growth of the Cambodian provincial administration, the establishment of an army camp, and a small amount of American aid to irrigation in the area have also produced some increase in the size of the urban population and in the amount of trade in the town.

The Chinese community in Siemréap is culturally less clearly defined than that of Phnom-Penh. By this I mean that a greater proportion of the Chinese in Siemréap have adopted aspects of Khmer culture, and it is consequently more difficult for the observer to determine which individuals are and which are not

[1] The 1961 census gives the population of the municipality of Siemréap as 10,230. Several areas of the town extend beyond the legal limits of the municipality, however, and there had of course been some growth in population during the two years between the census and my research there.

[2] The Chinese community in Siemréap included about seven families of Hakka (thirty individuals) and two families of Hainanese.

Chinese. In comparison with Phnom-Penh, the samples from the 1961 census show that twice as great a proportion of the Chinese in Siemréap were returned as Cambodian citizens, and twice as great a proportion gave Khmer as their mother tongue. Furthermore, while in Phnom-Penh only one Chinese in fifteen was married to a Cambodian, the comparable ratio in Siemréap was one in five. To give another indication, three times as great a proportion of Chinese households spoke Khmer in the home in Siemréap (13.6 per cent) as in Phnom-Penh (4.4 per cent). (The reader may refer to Appendix I for a more detailed comparison between the Chinese populations of the two communities.)

Although these figures may partly reflect the fact that the Chinese in Siemréap are a more settled population (if sex ratios and the percentage of children in the total population may be used as indices of settlement), they also reflect more frequent interaction between Chinese and Khmer in Siemréap. Contacts with government, to take an important example, involve interaction with Khmer, for it is my impression that there is a far lower proportion of Sino-Cambodians in the administration in Siemréap than in the capital. Even the people Chinese meet in the street are likely to be Khmer. Of paramount importance is the fact that most of their customers are Khmer. Chinese in Phnom-Penh deal primarily with Chinese customers in retailing, and almost entirely with Chinese in wholesaling; their economic relationships therefore lie within the Chinese community to a great extent. But in Siemréap, the Chinese merchant retails to the Khmer peasant, the Khmer soldier, the Khmer civil servant; only a small part of his business is with members of the Chinese community. He buys from wholesalers who are mainly in Phnom-Penh (and Battambang to a smaller extent).

In these circumstances, there is little occasion for vertical economic organization within the Chinese community in Siemréap, for all Chinese stores operate at approximately the same level and scale, in direct competition with other stores selling the same goods. Many shops previously carried on a two-way business with the peasants, buying their crops and selling them goods, but today the rice trade has been separated from retailing by the establishment of several large rice mills owned by businessmen from Phnom-Penh and Battambang, which buy through their own agents or directly from the peasants.[1] While there are, no doubt, some mechanisms among retailers for controlling access to goods and markets, there is no economic association with authority over the individual companies; as in Phnom-Penh, there appears to be a minimum of horizontal economic organization.

As in Phnom-Penh, religion serves to separate the Chinese in Siemréap from the rest of the population, both through self-identification and through the observation of Chinese religious behaviour by others. I did not observe any weddings, but informants asserted that they passed with little notice 'because the Chinese are poor here in Siemréap'. I was told that they usually involve a small feast, and marriages are seldom registered with the administration, the couple often writing their own marriage certificate. I attended two funerals, one poor and one rich. The rich one, that of a very old Hokkien lady whose grand-children had become acculturated to Khmer ways, was a mixture of recognizably Khmer and Chinese elements, including a cortège around the market and through the streets to a Khmer temple where the body was cremated.[2] Organized by the descendants of the deceased, the procession included most of the Chinese businessmen as well as a Chinese sports club. The other funeral – that of a poor Hakka bakery worker – was organized by the few Hakka in town with the aid of the same sports club. A very

---

[1] The list of industries provided by the Ministry of Industry includes only two rice mills in Siemréap Province (*Liste des Principales Industries* 1961, 47), but I was told by officials of the Ministry that the list was not comprehensive. Chinese in Siemréap told me there were five or six mills in the province in 1963. Siemréap Province was split in 1966, the northern part now forming a separate province.

[2] This funeral cortège was typically Chinese in its order and in the many Chinese banners it included. However, it also included one Western and one Khmer orchestra and several banners in Khmer script. Khmer priests and a Khmer *achar* (lay ritual practitioner) were in the cortège and led the ritual at the crematorium. The hearse was not that used in the poor funeral, which came from a Vietnamese temple, but one from a Khmer temple, which carried a coffin that is used repeatedly, the bottom burning out at each cremation but the sides being preserved by a metal lining inside. A typically Khmer ceremony was conducted at the crematorium while the Chinese master of ceremonies prepared a list of the banners and their donors. The daughters of the deceased and other female descendants shaved their heads and wore white *sampot* – Khmer mourning dress – while the male descendants, who were all grandchildren or further removed from the deceased, wore white suits rather than sackcloth or unbleached cotton. It was obvious to me that all the Chinese present were familiar with the procedure of a Khmer funeral.

small cortège, including only two of the Chinese leaders, accompanied the hearse to the Chinese cemetery.

None of the yearly festivals observed at Siemréap involves the Chinese in public ritual or occasions the participation of the Chinese associations.[1] *Yuan-Xiao* passes almost unnoticed, except for the many lanterns and family feasts that evening. Although *Qing-Ming* is the occasion for some Chinese to visit the cemetery, organization is unnecessary, for the cemetery is less than a mile from the market and easily reached on foot. The celebration of other festivals involves only family ritual; some of them also occasion visiting by the women to the Chinese temple. The temple itself is almost neglected by the community, its two old Hokkien caretakers eking out a bare living by begging. Only one Cantonese woman entered the temple during the day I spent there, which was the fifteenth of the lunar month.[2] Three stores donated banners to the temple at New Year, 1962, but none did the following year.

If there is little public ritual to distinguish the Chinese and evoke organization in this community, Chinese education serves both these functions, for many of the Chinese children attend a school established and maintained by the Chinese community. Indeed, the school is the most important of the few associations in the town.

The Chinese in Siemréap have run a primary school since 1925. Until the war, lessons were taught in three languages – Hokkien, Cantonese, and Teochiu – but since about 1950, the language of instruction has been Mandarin. In 1963 there were over two hundred pupils, representing about two-fifths of the Chinese

---

[1] In some other towns, public ritual is undertaken by the Chinese on certain holidays. Both Takhmau (Kandal Province) and Banam (Prey-Veng Province) hold 'god processions' at *Yuan-Xiao*, although Takhmau holds its procession on the sixteenth in order to avoid conflict with the major procession in nearby Phnom-Penh. In Kompong-Trach (Kampot Province), the Hainanese hold a 'god procession' on the twenty-second of the second month, involving mediums from three temples in the area. *Zhong-Yuan* (fifteenth of the seventh month) is celebrated in Tuk Méas (Kampot Province) with a public sacrifice of sweetmeats, money, and small commodities, all of which are scattered for the children at the end of the ritual. Finally, lion teams perform at Chinese New Year in some towns, the proceeds going to the local school, sports club, or mutual aid society.

[2] Teochiu celebrate on the second and sixteenth of the lunar month rather than the first and fifteenth; I was not in the temple on either the second or the sixteenth.

children of school age.[1] Each child paid a tuition fee that amounted to about half the average fee in Phnom-Penh's Chinese 'public' schools. The six classes met in a small building of only four rooms – a degree of crowding not uncommon among the Chinese schools I visited outside Phnom-Penh.

The school is run by a school board (dong-shi-hui) which consists of a head (dong-shi-zhang) and twelve members. The board hires a school principal, six Chinese teachers and two Cambodian teachers. Elections to the school board, held every second year, are in principle open to all Chinese, but a Cantonese who runs a stall in the market-place explained to me that he and other poorer men left 'those matters' to the richer businessmen of the community. In fact, the board member who topped the poll in 1963 received one hundred votes, which suggests that about half the heads of families voted in the elections.[2] All the Chinese to whom I spoke took great pride in their school, pointing it out as the main achievement of their community.

The Chinese in Siemréap also support two sports clubs, both of which were established after 1956. One of them was already moribund by 1963, but the other had many activities – including girls' and boys' table tennis and basketball teams – and its store-front clubroom was crowded almost every night with young people playing table tennis or engaging in other activities. While I was there, a visiting sports club from Kampot played a team match of table tennis and a game of basketball. Earlier in the year, the club in Siemréap had visited Kampot, Kompong-Trach, and Phnom-Penh, and had entered both male and female teams in the national table tennis tournament. The Siemréap provincial basketball team included several players from this club. The club apparently concentrated on sports activities, for it included no cultural or performing groups.

Like similar clubs in Phnom-Penh, the Siemréap sports clubs were led by elected executives of young people; each also had a

[1] In 1961 there were in Siemréap five hundred Chinese children between the ages of five and fifteen. Since the school provides only six years of schooling, it would be more realistic to consider three hundred children as of school age, which would mean that two-thirds of the Chinese children of school age attend the Chinese school. The figure of two-fifths is given in the text because it is comparable to the figures provided for Phnom-Penh in chapter 7. In 1963 there were five Chinese schools in Siemréap Province, one in each town.

[2] There were 230 Chinese households in Siemréap in 1961.

body of advisers, whose leader was given the title of director of the club (*hui-zhang*). The director and other advisers of the more active club were prominent businessmen in the town, contributing regularly to the expenses of the club, as well as making occasional contributions in kind (soft drinks, uniforms, equipment, or the loan of a lorry) to such events as annual parties or visits to other towns. The director took an active part in the affairs of the club, attending all its events, arranging games with other groups, and applying to the provincial administration for aid whenever the club wished to make a trip.

When I asked how many young people were involved in the sports clubs, the usual reply was, 'All of them.' It proved impossible to get an accurate figure, but my impression from talking with young men in their twenties was that the clubs were limited primarily to teenagers, with the exception of the stars on the basketball team. The one club event I attended, the tournament with Kampot, indicated to me that the few girls in the club were primarily Cantonese, while there were both Cantonese and Teochiu boys.

This club participated in both the funerals that took place during my stay. It provided the manpower to push the hearse at the poorer funeral. For the rich funeral, about a dozen members, the directors and two other advisers entered the cortège behind their club banner and bowed as a group before leaving the funeral pyre. The club also aided the provincial administration in such events as voluntary manual labour or the visit to Angkor of a foreign dignitary.

The only other association in the Chinese community of Siem-réap was the cemetery committee. Originally established in 1926 by the Cantonese, the cemetery admitted other speech groups after 1934. The Hokkien took no interest in it, however, preferring to bury their dead in private lots or cremate them at one of the Khmer temples. The committee therefore included no Hokkien.[1]

About ten men are elected annually to the cemetery committee. When I was there, most of the work related to the cemetery was carried out by the head of the committee, who had

[1] The earliest date in the Chinese cemetery is 1927 on a Cantonese gravestone; the earliest Teochiu stone was dated 1939, but the only Hainanese stone was set in 1934. Of the 159 graves in the cemetery, fifty-three were Cantonese, thirty-six Teochiu, six Hakka, one Hainanese, and sixty-three had no stones or did not indicate a place of origin.

held the post for several years. In fact, there was little for the committee to do. In 1962 the provincial administration had requested the Chinese to move their cemetery further from town, but the arrangements for obtaining a new site (provided by the administration) had been discussed and undertaken by the head of the committee in conjunction with other leaders in the community, rather than by the body of committee members. This suggests that the cemetery committee is of minimal importance in the Chinese community.

A mutual aid society (*hu-zhu-she*) that had existed during the final years of the *congrégation* had been disbanded two years before, ostensibly because aid had become available from the government for education and health; indigence has been rare among the Chinese since the tourist boom has come to Siemréap. When I asked why the two old Hokkien men living in the temple were not supported by a mutual aid society, an informant replied that the Chinese were no longer willing to contribute to mutual aid because of all the contributions expected of them for non-Chinese projects; he added that the two men made a better living by begging from store to store on their own than a society could provide. In the Chinese cemetery there are two gravestones dated 1961 that were erected by the mutual aid society.

LEADERSHIP AMONG THE CHINESE IN SIEMRÉAP

It makes little sense to speak of traditionist and modernist leaders in Siemréap, for the community is so small that differences are too idiosyncratic to typify in such terms, nor are there enough associations to form the basis of such a typology. The leaders of the active sports association, for instance, revealed in conversation a strong traditionist orientation that would certainly not have been shared by the 'progressive' youth they led.

Leadership among the Chinese in Siemréap operates in a somewhat wider area than in Phnom-Penh. Because of the much smaller scale of the community and the small number of associations, disputes among Chinese can be handled within the community and are therefore less likely to go to court. (I was told by a government official that he knew of no civil cases in the provincial court involving two resident Chinese.) The Chinese community is also called upon to participate in such events as voluntary manual labour, financial campaigns, and assistance in the preparations for visiting dignitaries.

Any matter affecting the Chinese as a whole is referred to the school board, which serves as the executive of the community. Although the head of the board denied that it discussed anything but school business, a Cantonese who ran a mobile soup-and-noodle stall told me that if there was any problem (*you mie shi*) it was taken to the school board. Another man of similar status, when asked if there was still a *hui-guan* in Siemréap, replied, 'No, there is no longer a *hui-guan*, only the school board.' Such remarks indicate that the Chinese look to the school board for community leadership. The school itself, being the only public building belonging to the Chinese (apart from the temple, which is too small and now inappropriate), is the meeting place for any assemblies of Chinese; that is, it becomes the modern *hui-guan* in the restricted sense of that term.

The importance of the school board in the political structure is evidenced also by the visit of President Liu Shao-chi to Angkor in May 1963. This visit involved rapid preparations by the Chinese because of the security precautions already explained (see chapter 10). Since many Chinese from neighbouring towns were expected to visit Siemréap to see the visitors from China, the Chinese in Siemréap were called upon to organize their welcome. Accordingly, a committee was established at a meeting held in the school on 30 May, two days after the similar committee had been formed in Phnom-Penh. The Chinese preparatory committee in Siemréap consisted of fifteen men, including all thirteen members of the school board. Of the two remaining members, one was a teacher elected secretary to the committee, the other was a Cantonese businessman who enjoyed good business connections with some of the government agencies in the town. The chairman had been head of the school board until the election several days before this meeting.

It is clear that the school board comprises the principal leaders in the Chinese community as well as serving as its leading body. The heads of the cemetery committee and of the active sports club are on the board, the latter having also served as one of the two vice-chairmen of the welcoming committee for President Liu. Three of the other advisers of the sports club are also on the school board.

Four of the thirteen members of the school board take a much more active part in community leadership than do the other nine. Among these four, it is not possible to distinguish an apex leader, however, for both the previous head of the board and the legal 'owner' of the school (*xiao-zhu*, the *répondant* required by law) emerge as powerful leaders. Informants could point to no single person as the leader of the community.

The absence of an apex leader is an exception to the usual situation among Chinese communities outside Phnom-Penh. One factor contributing to this situation is the indisposition of the previous *chef de congrégation*, who is too old and sick to participate in the politics of the community. Another important factor, distinguishing Siemréap from most other Chinese communities of similar size, is the presence of equivalent proportions of two speech groups. This distribution is reflected in the school board, where there are six Teochiu, five Cantonese, one Hakka and one Hainanese. Among the four most active leaders, two are Teochiu, one Cantonese, and one Hainanese. One of the Teochiu is an adviser to the active sports club, as are the Cantonese and Hainanese; the other Teochiu was chairman of the welcoming committee and until recently the head of the school board, in which latter position he was succeeded by the Cantonese. Although factions apparently cut across the Teochiu speech group, the possibility of a Teochiu minority finding allies among the other speech groups makes it more difficult for a single leader to emerge at the apex. The presence of more than one speech group also ensures that the four main leaders together do not form a power bloc, and for this reason the school board remains the highest executive body of the community.

In sum, then, the political structure of the Chinese community in Siemréap operates through a simple associational structure involving only three associations. The small size of the population allows more emphasis to be placed on informal relationships of friendship between leaders than is possible in Phnom-Penh. Nevertheless, the school board serves as the primary association for the community in all matters affecting it as a whole. The board includes the four main leaders, who together do not form a bloc and none of whom individually can claim over-all power in the community.

One might think that relations with the Chinese political structure in Phnom-Penh would affect power relations in the smaller town, but there are few formal relations outside the economic field between the Chinese communities in Siemréap and the capital. There are only four members of the Chinese Hospital Committee who live in Siemréap, two of whom are on the local Chinese school board. Some of the Cantonese belong to the appropriate locality associations in Phnom-Penh, but informants asserted that the vast majority, including most of the leaders, did not. One of the two most powerful leaders is the agent in Siemréap for the major Chinese newspaper in Phnom-Penh, but he belongs to no association in the capital. These few facts suggest that relations between the Chinese leaders in Siemréap and Phnom-Penh are largely economic in nature, involving transactions between individual companies in the two places; relations between the political structures as such are not apparent.

It is possible, of course, that a secret society forms the structure in both places and also the links between them, but I found no evidence whatsoever to support this idea. The nature of politics in the Chinese community – the fact that it has become divorced from economic issues – suggests that such an integration of political structures between different communities is unnecessary: the questions each deals with do not involve the other. Relationships based on kinship between the two places, although not studied in detail, of course provide non-economic ties, but my research suggests that they are not significant between the leaders in the two communities.

OTHER SMALL TOWNS

Research in the Chinese community of Siemréap indicated that today it is not typical of communities throughout Cambodia's small towns. Although the Chinese communities in the provinces of Battambang, Kampot, Kompong-Cham, and Svay-Rieng represent conglomerations of different speech groups in about equal proportions, those in all other provinces comprise a single speech group in each case with concomitant effects upon the social organization of the communities.

From interviews, from the data collected by an assistant, and from brief visits I made to six other towns, it appears that the typical small Chinese community, with one speech group predominating, is more closely integrated than that found in Siemréap. As in Siemréap, the school board usually acts as the executive of the community, but in most places there is an acknowledged leader who stands at the apex of the community structure. This man serves as head of the school board, as head of the sports club, and often as chairman of a mutual aid society or cemetery committee as well. In many cases this is the man who was *chef de congrégation* under the previous régime, and who remains the single richest and most powerful Chinese in the community.

It is not surprising that there should be a single leader at the head of many smaller Chinese communities, for, as I have already stated, the *congrégation* system in smaller centres operated in such a way as to make one man extremely powerful: the *hui-guan* focused on the *chef* to a much greater extent than in Phnom-Penh. Although this man's power was previously reinforced by his access to sanctions lying outside the Chinese community, nevertheless his emergence as unchallenged leader in those circumstances has often permitted him to continue in the leadership of his community after those sanctions were removed. In Siemréap, because the ex-*chef* was no longer on the political scene, either as an active leader or as a sponsor of a younger man, leadership was shared by a group of younger men, none of whom could command the entire community. I found a somewhat similar situation in some of the communities, such as Sisophon and Mongkol-borei (Battambang Province), where no single speech group dominates the community and where the ex-*chef* is no longer politically active. It is found in ethnically more homogeneous communities only when the ex-*chef* is dead, as in Kompong-Chhnang; otherwise these communities usually exhibit a single dominant leader.

One may conclude from the remarks in this chapter that the *congrégation* has left a greater imprint upon the smaller Chinese communities than it has upon that in the capital. It is evident that the *hui-guan* system continues in many smaller communities, albeit under the rubric of school boards. This may be due primarily to the smaller scale of the polity involved as compared to a political structure that directs activities for tens of thousands of Chinese in Phnom-Penh. It is also due to the fact that the polity has a wider field of operation in the smaller community. Certainly, the continuing power of individuals who now head their communities on the basis of having once been *chefs* indicates a legacy from the *congrégations* far stronger than in Phnom-Penh.

12

Comparisons with other Overseas Chinese Communities

The political organization of the Chinese community in Phnom-Penh today looks familiar to any student of overseas Chinese society. One observes in contemporary Phnom-Penh the same richness of associations with cross-cutting membership that is exhibited by most urban overseas Chinese communities all over the world. One can find a similar network of interlocking officers that provides the links between the associations, and one can demonstrate an equivalent structure of leadership operating through the associations in such a way that a small number of leaders can make their influence felt over a wide range of individuals.

An important difference between Phnom-Penh and other overseas Chinese communities is the recency of this associational structure, for the vast majority of associations have grown up within the last decade. I have argued that these associations did not arise earlier because of the presence of the *congrégation* system. The demonstration of their rise after the end of that system is a preliminary indication of the validity of my argument. However, a simple and obvious objection one could make to this thesis is that the recent rise of associations in Phnom-Penh follows directly from the great increase in Chinese population after the Sino-Japanese war, that associational complexity is a function merely of scale.

Freedman has suggested that 'the associations which in a small-scale and relatively underdeveloped settlement express social, economic, and political links in an undifferentiated form, tend, as the scale and complexity of the society increase, to separate into a network of associations which are comparatively specialized in their functions and the kinds of solidarity they express' (Freedman 1960, 47 f.). Following this suggestion, one might argue that the Chinese community in pre-war Phnom-Penh was 'small-scale' and 'underdeveloped', while the great post-war immigration of Chinese has resulted in a community of such scale and complexity as to produce a network of many associations. Freedman proposes a rough continuum of types of overseas Chinese urban communities. At one end stands Kuching[1] 'as the model of a simple and relatively small-scale overseas settlement', while 'Later Singapore is presumably the model of the most developed form of immigrant Chinese settlement in Southeast Asia' (Freedman 1960, 45).

The simplest test of a demographic explanation for the rise of voluntary associations in Phnom-Penh would be found in studying the history of Chinese associations in Saigon-Cholon, for that double city had a population of over two hundred thousand Chinese for most of the twentieth century.[2] Solely in terms of population, it would clearly fit at the Singapore end of the continuum. Yet prior to the Sino-Japanese war, Saigon-Cholon Chinese society was much like that of Phnom-Penh at the time: other than the *hui-guan* defined by the *congrégations*, there existed only the Cantonese locality associations, all of which were subordinate to the Cantonese *hui-guan*.[3] Although I did not visit Saigon-Cholon, I was able to interview a member of one of its more prosperous Chinese families, whose description of pre-war Chinese social organization corroborates what I have said except that he mentioned the existence at that time of a Chinese Chamber

[1] Freedman places Sarawak at one end of his continuum, but we may assume that he is referring to urban Sarawak, i.e. Kuching, for he has already made the point that in the rural areas of Sarawak solidarities of clanship and locality of origin are not expressed through associations because they appear in economic relationships, social status, and spatial distribution (Freedman 1960, 44; compare T'ien 1953, 35–68).

[2] The official figure for the Chinese population of Saigon-Cholon was given in 1909 as 72,152 ('Notice' 1909, 1071); but the same factors that produced underestimates of the Chinese in Cambodia were operative in Cochinchina (W Willmott 1967, 12 ff.), and we may therefore assume that this figure is a gross underestimation. Only ten years later, Coulet estimated over twice as many (Coulet 1929, 460). Since 1955 there have been about a million Chinese in South Vietnam, well over half of whom are probably in the capital and its twin city.

[3] It is quite possible that the Cantonese locality associations in Phnom-Penh were branches of similar associations in Cholon, for the number of Cantonese in Phnom-Penh may not have been sufficient to produce such associations independently. My informant asserted that there were five *congrégations* in Saigon and five in Cholon, all ten of which were represented on the council of *chefs* According to him, each *congrégation* supported its own hospital as well as school temple, and cemetery.

of Commerce in Cochinchina. The *congrégations* were dissolved
in 1960 ('South Vietnam's Chinese Problem' 1961, 148), but
unfortunately, the material on contemporary Chinese social
organization is not adequate to give an idea of the nature and
number of associations extant today. While we await further
studies, we may assume that the recent history of Chinese organization in Saigon-Cholon roughly parallels that of Phnom-Penh.

The attempt to delineate the factors involved in determining
the nature of social organization among the Chinese of Phnom-
Penh can be advanced by an examination of other overseas
Chinese communities concerning which a considerable literature
is available. In the following sections I describe comparable
aspects of Chinese social organization in Singapore, Bangkok,
Vancouver, Java, Manila and Borneo.

SINGAPORE

The history of Chinese associations outlined by Freedman for
Singapore forms a striking parallel to what I have described in
Phnom-Penh (Freedman 1960; see also Topley 1961). During
much of the nineteenth century, Chinese society in Singapore was
organized in a small number of secret societies, while today it
exhibits a multitude of voluntary associations based on the criteria
of kinship, clanship, common locality, common religious beliefs,
and various specific purposes such as education and sport (Freedman
1957, 92–8). In terms of the continuum, it has moved from some
point close to the simple end to the other extreme of complexity.

There are several similarities between this development and
what occurred in Phnom-Penh. In the first place, the secret
societies that ruled the Chinese in nineteenth-century Singapore
are analogous in some ways to the *hui-guan* in Phnom-Penh.
Freedman points out that they were not particularly voluntary,
for newly arrived immigrants found it essential to join one or
other of them for protection and for economic security and
contacts (Freedman 1960, 37). Of the nine secret societies, five
were organized within specific speech groups similar to the
hui-guan in Phnom-Penh.[1] Furthermore, the leaders of the secret

[1] Freedman 1960, 36. It may be, of course, that the five secret societies that
were based on speech groups were organized as *hui-guan* before the Ghee Hin
became active in Singapore.

societies had at their disposal sanctions extreme enough to provide them with considerable power over the membership. Finally, as with the termination of *congrégations* in Phnom-Penh, the end of secret society rule in Singapore coincided with the elimination from the Chinese community of the major economic aspects of political organization by the active intervention of the colonial power in the economics of the colony; today, voluntary associations in Singapore 'are relatively independent of economic groupings' (*ibid.*, 45).

But if the similarities are striking between Phnom-Penh and Singapore in terms of earlier forms and the historical development of Chinese associations, the differences are perhaps more important for my purposes here. The most important difference has to do with the nature of colonial rule over the Chinese community. In Phnom-Penh the French took definite steps to form a system of indirect rule from the start, but the secret societies in Singapore grew in a situation of relative inattention on the part of the British, and they were consequently without official recognition prior to the establishment of the Chinese Protectorate in 1877 (*ibid.*, 34 f.). While the great power of the *chef de congrégation* rested upon his right, unchallengeable within the Chinese community, of effecting deportation, the power of the secret society officer depended partly upon ritual solidarity and, in the final instance, upon violence (*ibid.*, 37 f.). The efficacy of violence as a sanction was no doubt continually impressed on the membership by the fighting that went on between the various societies, inter-associational conflict thus serving a definite function in maintaining the political structure of Singapore Chinese society in somewhat the same way that clan feuds, according to Gluckman, united Nuer society (Gluckman 1955, 1–26). The strength of the secret societies, enhanced by fighting each other, could be 'linked together in the face of external authority', for it 'expressed a solidarity of opposition to the state that cut across the opposition between communities' (Freedman 1960, 47).

Violence was unnecessary as a sanction in Phnom-Penh because the Chinese leaders had available to them the sanction of deportation. Deportation involved actions by the colonial administration, while violence as a sanction remained entirely within the Chinese community itself and could therefore be challenged by the organization of counter-violence. This fact may explain in part why secret societies in Singapore degenerated into 'small-scale criminal organizations' (Freedman 1960, 33), while the lack of violence as a sanction in Cambodia may account for the apparent ease with which the Chinese community of Phnom-Penh rid itself of secret societies.

Another important difference is evident between the two examples. It is apparent that within the Chinese community in nineteenth-century Singapore, no small number of secret societies could frustrate the growth of all other associations. Besides the five branches of the Ghee Hin representing the five speech groups, there were four other secret societies whose memberships (probably) cross-cut each other and those of the Ghee Hin societies (ibid., 36). Although Freedman emphasizes the fact that these nine societies were the major political groupings in the Chinese community, he gives evidence of the existence of clan and locality associations at the same time, and he quotes a contemporary Chinese resident as stating that some of them were 'able to hold their own' with the secret societies (ibid., 39). As the Chinese population grew, then, there appears to have been an unabated increase in the number of voluntary associations taking part in the political structure of the Chinese community.

That the secret societies could not effectively challenge alternative Chinese associations in Singapore is directly related to the fact that their power was based upon sanctions more or less available to any other association, aspiring or extant. Political segmentation, as Freedman suggests, apbears to be natural to the growing overseas Chinese community, provided there is no interference from outside.

BANGKOK

The Chinese community in Bangkok has been mentioned here several times already as one exhibiting a similar structure to that in contemporary Phnom-Penh. Its history, however, is quite different. The community appears to have been under indirect rule, probably based on speech groups, during the seventeenth century (Skinner 1957, 12–15); but there is no available record of the nature of its internal political organization at that time. As the Teochiu population grew to outnumber the earlier Cantonese and Hokkien settlers, the Thai kings did not develop the system of indirect rule, but seem to have left the Chinese to their own devices. The kings were mainly concerned with collecting revenue from the Chinese; during the eighteenth and nineteenth centuries this was accomplished through revenue farms, the most profitable of which were those for opium, gambling, lottery, and alcohol – all four 'based essentially on Chinese consumption' (*ibid.*, 120). Head tax, so important to the colonial government in Cambodia, appears to have diminished in importance in Siam after the seventeenth century, the kings following a deliberate policy of limiting head tax to encourage Chinese immigration and, hence, expenditure on the 'vices' from which heavy taxes were collected (*ibid.*, 124–5).

According to Skinner, the social structure of the Chinese community in Bangkok about 1890 'was fluid and rather amorphous' (*ibid.*, 134). By fluidity, Skinner means a high degree of social mobility, something not uncommon in overseas Chinese communities. By amorphousness, he apparently refers to the fact that many associations existed with little associational structure uniting them, there being a considerable amount of conflict between them. Secret societies were the most important, but by no means the only, associations. 'Far from providing a solid front against Thais or Westerners, secret societies constituted a divisive force within Chinese society' (*ibid.*, 141). While Skinner may have overlooked factors producing cohesion (cf. Freedman 1960, 47 n. 81), it is possible that secret societies were more divisive in Bangkok than elsewhere because the revenue farming system produced more conflicting interests among Chinese than did the *laissez-faire* attitude of the British, for instance, in earlier Singapore. The presence of many other associations, based on clanship, locality of origin, and other solidarities (Skinner 1957, 138 f.), provided the possibilities for the development of a more 'amorphous' social structure than existed in places where secret societies predominated.

Most important from the point of view of my thesis, there appear to have been no powerful leaders who could command large followings among the Chinese in Bangkok. Skinner states that 'the system of Chinese captains or headmen broke down during the nineteenth century' because of feuding and animosity within the Chinese community (*ibid.*, 141). It is clear from this that the system of indirect rule established in the seventeenth century did not survive the growth of the secret societies and other associations in subsequent centuries.

Twentieth-century Chinese society in Bangkok has developed from a long and rich history of Chinese associations. The associational structure that eventually replaced nineteenth-century anarchy and served as the political structure of a relatively united Chinese community, evolved from the conflict generated through the combination of a *laissez-faire* attitude on the part of the Siamese administration and the monopoly farming system that gave partial power to a large number of competing individuals. This history is similar to that of Chinese associations in Singapore, with two interesting exceptions. First, the conflict-ridden society of nineteenth-century Bangkok replaced a system of indirect rule that had existed some time before, while that in Singapore developed with the beginning of significant Chinese migration to the island. Second, the conflict may have been even more divisive in Bangkok because of the monopoly farming system, a method of finance not adopted by the British in Singapore.

VANCOUVER

The Chinese community in Vancouver, Canada, provides quite a different case.[1] While the Chinese population has never exceeded twenty thousand, the number of Chinese associations in Vancouver places it toward the complex end of the continuum suggested by Freedman, for there are today over eighty non-profit voluntary associations. The voluntary association was an accepted pattern in North American society by the time the Chinese arrived, and one which was therefore easy to repeat; in Southeast Asia, however, it involved innovation by immigrant groups. This may be an important contributing factor to the proliferation of associations in relatively small Chinese communities in the United States and Canada.

Another important difference between this community and that in Phnom-Penh is that the Chinese in Vancouver are almost without exception Cantonese, the vast majority coming from the

[1] I have studied the Chinese community in British Columbia during the years 1961–62 and 1965–69. The work has been supported by grants from the President's Committee on Research and the Institute of Social and Economic Research, both of the University of British Columbia, and by the National Museum of Canada.

district south and west of Canton city: *Si-yi, Shun-de, Zhong-shan,* and *Pan-yu*. Although language therefore could not be a criterion of recruitment, dialect and locality of origin were nevertheless utilized to distribute individuals among seven locality associations, termed *hui-guan*. Clanship was another important criterion, accounting for twenty-three of the associations existing today (W. Willmott 1964a, 34). Over-all political leadership, however, was vested in the Chinese Benevolent Association (*Zhong-Hua Hui-guan*), formed as a confederation of the seven locality associations. In 1962 this association was reorganized to include on its council representatives from most of the Chinese voluntary associations in the city (*Chinatown News*, x, 7, p. 30). The Chinese Benevolent Association served as an agent of communication between the Chinese and the federal, provincial, and municipal governments; to some extent it still performs this function today. It also served as the highest commission of reconciliation within the Chinese community. However, it was never given police powers, either formally or informally.

Unlike Phnom-Penh, Singapore, or Bangkok, the plurality of Chinese associations in Vancouver appears to date from soon after the Chinese community came into existence, and secret society rule was never absolute in the city. Only one Chinese secret society has been evident in Canada, known variously and at different times as the *Hong-men hui*, the *Zhi-gong Tang*, the *Min-zhi Dang*, and the Chinese Freemasons.[1] This society was founded in the goldfields of the Caribou, north-east of Vancouver, in 1862. For some years it was the only Chinese association in an area where the important problems for the Chinese community were the policing of gold claims, the settling of economic disputes, and solidarity in the face of severe economic exploitation and occasional violence (Lyman, W. Willmott, and Ho 1964). Prior to the advent of the Kuomintang, the secret society fulfilled the main organizational functions in the smaller communities in Canada, but has never stood alone or paramount in Vancouver. (In this regard, the situations parallel those in rural Siam and Bangkok; cf. Skinner 1957, 141–2.) Since the advent of Chinese immigrant families in large numbers after the second world war, the strength of the Chinese Freemasons within the

[1] There is no genetic relation between this Chinese secret society and Western Freemasonry (Lyman, W. Willmott, and Ho 1964).

community has been curtailed, although it is probably still the most powerful single Chinese association in Canada.

Two important points should be noted from this brief description of Chinese political organization in Vancouver. First, no leaders have been delegated power from outside the community. Second, although the Chinese population was small, it was organized by a large number of Chinese associations, whose criteria of recruitment produced cross-cutting memberships. Only in the anarchic situation of the goldmining town, where violence was a commonplace sanction, did the secret society flourish as the unique association and therefore as the government of the Chinese community. As in Singapore and Bangkok, one sees a strong tendency toward political segmentation in the urban setting of Vancouver. It is clear from this example that the complexity of the resulting associational structure is by no means a simple function of population size, nor of the presence of different speech groups in the same community.

None of the examples of overseas Chinese communities that I have treated so far in this chapter has involved a formal system of indirect rule (except seventeenth-century Bangkok, for which there is insufficient information). Such a system existed in other than French colonies, however, for in both Spanish Manila and the Dutch East Indies clearly defined systems of indirect rule operated through *gobernadorcillos de chinos* and *kapitans china* respectively.[1] The small body of literature on Chinese society in the Dutch East Indies indicates that the systems in Java and in West Borneo were so different that they must be treated separately.

JAVA

The Dutch East India Company adopted the practice of earlier rulers in Java by appointing a headman for each foreign community in Batavia, and later in each settlement where there were substantial foreign communities. The Chinese headmen were soon given the military title of Captain (later also Majors and Lieutenants, even Sergeants and Corporals), a system of

[1] The *congrégation* system was used to govern the Chinese in other French colonies, e.g. Madagascar (Tsien 1961), Tahiti (Coppenrath 1967).

nomenclature which continued until the 1930s.[1] The duties of these
Chinese Captains were 'to maintain peace and order in the
Chinese districts; to transmit the orders of the colonial government to the persons concerned; to keep the European administration informed of events in the Chinese quarters; and, finally, to
serve as advisors, guarantors, and spokesmen for their compatriots'
(Williams 1960, 124). It is significant that these duties included
neither control over immigration nor the collection of taxes. The
Dutch vacillated between policies of exclusion and free entry of
Chinese, but the Captains were so far from any control that they
at one time petitioned the Dutch East India Company to put a
complete halt to Chinese immigration (Cator 1936, 15). With
regard to revenue from the Chinese, the Dutch appear to have
concentrated on leasing farms rather than on the collection of a
special head tax, a policy similar to that followed by the Siamese
kings. Farms were leased to Chinese for the collection of head
tax from indigenes, bridge tolls, slaughtering taxes, gaming taxes,
market taxes, for the sale of fish, opium, and alcoholic liquors,
and for the operation of pawnshops (Kahin 1952, 12). In many
cases, farms were leased to Chinese Captains, making their
economic position paramount within their communities; the
first Chinese Captain appointed at Batavia was said to have been
the wealthiest among the four hundred Chinese in the city
(Cator 1936, 13).

I have been unable to find any clear description of the procedure for selecting a Captain in Java; some sources state that
they were merely appointed by the Dutch, while others assert
that they were nominated by their compatriots. Apparently
there was no legal procedure by which the Chinese could make
their choice of a candidate known to the administration; but it is
reasonable to assume that in most cases the Dutch appointed an
already recognized leader, for such a man would have more
possibility of maintaining peace and order (cf. D. Willmott 1960,
150).

One difference between the system of Chinese Captains in Java
and that of the *congrégations* in Phnom-Penh was the fact that only

[1] The system of Chinese Captains lapsed for three years, 1740–43, following the
massacre at Batavia and subsequent revolts throughout Java (Purcell 1965, 406).
The date of its final termination apparently varied between districts, for we know
that it ended in 1931 at Semarang (D. Willmott 1960, 152), while it continued until
1938 in Sukabumi (Tan 1963, 19).

one headman was appointed for each settlement in Java. This difference is more apparent than real, however, for during the first two centuries of Dutch rule the Chinese were overwhelmingly Hokkien (Purcell 1965, 387). The beginning of immigration of other speech groups in the latter half of the nineteenth century coincides with the rise of secret societies and the gradual emasculation of the Captaincies.[1]

Another difference can be seen in the relations between the colonial administrators and the Chinese. The French administrators (if not the *colons*) dealt cordially with the Chinese and permitted them considerable freedom of movement and association, both by law and informally. The Dutch, on the other hand, while recognizing that the Chinese were necessary as economic intermediaries between the native population and the company or colonial administration (Furnivall 1939, 46; Lasker 1946, 162), nevertheless considered it necessary to establish strict controls on their movements and also treated them with personal contempt.[2] The importance of this difference is apparent from the discussion of secret societies earlier in this chapter: the impetus for Chinese consolidation against Dutch oppression probably mollified forces tending toward segmentation within the community during the nineteenth century. The same solidarity is also indicated by the nature of the associations that arose around the turn of the century.

Unfortunately, I know of no description of Chinese social organization in nineteenth-century Java. There is therefore no way of determining the associational nature of the Chinese

[1] Williams describes Chinese attacks on Captains and the Captaincy between 1904 and 1916 (Williams 1960, 128–36). He suggests that the Captains never possessed much power, acting merely as agents of communication between the government and the Chinese: 'They barely deserve mention as instruments of indirect rule' (*ibid.*, 125). This may have been the case during the period Williams was studying (1900–1916), but Ong Tae Hae, a Chinese who visited Batavia in 1783, gives an account which indicates that the Chinese captains had considerable power at that time (Ong 1850, 4). See also D. Willmott 1960, 148 ff.
[2] Various authors describe the restrictive pass system whereby Chinese had to obtain a pass every time they wished to leave a city, the petty annoyances and insulting manner of Dutch administrators, and incidents of police brutality against the Chinese; see, for instance, Kahin 1952, 28; Purcell 1965, 406 and 418; van der Kroef 1953, 449; D. Willmott 1960, 6; Williams 1960, 40 f. But in another essay, Williams has suggested that the Dutch followed a policy of fostering the Chinese middle class until the introduction of the ethical programme about 1900 (Williams 1961).

communities at that time. However, we know from one historical
study and two monographs on twentieth-century communities
(Williams 1960; D. Willmott 1960; Tan 1963) that a large
number of Chinese associations of two distinct kinds were
established during the final years of the nineteenth and the first
decades of the twentieth centuries. On the one hand, the new
immigrants began to set up *hui-guan* for the various speech groups
in each town. On the other hand, the established Peranakan
businessmen formed chambers of commerce, educational, and
nationalist associations that quickly took over from the Chinese
Captains any vestige of community leadership still pertaining to
their status. The fact that these associations seem to have grown
up without conflict but under the accepted leadership of either
the Siang Hwee (*shang-hui*, chambers of commerce) or the Tiong
Hoa Hwe Koan (*Zhong-Hua Hui-guan*), a pan-Chinese nationalist
association, suggests that Chinese unity was promoted by the
harsh treatment received from the Dutch. Dutch attempts to
maintain the Chinese Captaincy in the face of these new community associations were completely ineffective.[1]

From the material I have outlined here, it is apparent that the
power of the Chinese Captains in Java was not comparable to
that of the *chefs de congrégation* in several important aspects. Since
they had no control over immigration, the Captains were not
given access to the sanction of deportation. Futhermore, in later
years they were expected to exercise their jurisdiction over
Chinese of other than their own speech group, so that they were
not supported by the solidarity of individual *hui-guan*. Indeed,
even in earlier times, some of them may have been appointed by
Dutch administrators without the approval of a majority of the
Chinese businessmen in the community (cf. D. Willmott 1960,
148–50), a situation that legally could not have occurred in
Phnom-Penh. In small centres, where personal relations between
the Dutch administrator and all the leading Chinese could be
developed with relative ease, such a system might have worked
with efficiency, despite the presence of various speech groups;
but in larger towns like Batavia, Semarang, and Surabaja, the

[1] Cator asserts that opposition to the Chinese Captains came from 'young
Chinese' who were moved merely by 'sentimental reasons' relating to the
absence of Captains from other minority groups (Cator 1936, 95). Much more
substantial sociological reasons can be invoked.

power of the Captains and other 'officers' diminished as diversity grew in the Chinese community. The system of indirect rule declined over several decades to disappear some time between the wars.

MANILA

Until the middle of the twentieth century, the Chinese community in Manila was almost entirely Hokkien with the exception of a very small group of Cantonese (called *macanistas* because many came through Macao) which numbered only 500 in 1850, about 3000 at the turn of the century; during the nineteenth century, they never comprised more than 5 per cent of the Chinese population of the Philippines (Wickberg 1965, 177). The Spanish attempted unsuccessfully to limit Chinese immigration at various times, and the total population of Chinese in the island was drastically reduced by periodic expulsions and 'government sponsored massacres in 1603, 1639, 1662, 1686, and 1762' (Weightman 1960, 74). By 1850 there were only six thousand Chinese in the Philippines, but rapid immigration during the half-century of economic development brought the total to about a hundred thousand by 1900.[1] Until 1850, almost all the Chinese were in Manila (Wickberg 1961, 55), and even in 1900 half of them, or about fifty thousand, resided in the main city (*ibid.*, 64).

Like the Dutch, the Spanish in Manila adopted a system of indirect rule over the Chinese community through a Chinese headman, called *gobernadorcillo de chinos*.[2] The duties of the *gobernadorcillo* were 'to act as judge in petty civil actions where both parties were Chinese, collect taxes for the Spaniards, keep order, and act as intermediary between the Chinese community and the Spanish government' (Wickberg 1965, 37), a list which

[1] My estimate based on Wickberg 1965, pp. 169–70. Curiously, Wickberg here accepts the official census figure of 41,035 for 1903, having pointed out on the previous page that the censuses in the 1890s probably counted only 'two thirds to three quarters of the total Chinese population'. In a note elsewhere in the book, he explains that the 1903 figure 'includes only Chinese nationals' (*ibid.*, 148 n. 5), which suggests to me that the figure of 100,000 is probably closer, particularly since Wickberg himself gives an estimate of 90,000–120,000 for 1890 and offers no explanation of a drastic drop in the following decade (*ibid.*, 170).

[2] This system lapsed for a few decades at the beginning of the nineteenth century, when the leaders of the occupational *gremios* held power. The system reverted to *gubernadorcillo* control by about 1830 (Wickberg 1965, 38).

closely resembles that of the duties of the *chefs de congrégation* in French Indochina. Like the French, the Spanish saw the Chinese as a special source of tax revenue and adopted a form of administration that would assure them of their return.

Although the Spanish leased monopoly farms on opium, cockpits, and taxes, revenues from the Chinese residents came primarily from annual head taxes, a policy that more closely resembled that followed in Indochina than the emphasis upon other taxes in Siam or Java. The Chinese paid at rates from four to twenty-one times as high as the *indios* (Filipinos), and were also subject to constant extortion from the Spanish tax authorities (Wickberg 1965, 9 f., 160, 165).

Immigration to nineteenth-century Manila, according to Wickberg, 'assumed two forms: coolie-broker and kinship-based; the relative amounts of each are not known' (*ibid.*, 170). It appears from Wickberg's account (*ibid.*, 195) that the *gobernadorcillo* had some control over coolies entering but perhaps little over immigrants who were sponsored by their kinsmen already resident in Manila, who did not need his approval to enter the country. The *gobernadorcillo* did not have the complete control over immigration enjoyed by his counterparts in Indochina.

Under the *gobernadorcillo*, the Chinese community was at first organized into a score or more of occupational groupings, called *gremios*, the leaders of which elected the *gobernadorcillo* annually. This system was changed in 1857, upon petition from the wealthier Chinese merchants; henceforth biennially the merchants in the top two commercial tax categories elected two candidates, to which was added the name of the incumbent, making a shortlist of three from which the Spanish governor selected the next *gobernadorcillo* (Wickberg 1965, 179 f.). As in Indochina, the choice of the governor was almost always that of the Chinese merchants themselves.

The switch from occupational guild organization to an over-all *hui-guan* for the Hokkien in Manila occurred during the first half of the nineteenth century. This *hui-guan* was known to the Spanish as the *Gremio de Chinos*.[1] Wickberg describes it as 'a kind of vaguely defined, supramunicipal corporate organization

---

[1] It is clear to me that the *Gremio de Chinos* is in fact a *hui-guan*, evidence for which is provided in the only Chinese document relating to it cited by Wickberg (1965, 209). Wickberg points out that most of his data come from Spanish sources (*ibid.*, 168), which may account for his not using the term *hui-guan*.

of the Chinese in the Manila area' headed by the *gobernadorcillo* (*ibid.*, 180). The Spanish made no attempt to interfere with this organization or to supervise its activities.[1] Apart from its political functions, the *hui-guan* undertook to safeguard the welfare of its members through a commission known as the Shan-chü Kung-so (*Shan-qu Gong-so*), which administered the Chinese cemetery, hospital, and school in Manila (*ibid.*, 185 f.). A Cantonese *hui-guan* was organized some time around 1850, which undertook the same functions of protection, welfare, and harmony for the much smaller Cantonese community in Manila (*ibid.*, 179).

This brief description of the Chinese community in nineteenth-century Manila suggests several similarities to that of Phnom-Penh. The presence of an elected leader, supported by a *hui-guan*, and with responsibilities toward a colonial administration that gives him power based on sanctions lying beyond his community, clearly resembles the situation in Indochina. But unlike the *chefs de congrégation*, the *gobernadorcillo de chinos* in Manila did not have complete control over Chinese immigration, and was unable, therefore, to block entry of potential opposition. This may explain an apparently larger rôle played by secret societies in Manila than in Phnom-Penh (Wickberg 1965, 39, 177–8). Nevertheless, the system of indirect rule enabled a *hui-guan* to discharge effectively many functions for the Chinese community.

Another difference lies in the animosity experienced by the Chinese in Manila. Like the Dutch, the Spanish treated the Chinese with contempt, and unlike even the Dutch, the Spanish carried out successive massacres of the Chinese during the seventeenth and eighteenth centuries which laid the background for continuing ill-will throughout Spanish rule.[2] The Chinese also suffered much more serious limitations on movement and residence in the Philippines than in Indochina. As in Java, discrimination and animosity tended to militate against the development of opposing factions within the Chinese community, thus reinforcing the control of the *hui-guan*. It is significant in this regard that no clan associations developed in Manila prior to 1898 (Amyot 1960, 104; Wickberg 1965, 174).

---

[1] The Spanish explicitly refused to recognize the *hui-guan* in law in 1882, when it petitioned for legal recognition (Wickberg 1965, 196 f.).

[2] For a detailed discussion of Spanish prejudice and discrimination with regard to the Chinese in the Philippines, see Margaret Wyant Horsley's Ph.D. dissertation (1950).

I have not been able to find any account of the end of the *gobernadorcillo* system in Manila. Presumably it ended soon after the American occupation, perhaps partly due to pressure from the recently established Chinese Consulate and the development of Chinese nationalism, leading eventually to Kuomintang control of the community (cf. Jensen 1956, *passim*). A Chinese Commercial Council was established in 1904, replacing the Hokkien *hui-guan* in power (Weightman 1960, 337 ff.). Today, Manila Chinese are organized into a multitude of associations based on clan, region, and language.[1]

KONGSIS IN BORNEO

The Chinese found in Java a settled agricultural society (or societies), and they created rôles of importer, middle-man, and artisan that could realize a profit in such a society. In West Borneo, however, they found a relatively sparse and uncivilized population with whom only a very limited trade was possible. There was ample land for the Chinese to establish mining, lumbering and planting enterprises. The typical Chinese enterprise in this area was the kongsi (*gong-si*), whose uniqueness as a form of business firm resulted from three factors: its composition, its size, and its territory.[2] While Chinese migrated to Java as individuals and small groups, it was typical in Borneo for a kongsi to be established by the migration of an entire lineage or segment

[1] Weightman mentions separate *hui-guan* for Chinese from Foochow, Teochiu, and Hainan (Weightman 1960, 336). Amyot, however, asserts that there are only Cantonese and Hokkien in Manila, 'except for a small smattering of Hakka speaking people' (Amyot 1960, 103). In a private communication, Skinner suggests that in 1962 the Chinese population of the Philippines divided as follows: Hokkien 70 per cent, Cantonese 20 per cent, Teochiu 4 per cent, Hakka 4 per cent, Hainanese 2 per cent.

[2] The main source on the kongsis of West Borneo is De Groot's *Het Kongsiwezen van Borneo*. One French and one English source basing themselves primarily upon De Groot were available to me (Schlegel 1885; Ward 1954). Professor Lo Hsiang-lin has written a history of the Lanfang Kongsi (Lo 1961). It is clear from Cator's description that the kongsis at Billiton were not comparable, being smaller associations of workers in a single mine, comprising only men, and without a territorial organization (Cator 1936, 191–3). Although Boeke speaks of tobacco planted by Chinese kongsis at Deli in Sumatra (Boeke 1953, 220), Cator states that the planters were working for foremen appointed by the management and were not organized into kongsis (Cator 1936, 225). Finally, the 'panglongs' along the northeast coast of Sumatra, lumber camps serving Singapore and involving capital and labour from that city, were business enterprises along modern lines, not kongsis (*ibid.*, 217–22).

of a clan, uprooted as a body from China; each kongsi therefore contained a nucleus of agnatic kinsmen that provided the original organization. The kongsi had anywhere from several hundred to twenty thousand members, the largest being the Lanfang Kongsi (*Lan-fang Gong-si*), which controlled about 10,000 square miles administered in seven districts. Finally, each kongsi controlled a rather large area of land, within which all inhabitants belonged to the kongsi.

It is self-evident that the community organization in such a commercial enterprise would have been entirely different from that in any other of the overseas Chinese settlements I have discussed. Because it included the entire population of a territory, the kongsi performed all the functions of government within its boundaries. Whether or not it paid tribute to an outside authority was relatively insignificant to its political structure. The Lanfang Kongsi, which was the only one to survive the Dutch campaign of 1857 (and that because the Dutch had replaced its head with their own pro-Dutch nominee in 1849), maintained the same internal structure until its demise in 1884.

Lo writes as if the Lanfang Kongsi were independent until it 'was finally overthrown by the Dutch invading force in 1884 immediately following the death of the tenth president' (Lo 1961, 8). Ward and Schlegel, however, indicate that the Dutch in fact conquered the area during the 1850s, sparing only the Lanfang Kongsi because its head, *Liu A-sheng*, was a Dutch nominee (Ward 1954, 364; Schlegel 1885, 458 f.). In fact there were three periods of different rule: when it was first settled, in 1775, the Kongsi was under the sultan at Pontianak (Ward 1954, 449); from 1777 to 1849, it was independent; and from 1850 to 1884, it was under the rule of the Dutch. There appears to have been little change in its political organization through all these changes. Although theoretically authority was delegated up from the bottom before 1850 and down from the top under the Dutch, in fact the top leaders had great power from the beginning, and popular consent was sought for appointments at every level until the end.

The kongsi is therefore not at all typical of overseas Chinese communities, but represents a form of extreme independence which goes beyond indirect rule to almost complete autonomy.[1]

---

[1] The founder of the Lanfang Kongsi apparently tried unsuccessfully to make it part of the Chinese Empire by offering tribute to Peking (Ward 1954, 363).

In such circumstances, there appear to have been no associations alternative to the structure of the kongsi; economic and political organization was congruent, and the unity of the kongsi was assured both by the necessity of economic cooperation and by the need for protection against other kongsis and non-Chinese outsiders.

Another rather unusual form of overseas Chinese community is the rural village, an example of which has been described by Newell. While there may be important similarities between Treacherous River in Province Wellesley (Malaya) and some of the Hainanese pepper-planting villages in Kampot Province, there is so little in common between it and Phnom-Penh that a detailed discussion would be out of place here. Treacherous River comprises twelve hundred Chinese from the southern area of Teochiuland, all of whom grow vegetables and enjoy a somewhat similar standard of living. The only associations in the village are the school and two 'religious societies', none of which, according to Newell, distinguishes a sub-group within the village (Newell 1962, 125). The school principal serves as mediator in some disputes, but it is evident that the political organization of the community derives from exchange relations and the organization of work rather than from the associations. Unfortunately, the analysis is not carried far enough for any pattern to emerge, and only a hazy picture of power relations is provided.[1]

Schlegel likened the kongsi to the village in China, but there is little similarity, for it was a much larger unit enjoying few relations with neighbouring kongsis (other than war), and the entire population of the kongsi was united in a cooperative economic enterprise that went far beyond the cooperation found in the Chinese village. A Chinese writing in 1948, relating how his grandfather had described the kongsi in Borneo, states that it was 'the ideal form of commonwealth': members worked together, gold was shared equally, and the entire kongsi was self-supporting except for salt and a few imported goods (ibid., 369 n. 51).

[1] A recent study of the Chinese community at Alor Janggus, Kedah State, Malaysia, by Kiyoshige Maeda is disappointingly sparse in information on community structure. The author, 'whose major field of endeavour is modern Chinese languages' (Maeda 1967, 3), devotes only four pages to a discussion of 'administration' of the community (ibid., 33-6). From this brief account, the impression gleaned is of a political structure involving a small, informal clique of four businessmen, one of whom is paramount because he is wealthiest, and whose leadership has been legitimated by election to the position of chairman of the school board. No other association is described, although Cantonese and Hokkien hui-guan are mentioned (as 'clan associations') in respect to the two Chinese cemeteries. The community numbers only 481 Chinese in all.

CONCLUSION

All the examples of overseas Chinese communities discussed in this chapter, with the exception of the kongsis of West Borneo and the rural village in Malaya, exhibit a political structure that depends on associations. Not only do associations provide aspiring individuals the means to achieve a certain measure of power, they also provide the framework through which policy is determined and communicated to the population and disputes are settled. The examples further indicate that the segmentation of the community through the establishment of more associations occurs in all overseas Chinese communities. The resulting associational structure varies from one community to another, and from the comparison of examples it has become apparent that several factors determine its pattern.

The most obvious factor is the size of the community. A community of a thousand does not require, nor can it produce, the elaborate associational structure that one might find in a community of a hundred thousand. But two examples indicate that scale alone cannot account for the relative lack of associations in Phnom-Penh under the French. In Vancouver, a Chinese population of fifteen thousand has produced over eighty associations, the relations between which form a highly complicated associational structure. At the other extreme, political organization among the hundreds of thousands of Chinese in pre-war Saigon-Cholon was provided almost entirely by ten *hui-guan* and fifteen Cantonese locality associations.

The nature of Chinese migration is a second factor. Migration by a lineage as a unit to West Borneo can be contrasted, in the type of community organization it produced, with the relatively individualized migration of Chinese to other parts of Southeast Asia. More important, the migration of various speech groups to Bangkok and Singapore produced a more complicated structure than was evident in the purely Hokkien communities of pre-twentieth-century Java and Manila. One might expect that the diverse immigration to Phnom-Penh throughout a century would have produced a proliferation of associations during that time, as it did in Java at the turn of the century.

Yet another factor affecting associational structure is the presence or absence of a perceived threat to the Chinese. The anti-Chinese policy of the Dutch and Spanish united communities that might have segmented much earlier into more associations, while the *laissez-faire* attitude of the Siamese rulers allowed segmentation to proceed more quickly. Similarly, the goldfields of British Columbia, with their lack of recognized legal order, forced the Chinese to unite in a single secret society, while the established authority of police and courts in Vancouver permitted the community to segment on the basis of various criteria. Applied in isolation to Phnom-Penh, this factor would also lead one to suggest a high rate of segmentation throughout the period of French rule.

A fourth factor, and the one on which most stress has been laid in this study, is the nature of rule over the Chinese community by the non-Chinese administration. Where the political organization of the Chinese community has been of little concern to outside authorities, as in Bangkok, Singapore, and Vancouver, segmentation has proceeded unabated to produce myriad associations based on criteria that permit cross-cutting memberships. Even under some systems of formal indirect rule, segmentation has proceeded apace. In Java this was so because the Captains were not provided with sanctions to stop alternative leaders and because their constituency was, for the Chinese at the time, an unnatural grouping comprising more than one speech group.

It is this fourth factor that clearly distinguishes the situation in twentieth-century Phnom-Penh from that in the other cities discussed here, with the possible exception of nineteenth-century Manila. The comparisons suggest that the crucial factor in inhibiting the elaboration of an associational structure for the community in Phnom-Penh was the presence of a system of indirect rule that was more or less unique to French Indochina, and entirely unique in its effective extension into the third and fourth decades of the twentieth century. The removal of that system allowed an associational structure to develop in Phnom-Penh that is consistent with that of overseas Chinese communities elsewhere.

13

Beyond a Conclusion

Having completed a formal demonstration of my thesis and provided a description of the social organization of the Chinese community in Cambodia, I wish now to move to a discussion of the traditional Chinese trading city. The exercise can be justified simply by the lack of sociological literature on Chinese urban society. Because social scientists in the past have held the view that traditional Chinese society was the sum of its villages, united by an Imperial Administration, they believed that our understanding of it would advance by the multiplication of anthropological village studies, on the one hand, and historical studies of the central government on the other. A concept of the economic and social integration of villages into larger social units, although hinted by at least one of the village studies (M. Yang 1948, 190–202), was nevertheless neglected until very recently. Organic solidarity in the Chinese situation was seen to end at the village level.

To a large extent this preoccupation with village and Empire reflects the Chinese ideal view of society. Chinese cities lacked the self-conscious bourgeoisie of Western cities (Balazs 1964, 66), and therefore even those living in cities participated in an ideology that provided them no status. The city was not thought by the Chinese themselves as an important and distinct part of their society.

Among scholars, the problem has been perpetuated, of course, by a disciplinary division of labour (cf. Freedman 1963, 3 f.): anthropologists were equipped to do village studies, yet historians were not trained to ask the kinds of sociological questions that would have directed research toward the city. At the risk of falling between both, I venture to suggest that the analysis I have presented in this study leads one to pose some interesting socio-logical questions about traditional Chinese urban society, a crucial link in the integration of Chinese society.

I use the term 'traditional Chinese trading city' to indicate that I am excluding three kinds of urban communities in China: (1) pre-Sung cities; (2) market towns in traditional China; and (3) Shanghai.

Pre-Sung cities were collections of villages (*li*) that were gathered together into walled areas for protection and in order to provide retainers for the ruling officials. They exhibited several of the characteristics of cities that Coe has described as 'unilateral' (Coe 1961, 67 f.), for they included cultivated fields within their walls and the solidarity that held them together was the power of the officials rather than economic interdependence with the surrounding countryside. Much of the population in pre-Sung cities either was forced by the army to reside within the walls or else moved there for protection. The various 'villages' making up the city had little contact between them, being separated by walls in which the gates were closed every night (Katô 1932, 48 n. 2; Balazs 1964, 67–71; Eberhard 1956, 257).

Fei Hsiao-tung distinguishes cities from towns in traditional China, the towns being market centres serving the villages, while the cities were administrative centres exploiting the villages (Fei 1953, 91–107). (In fact the cities did more than exploit, for the merchants who carried out inter-district trade lived there.) The standard market town can be conveniently ignored in my discussion because it is an integral part of rural China (cf. Skinner 1964).

Finally, Shanghai represents an essentially non-Chinese phenomenon. Murphey describes it as a 'replica of the nineteenth century Europe which had built it, and in time of the twentieth century America which was also a prominent contributor... Modern Chinese banking and finance, manufacturing, and commercial organization (and the new class of Chinese associated with them and divorced from traditional China) all got their start there' (Murphey 1953, 3; see also Murphey 1954, 354, and Levy 1949a, 15). Shanghai was in no way a traditional Chinese trading city.

Among sociologists, interest in the traditional Chinese trading city has usually been confined to the problem of explaining why China did not advance toward an industrial revolution at the same time as, or earlier than, Europe. Only cultural answers to this question have been provided, relating it to the Chinese value system and its rationalizing Confucian ideology. Mayborn, for instance, has suggested that the emphasis upon familism led to a priority on mutual aid rather than on self-reliance among merchants (Mayborn 1925, 186). A more sophisticated, but nonetheless exclusively cultural explanation has been provided by Levy in his discussion of the Chinese family system (Levy 1949b). Explanations remain cultural because there has been little sociological analysis of that area of Chinese society which is crucial to answering questions about Chinese 'stagnation': namely, the structure of the city. My treatment here does not relate specifically to this question, but I believe it will contribute toward providing a sociological answer.

TRADITIONAL CHINESE CITIES AND OVERSEAS COMMUNITIES

Three similarities between the overseas and the Chinese urban situations come immediately to mind. It is significant that these three characteristics distinguish urban from village social organization; they cannot, therefore, be illuminated by any number of village studies in China.

In the first place, the population of the Chinese city consisted in large measure of immigrant 'foreigners' (cf. Eberhard 1956, 265): workers from the surrounding countryside and merchants from other cities and towns. The merchants in particular were in many cases from areas of China remote in language and customs from their place of residence. Gernet writes that the quarter of thirteenth-century Hangchow (*Hang-zhou*) where many merchants resided (Phoenix Hill) was called colloquially 'the hill of the foreigners' (Gernet 1962, 82). According to Morse, 'The Cantonese is as much an alien in Shanghai as the Portuguese were in Spain when Philip II was sovereign over both countries' (Morse 1932, 42). Levy describes the merchants as 'outlanders' in an ideal sense (Levy 1949a, 5). The mandarins, too, were 'foreigners', for they were not permitted to serve in their home districts.

The second similarity, and one which follows partly from the first, is that kinship was not the primary principle of social organization in the Chinese city. Much of the population, both rich and poor, probably maintained ties with lineages in their rural areas of origin. Urban conditions in any case made it difficult to maintain corporate kin groups except among the most wealthy. Since the mandarins were posted to foreign districts and moved frequently, there was little possibility in the city for the elaboration by marriage and descent of kin links between them. All this suggests that criteria other than kinship were employed to form groupings in the Chinese city as in the overseas Chinese community. It is significant in this regard that Morton Fried, who studied a market town rather than a village, placed his emphasis upon relationships other than kinship (Fried 1953). Until his study appeared, village studies had led most social scientists interested in China to describe Chinese social structure almost exclusively in terms of kinship.

A third and related similarity is the structuring of a large part of the community in terms of voluntary associations (cf. Tao 1915, 83). The several studies of 'guilds' indicate that there were various types of associations into which migrants to the city were recruited on the basis of different criteria. The organization of these guilds and their relationship to each other may have exhibited considerable similarity with the associational structure of overseas urban Chinese communities. My material also suggests that the examination of the relationship between these associations and the administration may be useful in leading us to understanding of the political structure of the traditional Chinese urban community.

ASSOCIATIONS AND ASSOCIATIONAL STRUCTURE OF THE CHINESE TRADING CITY

The similarity between the 'provincial guilds' in the Chinese cities and the *hui-guan* in Phnom-Penh is immediately apparent. Indeed, the provincial associations were called *hui-guan*, and they probably provided the models for overseas Chinese *hui-guan*: immigrants to Phnom-Penh from Canton were probably aware, for instance, of the Cantonese *hui-guan* in Foochow. There is little information on these provincial *hui-guan* in urban China, for the studies have focused on the commercial and handicraft guilds.[1] They grouped practically everyone in the city from the

[1] The main study of Chinese guilds was conducted in Peking by Burgess and Gamble (Burgess 1928 and 1930; Gamble and Burgess 1921, 163–222). The emphasis these sociologists placed on the craft guild can be traced to the fact that

particular districts for which they were organized. Membership in them was almost mandatory for those wishing to live in the city, not because of the law, but because an immigrant was without security or contacts unless he joined (Morse 1932, 14 f.; Doolittle 1866, 151). The provincial guilds occupied themselves with matters of welfare among their *Landsmänner*, particularly with matters related to funerals and the shipment of bones back to the home district; many of them maintained cemeteries near the city (MacGowan 1886, 144; Morse 1932, 45). They usually owned a temple, where common worship was undertaken at least once a year and sacrifices made to the patron saint periodically (Morse 1932, 45; Allen 1872, 402). Finally, each provincial *hui-guan* settled disputes between its members as well as supporting any member in a just suit against an outsider (Morse 1932, 49 f.; Allen 1872, 400).

The structure of the provincial *hui-guan* in the Chinese city was probably not very different from that of the *hui-guan* in pre-war Phnom-Penh. (The descriptions of craft guild structure are also strikingly similar to my description of the *hui-guan* in Phnom-Penh.) A nominally democratic elective system was in fact controlled by the richer merchants, whose donations supported the *hui-guan* and from among whom its officers were chosen. Morse states that the *hui-guan* could not be democratic because its members placed considerable emphasis upon solidarity in a 'hostile territory' (Morse 1932, 43). The power of the *hui-guan* over its members may have been just as strong in the Chinese city as in pre-war Phnom-Penh, although in the one case it derived from the control of trade and in the other from control of immigration.

But not all the urban population was 'foreign', and, besides the provincial *hui-guan*, various other kinds of associations were present in the Chinese city. Burgess provides four other categories of 'guilds': religious fraternities, professional guilds, craft guilds,

Peking was a somewhat unusual Chinese city, for Peking and Chengtu were the main centres of small-scale industry (non-peasant handicrafts) in China (Liao 1948, 89 f.). Chengtu and Peking are both in areas of relatively prosperous and homogeneous agriculture; each was near another large city that was better situated for trade: Tientsin near the coast of the Yellow Sea, and Chungking on the Yangtse. Although the handicraft guilds that dominated the commercial life of these two cities were similar to the *hui-guan* in many ways, neither city was typical of traditional urban China.

and commercial guilds.[1] It is apparent from the descriptions, however, that the memberships of these different kinds of associations did not overlap. Because of occupational specialization along ethnic lines, it would have been unlikely if not impossible that a Cantonese resident of Ningpo, for instance, belonged at the same time to the Cantonese *hui-guan*, to the guild of sugar merchants, and to a fraternity worshipping the sage Lu Pan. The rules of the Cantonese *hui-guan* indicate that its members were all merchants (K 1883, *passim*; Allen 1872, *passim*); the guild of sugar merchants comprised only Hokkien (MacGowan 1886, 138); while the worshippers of Lu Pan would probably be limited to members of the building trades: carpenters, masons, cabinet-makers, and painters (Burgess 1928, 100 f.).

I have suggested that overseas Chinese exhibit a strong belief in the efficacy of combination, a belief that makes individuals willing to give considerable power to their leaders. Even among merchants struggling to get ahead of each other, the power of leaders to determine policy appears to be accepted readily. This same emphasis upon solidarity is seen in accounts of conflict with guilds in the earliest treaty ports in China (MacGowan 1886, 154–67).

Both in China and abroad, the solidarity of Chinese merchants finds ritual expression in periodic religious practices involving all the members of the *hui-guan*. The object of worship is sometimes a sage or deity related to the home district; more often it is *Guan Gong*, the supernatural personification of non-kin solidarity.[2]

---

[1] Burgess 1928, 16. The religious fraternity is mentioned in Morse, 9 f. The distinction made by Burgess between professional and craft guilds merely indicates that some guilds 'sell their services rather than manufactured goods' (Burgess 1928, 16); they are not different in structure or purpose. Burgess also distinguishes between social and economic 'provincial guilds', a distinction which probably derives from the special nature of Peking (see p. 164 n. 1); Burgess was familiar with the *hui-guan* in Peking, which had primarily non-commercial functions as inns for visiting students and officials, while the descriptions of *hui-guan* in other cities suggested to Burgess that their functions were primarily economic. It is unlikely that there were two separate kinds of *hui-guan*, such that one of each could be present in a city for men from the same district. The distinction between economic and social *hui-guan* is therefore as arbitrary as that between professional and craft guilds. The main material in English on *hui-guan* are in Morse, Mac-Gowan, and two complementary sets of rules for the Cantonese *hui-guan* in Foochow about 1870 (Allen 1872; K 1883).

[2] *Guan Gong* was a hero of the Three Kingdoms period, who entered into a sworn brotherhood with two of his lieutenants, *Liu* and *Zhang*. Because this act symbolizes non-kin loyalty, *Guan Gong* is often chosen as the patron saint of such

That the Chinese are well aware of the sociological implications of group worship is evidenced by statements from various guild officers interviewed by Burgess's assistants in Peking. A member of the guild of leather merchants stated, 'Worship is an unimportant thing, but the group spirit created through the meetings is very useful'; a mason said, 'But for the religious bond, the guild might not have lasted so long.' The recognition of the social control provided by ritual is expressed in this statement from the manager of the awning-makers' guild: 'The relation between the religious rights [sic] and the solidarity of the guild is very close, for offenders are brought to the master and are fined incense money' (Burgess 1928, 183 f.). The Chinese recognize that group ritual reinforces the solidarity they seek in association.

The solidarity among the members of a Chinese guild has been attributed by some writers to an innate tendency toward 'clannishness' on the part of all Chinese (e.g. d'Enjoy 1907; Mayborn 1925, 186). A sociological explanation may relate it to the need for such solidarity in order to survive both the demands placed upon the merchants by the imperial administration and the hostility of the local population and other guilds. I shall return to this question in the next section, but it is already evident that the willing submission of Chinese merchants to powerful leaders is not an overseas innovation, for it was present in the *hui-guan* in China as well. It produced a situation in the Chinese city in which almost every individual belonged to some kind of corporation. Unlike Western cities, the Chinese city exhibited little sociological *anomie*. Therefore, the political organization of the city may well have comprised an associational structure comparable to some of the overseas examples I have given.

Two diverse examples of associational structure have been provided for Phnom-Penh. During the period of *congrégations*, a small number of *hui-guan* with discrete memberships had a minimum of connections between them, any problems or conflict being solved by an overarching body consisting of the top leaders from each association. In contemporary Phnom-Penh there are many Chinese associations, the political relationships between which are realized through overlapping memberships

overseas associations as secret societies. A single clan association in Vancouver (and elsewhere) embraces the three names *Guan*, *Liu*, and *Zhang* (cf. W. Willmott 1964a, 35, Table 1).

and in particular through linking officers. Neither of these suggests itself as a perfect model of the associational structure of the Chinese city, for although there were many associations, they appear to have been discrete. Furthermore, an important function served by the Chinese associational structure in Phnom-Penh was the preservation of Chinese solidarity in the face of an alien culture as well as a colonial administration. While each individual *hui-guan* in the Chinese city may have served this function, no cultural solidarity would have united the 'foreign' Chinese as a body (except, perhaps, at the beginning of the non-Han dynasties).

The presence of many non-overlapping associations and the lack of solidarity among them provides the possibility of frequent conflict between members of different associations. Indeed, it has been suggested that this is one reason why the merchants in the Chinese city were never united against the administration (Gernet 1962, 94). However, the similar economic interests of members of different guilds and the desire of all of them to avoid litigation whenever possible (cf. Arnold 1930, 149) leads one to speculate that there may indeed have been some associational structure in the Chinese town that could deal at least with conflict between members, if not with conflict between associations and the administration. The leaders of the various guilds may have met as a reconciliation commission when needed.

A recently published study of a trading town near the island of Hongkong provides some evidence that the questions I have been dealing with are not far off the mark. The article also indicates that material is available to the imaginative scholar for the study of associations and associational structure in Chinese cities. I refer to the article by J. W. Hayes on the town of Cheung Chau in the late nineteenth century. Although the town was too small to include merchants engaged in other than relatively local trade, nevertheless the urban population comprised traders from various parts of Kwangtung with sufficient differences in loyalties to allow the establishment of four *hui-guan*. It is interesting that a single *hui-guan* in Cheung Chau united the Teochiu with Cantonese from *Hui-zhou*, both districts being in north-eastern Kwangtung. This combination suggests that the geographic unit upon which the *hui-guan* is based is relative to the location of the city and the nature of its population. In the case of Cheung Chau, the extent of the geographic unit for each *hui-guan* varied according to its distance from the town, a *hui-guan* representing a smaller area if it was closer. This was probably true in most cities.

Hayes deduces from his evidence – three stone tablets commemorating events involving community cooperation – that the associations together provided the administrative leadership for the town. He indicates that they cooperated in such things as town defence, hospital facilities, and welfare matters. For some of these, they united in an 'organisation of local leaders' called 'gaai fong' in Cantonese (*jie-fang*). According to Hayes, it had an 'informal constitution and its leaders were generally those persons who were already playing a leading part in the affairs of the four district associations' (Hayes 1963, 98). From Hayes's account it is apparent that most matters pertaining to the town were left by the magistrate to the associations and the structure uniting them.

The comparisons among overseas Chinese communities made in chapter 12 indicate that an important factor in determining the associational structure of a community was the political relationship between the community and the non-Chinese authorities: different kinds of direct or indirect rule produced diverse associational structures. While we cannot speak of the authorities in the Chinese city as being non-Chinese throughout the traditional period in China, nevertheless I have outlined two characteristics of urban associations in China which suggest that a system of indirect rule may have been present in the traditional Chinese city: first, the discreteness of membership would have allowed no ambiguity about responsibilities over individuals; and second, the willingness of merchants to submit to powerful leaders in the interests of solidarity would have made such a system workable.

MERCHANTS AND MANDARINS

From the point of view of political anthropology, perhaps the most interesting thing about the Chinese community in Phnom-Penh is the formal separation of political from economic power. This is characteristic of most overseas Chinese communities: a leader can achieve political power in the associational structure which does not provide concomitant economic power. In Phnom-Penh, this is true both during the life of the *congrégations* and at the present time. In both situations economic power can be translated into political power, for wealth is the main condition for access to office; but in neither situation does the accession to political office lead directly to the acquisition of wealth. It may be that the control of movement in the hands of the *chef de congrégation* could be used to advance his own economic interests – for instance, by denying a business rival access to a particular provincial market – but it is clear from the data that such practices would have been considered *ultra vires*, and it is unlikely that they would have been tolerated as a regular procedure. All my informants agreed that there was no economic advantage to be gained from being a *chef de congrégation*. In the situation today it is even less likely that office in the Chinese voluntary associations can provide direct economic power. Office in voluntary associations of course provides contacts and prestige – both of which can be translated into economic advantage – but it does not give a Chinese businessman authority or power over the economic actions of others. In short, one may say that those who aspire to leadership among the Chinese in Phnom-Penh are interested in the prestige of power rather than in the power of prestige.

The Chinese city, too, exhibited a formal separation of political from economic power, but at a somewhat different level: the merchants took no official part in the administration of the city. Indeed, Chinese cities lacked a municipal administration as such, the officials of the district being responsible for the entire rural as well as urban area, and the administrative structure being designed essentially for rural administration. On the other hand, office in an association probably provided the merchant both economic and political power over his members; the leaders of the *hui-guan* were not only elected from among the richest merchants, but may have been able to turn their authority into further economic advantage. The difference between the two situations lies in the fact that the mandarins were interested in the merchants only in so far as they could extract profit from them (Murphey 1954, 358). Indeed, official demands and requisitions were so great as to ruin a significant proportion of merchants periodically (Katô 1932, 62 ff.; Balazs 1964, 77). In such circumstances, office in a *hui-guan* may have provided some economic advantage through the power of distributing requisitions. It seems likely that the merchant in the Chinese city was as interested in the power of prestige as in the prestige of power.

I have already suggested that the heads of the *hui-guan* in the

Chinese cities could be seen as agents of the imperial administration in a system of indirect rule over their followers. Gernet writes that at Hangchow (*Hang-zhou*) in the thirteenth century, the heads of the guilds 'exercised a general control over their members, came to the aid of those in need or who had no family, and insisted upon each member's absolute integrity' (Gernet 1962, 87 f.). Marco Polo remarked (as did the first European traders in Canton; cf. Hunter 1882) that the word of a Chinese merchant could be trusted, a fact that no doubt derived from the power exercised by the *hui-guan*, in the person of its head, over each member. MacGowan reports that the guilds did some policing in matters of theft, tax delinquency, and fictitious buying (Mac-Gowan 1886, 143). Finally, Gamble states that the officials found the guilds 'useful', for they could consult the headmen on the enforcement of new policy; furthermore, 'the guild has often accepted the responsibility for enforcing the rules and even for the taxes' required by the administration (Gamble and Burgess 1921, 165). These few facts suggest that the head of the guild occupied a position in the political structure of the Chinese city somewhat analogous to the position of *chef de congrégation* in French Cambodia.

The powers of the *chef de congrégation* in Phnom-Penh comprised two distinct elements. On the one hand, control over the movements of his *congréganistes* derived from French colonial law. On the other hand, control over the activities and expenditures of the *hui-guan* derived from the voluntary obedience of his followers. These two aspects of his power were in a real sense contradictory, for their legitimation involved disparate systems of belief. The *chef* was therefore caught between two belief systems: that of the French and that of the Chinese. As a cultural problem, the ambivalent position of the overseas Chinese leader in situations of indirect rule (formal or informal) has been compared to that of the foreman in industry, who must accept two disparate systems of values in order to accomplish his tasks (Skinner 1968).

By analogy one is led to suggest that the head of the guild in the traditional Chinese city was caught in a similar dissonance of authority. There is an important difference between the two situations, however: while the *chef de congrégation* was a status defined by law, the position of guild head was entirely outside the legal structure in China. The incongruity appeared not between the law and minority beliefs, but between the interests of the officials and those of the merchants. The head of the guild may have been in a position of ambivalent loyalty, but it was not based on separate systems of beliefs about authority.[1]

The fact that merchants participated in the value system of the officials led them to seek the legitimate prestige and power of office wherever possible by the purchase of degrees (and of office in the late nineteenth century) and also by developing kin links with officials, either through descent or marriage. Socially (not culturally) this is comparable to assimilation in the overseas situation, with one major qualification: the merchant was aware of his low status in traditional China, while few Chinese in Southeast Asia consider themselves of lower status than the indigenous population.[2] The discrepancy between ideally low status and great economic power makes the merchant's relationship to the official in China a particularly interesting one to examine.

Eberhard suggests that many of the merchants were younger sons of officials, and hence could not develop an 'entrepreneurial spirit' because of the patronage of elder kinsmen (Eberhard 1956, 267 f.). The traditionally low status of the merchant suggests that a man, once having achieved office, would not turn to trade to make more wealth. Furthermore, the great opportunities for gain available to the official would probably have led few to seek further wealth in trade (cf. Chang 1955, 43–51). Although Chang Chung-li gives several examples of officials turned merchant, most of these traded in items monopolized by the government: salt brokering, and pawnshops (at some times). His biographies of officials who were businessmen are mainly of officials who achieved their position through trade rather than vice versa (Chang 1962, *passim*). After the middle of the nineteenth century, the situation changed, beginning at Shanghai. From then on, officials went into business more and more frequently (*ibid.*, 155

[1] Many guilds hired a general secretary from among the gentry, for only a literatus could petition the mandarins (Morse 1932, 17; Allen 1872, 400). In the overseas community, the interpreter was in an analogous position, although the leaders of the Chinese community themselves might enjoy direct contact with the authorities, as in the case of the Chinese Captains and some of the *chefs de congrégation* (cf. Skinner 1968; D. Willmott 1960, 148 f.).

[2] In fact, two contradictory traditional values confronted the overseas Chinese businessman: on the one hand his self-image was low as a merchant, on the other, it was high as a Chinese. A motivation to assimilate to the indigenous population involved some balancing of these conflicting values.

and 160–70). The explanation for the absence of an entrepreneurial spirit in the Chinese city is perhaps to be found in the political relationships between merchant and official; the kin links uniting them form only one aspect of this relationship.

Put most simply, three different power relationships are possible between merchant and mandarin: (1) the mandarin was subordinate to the merchant; (2) the merchant was subordinate to the mandarin; or (3) a relationship existed between them on the basis of equivalent power operating in different fields. The first possibility is not consistent with either the low ideal status of the merchant or the fact that the mandarin could call upon the might of the Imperial Administration – in local and immediate terms, the garrison. There is more possibility of the opposite relationship obtaining, but two factors suggest that it, too, is unlikely: (a) the merchants were combined in associations that made boycott an effective weapon against repressive measures; and (b) the mandarin's career depended on his ability to avoid trouble of any kind in his district. It is far more likely, therefore, that the merchants and mandarins lived in a relationship involving constant compromise and struggle, a process that was symbiotic in providing advantages to both. Levy has likened this relationship to that between gangster and politician in some American cities during the first decade of the twentieth century (Levy 1949a, 6 f.).

But the relationship between merchant and mandarin was complicated by the presence of a third powerful class in the Chinese city, for which there is no analogy in overseas Chinese communities. I refer to the gentry, that body of landed families some of whom were rich and many of whom held degrees. The relationship of the gentry to both merchants and officials has been discussed at length by Chang Chung-li, and Fei has discussed the latter relationship briefly (Chang 1955 and 1962; Fei 1953, 17–32). Even if we follow Chang's very narrow definition of the gentry, only about ten per cent of them held office at any time during the nineteenth century, and the proportion was probably even lower during Ming and earlier Ch'ing times.[1] The vast majority

[1] This percentage is estimated from figures given by Chang Chung-li in different parts of his book (Chang 1955). On page 120 he gives figures for the 'total of officials and holders of official titles' of 80,000 before the Taiping rebellion and 150,000 after; on page 165, in Table 32, he gives the figures for the total size of the gentry (not including their families) of 1,095,000 before the Taiping rebellion and 1,444,000 after. But if we limit the figures to 'regular'

of the gentry were therefore living in their home districts, where their influence both in business and in official affairs was of great weight.

The study of traditional Chinese urban social organization thus leaves the overseas material behind. Perhaps the questions I have raised will impel other students, as they impel me, to seek whatever data are available on the political structure of the Chinese city in order to attempt to formulate some answers to the questions and suggestions I have raised. It is my belief that the more we study the Chinese city the less foreign to China will appear the social organization of overseas Chinese communities.

gentry, only about 3 per cent gained office (*ibid.*, 118). The proportion of 'regular' and 'irregular' degrees and titles or offices was less during the Ming dynasty and rose throughout the Ch'ing dynasty (Ho 1959, 46 f., 104). Chang defines 'gentry' as those men who have received at least one degree through examination or purchase (Chang 1955, 3). Occasionally he broadens the definition to include the families of such men, thus coming close to the definition used by Fei Hsiao-tung (Fei 1953, 17). Ho provides an even narrower definition of 'official class', but does not himself use the term 'gentry' (Ho 1959, 34–41).

APPENDIX I

Some Statistics on the Chinese in Phnom-Penh and Siemréap

The following table is based on material from the 1961 census which was made available to me by the *Direction de la Statistique*. Two decks of census cards were purchased from the census bureau: one deck of 7445 cards represented the entire urban population of Siemréap with the exception of those tracts (001, 003, 005, 007, 008) which comprise institutions alien to the local population (army camps and prison) and which it was known through research included no Chinese. The other deck of 1987 cards represented three city blocks in the centre of Phnom-Penh that were known to be almost solidly Chinese.

Only two questions in the census relate directly to the question of ethnicity: nationality and native language (*langue maternelle*). In both samples, it was assumed that all those of Chinese nationality as well as those whose native language was Chinese are ethnic Chinese. The figure for Siemréap was therefore 1306 Chinese, and for the Phnom-Penh sample, 1592. In fact, the number of Chinese may be somewhat higher, as I have argued elsewhere (W. Willmott 1967, Appendix ii).

TABLE 5. Statistics on the Chinese, based on 1961 Census Samples

Item	Siemréap Absolute	Percentage	Phnom-Penh Absolute	Percentage
1. Age:				
under 15	638	48.8	635	39.9
15 to 45	506	38.8	716	44.9
over 45	162	12.4	241	15.2
2. Women per 100 men (15–45)	86		78	
3. Place of birth:				
China	293	22.6	405	25.6
Indochina	1007	77.2	1161	72.9

TABLE 5 (contd.)

Item	Siemréap		Phnom-Penh	
	Absolute	Percentage	Absolute	Percentage
4. Nationality:				
Cambodian	96	7.4	48	3.0
Chinese	1210	92.6	1444	97.0
5. Native language:				
Chinese	1247	95.5	1573	98.8
Khmer	16	1.2	8	0.5
Other	43	3.3	11	0.7
6. Average size of household:				
all individuals		6.35		6.65
kin only		6.01		6.04
7. Language of household:*				
Chinese	192	83.8	218	95.6
Khmer	31	13.6	10	4.4
Vietnamese	6	2.6	0	–
8. Place of birth of couples:				
Husband *Wife*				
China China	64	28.0	80	38.8
China Indochina	75	32.8	55	26.7
Indochina China	16	7.0	18	8.8
Indochina Indochina	74	32.3	53	25.7
9. Nationality of couples:				
Chinese Chinese	158	67.2	205	87.0
Chinese Cambodian	50	21.3	16	6.9
Cambodian Chinese	11	4.7	8	3.4
Cambodian Cambodian	6	2.5	0	–
Chinese Vietnamese	8	3.4	0	–
Vietnamese Chinese	2	0.9	0	–

* For these statistics only those households including a married couple were counted; for Siemréap, 229, and for Phnom-Penh, 233. Information was lacking for some couples.

Newspapers in Phnom-Penh, 1962–63

In 1962–63 there were thirteen daily newspapers published in Phnom-Penh, distributed between the speech groups as follows (one of the French papers appeared only thrice weekly):

		Circulation
Four Khmer Papers		10,100
Three French papers		7,900–8,400
Vietnamese paper		4,600
Chinese papers:		
Mian-Hua Ri-bao	6,000	
Gong-Shang Ri-bao	6,000	
Mei-Jiang Ri-bao	7,200	
Sheng-huo Wu-bao	3,500	
Xin Bao	6,000	
Total Chinese papers		28,700
Total Circulation		51,300–51,800

(Circulation figures from the Press Bureau of the Ministry of Information.) All these newspapers had a nationwide circulation, being the only dailies published in the Kingdom. The preponderance of Chinese is therefore not necessarily representative of the relative reading populations in Phnom-Penh itself.

By April 1967, the Ministry estimated that the circulation of daily newspapers had risen to 70,000, of which 25,000 were thought to be Chinese. The drop can be explained by the closing of the *Xin Bao* in the interim.

In September 1967, when there was a government crisis of some proportions, all private newspapers in the kingdom were closed down permanently, including, of course, all the Chinese newspapers.

The 'Procession of Gods' at *Yuan-Xiao*, 1963

The following is a list of the items in order of march making up the procession on the principal day of *Yuan-Xiao* (fifteenth of first month), February 1963 (see pp. 98–102 for a description of the parade).

Two great paper lanterns flanking a banner on which was written (in Chinese) 'Phnom-Penh Overseas Chinese Salute *Yuan-Xiao*' (*Jin-bian Hua-qiao Qing-zhu Yuan-Xiao*).

Cortège of the Teochiu temple, including banners, flags, wooden signs, a small traditional orchestra, a horse, and a soft-drinks van carrying refreshments; about one hundred people, no medium.

A lion team from Kratié.

Cortège of a Phnom-Penh lion team, led by a banner stating *Lao-xian shi-miao*, a huge papier mâché head of a stag, four lanterns with the characters *Ren-de Shan Tang*, followed by many lanterns, flags, and banners, then the team itself; about one hundred people.

Twelve paper lanterns in the shape of fish, carried on the ends of upright poles by costumed men.

About fifty large satin banners, each carried by two girls in satin uniform, each presented by a company (all Teochiu according to an informant).

A Teochiu opera company, consisting of about thirty costumed actors and actresses.

Three dance troupes of small girls in costume doing folk-dances.

Orchestra and dance troupe of the *Ren-de Shan Tang*, thirty people.

Cortège of about a hundred people surrounding a possessed medium standing on a sedan and followed by a great papier mâché bird.

Cortège of a Vietnamese medium.

Cortège including an adult and a children's dance troupe and a possessed medium; about a hundred people.

Cortège of the Hainanese temple, about four hundred people, including a traditional orchestra, a cart carrying refreshments, and a female medium.

Cortège of another medium.

Cortège of the Hakka temple, about fifty people, no medium.

Cortège of the Association of Dental Technicians, including a dragon team of about twenty men.

Cortège of the Cantonese temple, including the *Huang-shao-shi* lion team and about fifty people, no medium.

Cortège of one of the *Ben-tou-gong* temples, including a children's percussion band in costume, two mediums.

Thirty-two cortèges including forty-two male mediums.

Cortège of a Khmer-loeu male medium.

Eighteen cortèges including thirty female mediums.

Cortège of the Hokkien temple, including wooden signs, a horse, and three sedan chairs holding idols, on the last of which stood an elderly medium dressed in white apron and red bib; about three hundred people.

Cortège of the *Wu-bang hui-guan* temple, including two sedan chairs, on the second of which stood a male medium similarly dressed; about two hundred people.

Fourteen vans advertising soft drinks and sauces, each with its own loudspeaker and each surrounded by men distributing advertising circulars.

LIST OF CHINESE CHARACTERS

(Words in italics do not conform to the system of
romanization used throughout the text.)

ai-si-ting 哀思亭

bai 拜

bang 幫

bang-hui 幫會

bang-zhang 幫長

Ba Xian Jia Xi 八仙賀喜

Bao-an 寶安

Bao-sheng Da Di 保生大帝

Bao-Xing 寶興

Bei-ji Da Di 北極大帝

Ben-tou Gong 本頭公

Bo-luo 博羅

Chang-jiang Ju Luo Ban Gu 長江局鑼班鼓

Chao-Qiong-Ke Xue-xiao 潮瓊客學校

Chao-yang 潮陽

Chao-zhou hui-guan 潮州會館

Chen 陳

Chen Chi-lu 陳奇祿

Chen Guang-yu 陳光玉

Chen Shun-he 陳順和

Chong-Jiu 重九

Chong-Yang 重陽

Chou En-lai (Zhou En-lai) 周思來

da-ji 大祭

Da-sheng Fo-zu 大聖佛祖

da-shou 大壽

de 德

De-Fong 德豐

De-Hua 德華

De-Long 德隆

De-Xing 德興

diao-jie 調解

Dong-fang　東方

Dong-guan　東莞

Dong-Hua Yi-yuan　東華醫院

Dong-Jie　冬節

dong-shi hui　董事會

dong-shi zhang　董事長

Duan-Hua Zhong-xue　端華中學

er-pan　二盤

Foochow (Fu-zhou)　福州

fu (*district*)　府　　(*charm*)　符

fu-zhang　副長

Gao-ming xian　高明縣

Gao-yao　高要

gong-ci tang　公祠堂

gong-ji　公祭

gong-ji tang　公祭堂

gong-li　公立

gong-si　公司

Gong-Shang Ri-bao 工商日報

gong-so 公所

gu-wen 顧問

Guan Gong 關公

Guan Sheng Da Di 關聖大帝

Guang-Zhao-Hui Hui-guan 廣肇惠會館

Guang-zhou 廣州

Guo 郭

Hainan 海南

Hakka (Ke-jia) 客家

Hang-zhou 杭州

Hao-shan 鶴山

Hokkien (Fu-jian) 福建

hong-bang 洪幫

hong-bao 紅包

Hong-men Hui 洪門會

Hong-men Tuan-ti 洪門團體

hu-zhu-she 互助社

Hua-qiao 華僑

Hua-xian 花縣

Huang 黃

Huang Bang-zhang 黃幫長

Huang shao-shi 黃少獅

Huang-shi zong-qin tong-ren 黃氏宗親同人

hui 會

hui-guan 會館

hui-zhang 會長

Hui-zhou 惠州

Jie-fang 街坊

Jie-yang 揭陽

Jin-bian Hua-qiao Qing-zhu Yuan-Xiao 金邊華僑慶祝元宵

jin-bu 進步

Jin-shui Xian Gong 金水仙公

Jiu-jiang xiang 九江鄉

Kang Zhen Jun 康真君

Kuomintang (Guo Min Dang) 國民黨

Kwangtung (Guang-dong) 廣東

Lai Die-cha 賴迭差

Lan-fang Gong-si 蘭芳公司

Lao xian-shi miao 老仙獅廟

Li 李

Lian-you Hu-zhu-she 聯友互助社

Lin 林

Liu 劉

Liu A-sheng 劉亞生

Liu Shao-chi (Liu Shao-qi) 劉少奇

Lu 盧

Luo 羅

lu-xing jie-hun 旅行結婚

man yue 滿月

Mei-jiang Ri-bao 湄江日報

men shen 門神

Mian-Hua Qiao-Jiao 棉華僑教

Mian-Hua Ri-bao 棉華日報

miao 廟

Min-zhi Dang 民治黨

Ming-xiang 明香

mu pu-sa 木菩薩

Nan-hai 南海

Nan-hai Jiu-jiang 南海九江

pan 盤

Pan-yu 番禺

qi-fu 七府

qi-fu gong-so 七府公所

qi-xie qi-shi 泣謝啓事

Qing-Ming 清明

Qing-yuan 清遠

Ren-de Shan Tang 仁德善堂

San-he Hui 三和會．三河會

san-pan 三盤

Shan-qu gong-so 善舉公所

San-shui 三水

shang-hui 商會

Shang-wu Yin-shu Guan 商務印書館

shang-yue 賞月

Sheng-huo Wu-bao 生活午報

Sheng Mu 聖母

Shui-wei Sheng-Mu 水尾聖母

Shun-de 順德

si 寺

Si-hui 四會

Si-jiao Hao-ma Xin Ci-dian 四角號碼新詞典

Si-ming Zao Jun 司命灶君

Si-yi 四邑

tang 堂

tang-yuan 糖圓

Teochiu (Chao-zhou) 潮州

ti-yu hui 體育會

Tian-di Fu-Mu 天地父母

Tian-hou Sheng Mu 天后聖母

tong-xiang hui 同鄉會

tong-xing hui 同姓會

tong-xing qin-hui 同姓親會

tu-di zhi shen 土地之神

tuan-ti 團體

Wang 王

Wu 吳

wu-bang 五幫

Wu-bang diao-jie wei-yuan hui 五幫調解委員會

Wu-bang gong-so 五幫公所

Wu-bang hui-guan 五幫會館

Wu-fang Wu-tu Long-shen 五方五土龍神
Qian-hou Di-zhu Cai-shen 前後地主財神

Xi-fang Nian-fo She 西方念佛社

xian 縣

Xian-tian Da Dao 先天大道

xiang 鄉

xiao-zhu 校主

Xie 謝

Xie-shi Xian-qiao Gong-mu 謝氏先僑公墓

Xie-tian Da Di 謝天大帝

Xin Bao 新報

xing 姓

Xu 許

Xuan-tian Shang Di 玄天上帝

Yang 楊

Yao-ming 曜明

Ye Bao-xing 葉寶興

Ye Pei-chen 葉沛臣

you mie shi 有乜事

you-shen 遊神

Yuan-Xiao 元宵

yue-bing 月餅

yue-shui 樂稅

Zeng-cheng 增城

Zhang 張

Zhang-shi zong-zu 張氏宗族

Zhao-zhou 肇州

Zheng 鄭

Zhi-gong Tang 致公堂

zhi-gu 執骨

zhi-shi-hui 值事會

Zhong-hua hui-guan 中華會館

Zhong-hua li-shi hui-guan 中華理事會館

Zhong-hua Yi-yuan yan-ge xiao-shi 中華醫院沿革小史

Zhong-hua Yi-yuan Yi-liao Xie-zhu Hui 中華醫院醫療協助會

Zhong-hua Zheng-jue Si 中華正覺寺

Zhong-Qiu 中秋

Zhong-shan 中山

Zhong-Yuan 中元

zhou 州

Zhou Jie-gang 周節剛

Zhu-sheng Niang-niang 注生娘娘

zong 粽

LIST OF WORKS CITED

Abbreviations used in the text: AKP   *Agence Khmère Presse*
                         An. du Camb.   *Annuaire du Cambodge*
                         JOC   *Journal Officiel du Cambodge*
                         JOIF   *Journal Officiel de l'Indochine
                                      Française*

Agence Khmère Presse (directeur: Tep Chhiu Kheng), Ministry of Information, Phnom-Penh, August 1962–July 1963 (daily information bulletin).

ALLEN, C. F. R. (trans.), 1872. 'Regulations of the Canton guild at Foochow' in *A vocabulary and hand-book of the Chinese language, romanised in the mandarin dialect* (2 vols.) by Rev. Justus Doolittle, Foochow and London.

ALMOND, GABRIEL, 1960. 'Introduction', *The politics of the developing areas* (G. Almond and James S. Coleman, eds.), Princeton, pp. 3–64.

AMYOT, JACQUES, 1960. *The Chinese Community of Manila: a study of adaptation of Chinese familism to the Philippine environment*, Philippine Studies Program Research Series, no. 2, University of Chicago.

Annuaire du Cambodge, 1892, 1893 and 1894.

ARNOLD, JULEAN, 1930. 'The commercial problems of Chinese', *Annals of the American Academy of Political and Social Science*, **152**, pp. 142–59.

BALAZS, ETIENNE, 1964. *Chinese Civilization and Bureaucracy, variations on a theme* (trans. H. M. Wright, Arthur F. Wright, ed.), New Haven.

BEAUCHATAUD, JEAN-PIERRE, n.d. *La minorité vietnamienne du Cambodge* (unpublished *mémoire de stage*), Ecole Nationale de la France d'Outre-Mer (Institut des Hautes Etudes d'Outre-Mer).

BEERSKI, P. JEANNERAT DE, 1923. *Angkor: ruins in Cambodia*, London.

BLYTHE, W. L., 1941. 'Foreword' in *Triad and Tabut* by Mervyn Llwelyn Wynne, Government Printing Office, Singapore.

———, 1969. *The Impact of Chinese Secret Societies in Malaya*, Oxford.

BOEKE, J. H., 1953. *Economics and economic policy of dual societies as exemplified by Indonesia*, Haarlem.

BOUDET, PAUL, 1942. 'La conquête de la Cochinchine par les Nguyên et le rôle des émigrés chinois', *Bulletin de l'Ecole Française d'Extrême-Orient*, **xlii**, pp. 115–32.

Bulletin Administratif du Cambodge (monthly publication during the French Protectorate), Phnom-Penh.

BURCHETT, WILFRED G., 1959. *Mekong Upstream, a visit to Laos and Cambodia*, Berlin.

BURGESS, JOHN STEWART, 1928. *The guilds of Peking*, New York.

———, 1930. 'The guilds and trade associations of China', *Annals of the American Academy of Political and Social Science*, **152**, pp. 72–80.

Cambodge, 1962. Ministry of Information, Phnom-Penh.

CATOR, W. J., 1936. *The Economic Position of the Chinese in the Netherlands Indies*, Oxford.

CHANG, CHUNG-LI, 1955. *The Chinese gentry, studies on their role in nineteenth century Chinese society*, Seattle.

———, 1962. *The income of the Chinese gentry*, Seattle.

CHAU KON [ZHOU JIE-GANG], 1961. *Zhong-Hua Yi-yuan yan-ce xiao-shi*, Phnom-Penh (in Chinese).

——— (ed.), 1963. *Recueil des règlements en vigueur relatifs aux opérations d'import et d'export au Cambodge, 1962* (Numéro spécial du Journal Mekong Yat Pao), Phnom-Penh.

Chinatown News (fortnightly magazine, Roy Mah, ed.), Vancouver.

CLAIRON, MARCEL, 1962. *Droit Khmer, code de commerce (édition mise à jour au 30 septembre 1961)*, Phnom-Penh.

COE, MICHAEL, 1961. 'Social typology and tropical forest civilisations', *Comparative Studies in Society and History*, **iv**, no. 1, pp. 65–85.

COMBER, LEON, 1957. *An introduction to Chinese secret societies in Malaya*, Singapore.

COPPENRATH, GÉRALD, 1967. *Les Chinois de Tahiti, de l'aversion à l'assimilation, 1865–1966*, Publications de la Société des Océanistes, no. 21, Paris.

CORDIER, M. H., 1888. 'Les sociétés secrètes chinoises', *Revue d'Ethnographie*, **7**, pp. 52–72..

COUGHLIN, RICHARD J., 1960. *Double identity, the Chinese in modern Thailand*, Hongkong.

COULET, G., and P.B. [PAUL BOUDET], 1929. 'Les Chinois en Indochine', *Extrême-asie, Revue Indochinoise*, n.s., no. 35, pp. 457–64.

DE GROOT, J. J. M., 1886. 'Les fêtes annuellement célébrées à Emoui (Amoy), étude concernant la religion populaire des Chinois' (trans. from Dutch by C. G. Chavannes), *Annales du Musée Guimet*, vols 11 and 12.

DE LA PORTE, L., 1880. *Voyage au Cambodge, l'architecture khmer*, Paris.

D'ENJOY, P., 1907. 'Associations, congrégations, et sociétés secrètes chinoises', *Revue Indochinoise*, n.s., no. 55, pp. 440–52.

Dépêche, La (directeur Chau-Seng) (daily newspaper), July 1962–July 1963, Phnom-Penh.

DOOLITTLE, REV. JUSTUS, 1866. *Social life of the Chinese: some account of their religious, governmental, educational, and business customs and opinions, with special but not exclusive reference to Fuhchau*, London.

'Dragon in the Reeds', *Far Eastern Economic Review*, **lvi**, no. 10 (8 June 1967), pp. 613 ff.

DUBREUIL, RENÉ, 1910. *De la condition des Chinois et de leur rôle économique en Indo-Chine*, Bar-sur-Seine.

DURAND, MAURICE, 1959. *Technique et panthéon des médiums viêtnamiens (Dông)*, Publications de l'EFEO, **xlv**), Paris.

EASTON, DAVID, 1959. 'Political Anthropology', *Biennial Review of Anthropology 1959* (Bernard J. Siegel, ed.), Stanford.

EBERHARD, WOLFRAM, 1956. 'Data on the structure of the Chinese city in the pre-industrial period', *Economic Development and Cultural Change*, **iv**, no. 3, pp. 253–68.

EISENSTADT, S. N., 1959. 'Primitive political systems: a preliminary comparative analysis', *American Anthropologist*, **61**, no. 2, pp. 200–20.

ELLIOT, ALAN J. A., 1955. *Chinese spirit-medium cults in Singapore*, London School of Economics Monographs on Social Anthropology, no. 14, London.

FALL, BERNARD B., 1958. 'Vietnam's Chinese Problem', *Far Eastern Survey*, **xxvii**, no. 5, pp. 65–72.

FEI, HSIAO-TUNG, 1953. *China's gentry: essays in rural-urban relations* (Margaret Redfield, ed.), Chicago.

FIRTH, RAYMOND, 1951. *Elements of Social Organisation*, London.

——, 1955. 'Some principles of social organisation', *Journal of the Royal Anthropological Institute*, **85**, pp. 1–18.

——, 1959. *Social change in Tikopia*, London.

FISHER, CHARLES A., 1964. *South-east Asia, a social, economic, and political geography*, London.

FORTES, MEYER, and EVANS-PRITCHARD, E. E., 1940. *African Political systems*, London.

FREEDMAN, MAURICE, 1957. *Chinese family and marriage in Singapore*, Colonial Research Studies, no. 20, London.

——, 1960. 'Immigrants and associations: Chinese in nineteenth century Singapore', *Comparative Studies in Society and History*, **iii**, no. 1, pp. 25–48.

——, 1963. 'A Chinese phase in social anthropology', *British Journal of Sociology*, **xiv**, no. 1, pp. 1–19.

FREEDMAN, MAURICE, and TOPLEY, MARJORIE, 1961. 'Religion and social realignment among the Chinese in Singapore', *Journal of Asian Studies*, **xxi**, no. 1, pp. 3–23.

FRIED, MORTON, 1953. *Fabric of Chinese society, a study of the social life of a Chinese county seat*, New York.

FURNIVALL, J. S., 1939. *Netherlands Indies, a study of plural economy*, Cambridge.

GAMBLE, SYDNEY D., and BURGESS, JOHN STEWART, 1921. *Peking, a social survey conducted under the auspices of the Princeton University Center in China and the Peking Young Men's Christian Association*, London.

GASPARDONE, EMILE, 1952. 'Un Chinois des mers du sud, le fondateur de Hà-Tiên', *Journal Asiatique*, **240**, no. 3, pp. 363–85.

GERNET, JACQUES, 1962. *Daily Life in China on the eve of the Mongol invasion, 1250–76* (translated by H. M. Wright), New York.

GINSBURG, NORTON S., 1955. 'The great city in southeast Asia', *American Journal of Sociology*, **lx**, no. 5, pp. 455–62.

GLUCKMAN, HERMAN MAX, 1955. *Custom and conflict in Africa*, Oxford.

GROSLIER, B.-P., 1954. 'Une enquête démographique et sociale sur un quartier de Saigon-Cholon', *Bulletin de la Société des Etudes Indochinoises*, n.s., no. 1, pp. 5–21.

——, 1958. 'Angkor et le Cambodge au XVIe siècle d'après les sources portuguaises et espagnoles,' *Annales du Musée Guimet*, lxiii, Paris.

HAYES, J. W., 1963. 'Cheung Chau 1850–1898, information from commemorative tablets', *Journal of the Hong Kong Branch of the Royal Asiatic Society*, **3**, pp. 86–106.

HEPP, MAURICE, 1928. *L'immense Indo-Chine, une vue cavalière de l'Indo-Chine, les Chinois et l'Indo-Chine, questions indo-chinoises*, Paris.

HO, PING-TI, 1962. *The ladder of success in Imperial China*, New York.

HORSLEY, MARGARET WYANT, 1950. *Sangley: the formation of anti-Chinese feeling in the Philippines, a cultural study of the stereotypes of prejudice* (unpublished Ph.D. dissertation), Columbia University.

[HUNTER, WILLIAM C.,] An Old Resident, 1882. *The fan-kwae at Canton before treaty days, 1825–1844*, London.

JENSEN, KHIN KHIN MYINT, 1956. *The Chinese in the Philippines during the American régime: 1898–1946* (unpublished Ph.D. dissertation), University of Wisconsin.

Journal Officiel de l'Indochine Française, Saigon and Hanoi.

Journal Officiel du Cambodge, Phnom-Penh.

K, 1883. 'Chinese guilds and their rules', *China Review*, 12, pp. 5–9.

KAHIN, GEORGE McT., 1952. *Nationalism and revolution in Indonesia*, Ithaca.

KATÔ, SHIGESHI, 1932. 'On the hang or the associations of merchants in China, with especial reference to the institution in the T'ang and Sung periods', *Memoirs of the Research Department of the Toyo Bunko*, viii, pp. 45–83.

LAFARGUE, JEAN-ANDRÉ, 1909. *L'immigration chinoise en Indochine, sa réglementation, ses conséquences économiques et politiques*, Paris.

LASKER, BRUNO, 1946. 'The role of the Chinese in the Netherlands Indies', *Far Eastern Quarterly*, 5, no. 2, pp. 162–71.

LECLERE, ADHÉMARD, 1898. *Les codes cambodgiens* (2 vols.), Paris.

——, 1907. 'Histoire de Kampot, et de la rébellion de cette province en 1885–1887', *Revue Indochinoise*, nos. 60 and 61, pp. 828–41 and 933–52.

LEVASSEUR, G., 1939. *La situation juridique des Chinois en Indochine depuis les accords de Nankin (problème de droit international privé)*, 2nd edition, Hanoi.

LEVY, MARION J., 1949a. 'The social background of modern business development in China', in *The rise of the modern Chinese business class: two introductory essays*, by Marion J. Levy and Kuo-heng Shih, Institute of Pacific Relations, New York.

——, 1949b. *The Family Revolution in Modern China*, Cambridge, Mass.

LIAO CHIH-WEI, 1948. 'The apprentices in Chengtu during and after the war', *Yenching Journal of Social Studies*, iv, no. 1, pp. 89–106.

Liste des Principales Industries, 1961, Ministry of Industry, [Phnom-Penh].

LO HSIANG-LIN, 1961. *A historical survey of the Lan-fang presidential system in Western Borneo, established by Lo Fang-pai and other overseas Chinese*, Institute of Chinese Culture, Hongkong.

LO HSIANG-LIN et al., 1963. *Hongkong and its external communications before 1842*, Institute of Chinese Culture, Hongkong.

LYMAN, STANFORD M., WILLMOTT, W. E., and HO, BERCHING, 1964. 'Rules of a Chinese secret society in British Columbia', *Bulletin of the School of Oriental and African Studies*, 27, no. 3, pp. 530–9.

MACGOWAN, D. J., 1886. 'Chinese guilds, or chambers of commerce and trade unions', *Journal of the China Branch of the Royal Asiatic Society*, n.s., xxi, pp. 133–92.

MAEDA, KIYOSHIGE, 1967. *Alor Janggus, a Chinese community in Malaya* (Social Science Series S-1), Kyoto University Centre for Southeast Asian Studies, Kyoto.

MAYBORN, PIERRE B., 1925. *Essai sur les associations en Chine*, Paris.

Mei-Jiang Ri-bao (Chinese language daily newspaper), Phnom-Penh.

Mian-Hua Qiao-Jiao (Lai Die-cha, ed.), [Phnom-Penh], n.d. (1957?) (in Chinese).

Mian-Hua Ri-bao (Chinese language daily newspaper), Phnom-Penh.

MIDDLETON, J., and TAIT D., 1958. 'Introduction', *Tribes without rulers*, London, pp. 1–31.

MILLS, C. WRIGHT, 1959. *The Sociological Imagination*, New York.

MONOD, G. H., 1931. *Le Cambodgien*, Paris.

MORGAN, W. P., 1960. *Triad societies in Hongkong*, Hongkong.

MORSE, HOSEA BALLOU, 1932. *The guilds of China, with an account of the guild merchant or co-hong of Canton* (2nd edition), London.

MURPHEY, RHOADES, 1953. *Shanghai, key to modern China*, Cambridge, Mass.

——, 1954. 'The city as a center of change: western Europe and China', *Annals of the Association of American Geographers*, **44,** pp. 349–62.

MURRAY, DOUGLAS P., 1963. *A survey of Chinese education in southeast Asia*, Department of Asian Studies, Victoria University, Wellington.

NEWELL, WILLIAM H., 1962. *Treacherous River, a study of rural Chinese in North Malaya*, Kuala Lumpur.

NGUYEN QUOC DINH, 1941. *Les congrégations chinoises en Indochine française*, Paris.

'Notice sur la situation des Chinois en Indochine', *Revue Indochinoise*, n.s., **xi** (1909), pp. 1063–100.

ONG TAE HAE, 1850. *The Chinaman abroad, an account of the Malayan archipelago, particularly of Java* (trans. W. H. Medhurst, D.D.), London.

POREE-MASPERO, EVELINE, 1962 and 1964. *Etude sur les rites agraires des Cambodgiens* (Le monde d'outre-mer passé et présent, no. xiv), Ecole Pratique des Hautes Etudes, VIe section, Sorbonne, Paris (2 vols.).

'Prince réfute les critiques injustifiées contre sa politique, Le', *La Dépêche*, 26 November 1957.

PURCELL, VICTOR, 1951. *The Chinese in Southeast Asia*, London; 2nd ed. 1965.

PYE, LUCIAN W., 1960. 'The politics of southeast Asia', in *The politics of the developing areas* (Gabriel A. Almond and James S. Coleman, eds.), Princeton, pp. 65–152.

RADCLIFFE-BROWN, A. R., 1940. 'Preface' to *African Political Systems* (M. Fortes and E. E. Evans-Pritchard, eds.), London.

Réalités Cambodgiennes (directeur: Nhiek Tioulong) (weekly magazine), Phnom-Penh, nos. 314–403, July 1962–June 1964.

Recueil général de la législation et de la réglementation de l'Indochine (à jour au 31 decembre 1925); deuxieme partie: arrêtés, décisions et circulaires du gouverneur général et des chefs d'administration locale, vol. 1, Service de legislation et d'administration du Gouvernement Général, 1927, [Hanoi].

RUSSIER, HENRI, 1914. *Histoire sommaire du Royaume de Cambodge des origines à nos jours*, Saigon.

SCHAPERA, I., 1956. *Government and Politics in Tribal Society*, London.

SCHLEGEL, G., 1885. 'Les Kongsis chinoises à Bornéo', *Revue Coloniale Internationale*, **I**, pp. 448–65.

Si-jiao Hao-ma Xin Ci-dian, Hongkong, Shang-wu Yin-shu Guan, 1958.

SIMON, G. EUG., 1868. 'Note sur les petites sociétés d'argent en Chine', *Journal of the China Branch of the Royal Asiatic Society*, n.s. **v**, pp. 1–23.

SKINNER, G. WILLIAM, 1957. *Chinese society in Thailand: an analytic history*, Ithaca.

——, 1958. *Leadership and power in the Chinese community of Thailand*, Ithaca.

——, 1964. 'Periodic marketing and social organization in rural China, Part 1', *Journal of Asian Studies*, **24**, no. 1, pp. 3–43.

——, 1968. 'Overseas Chinese Leadership: paradigm for a paradox' in *Leadership and Authority* (Gehan Wijeyewardene, ed.), Kuala Lumpur.

SMITH, M. G., 1956. 'On segmentary lineage systems', *Journal of the Royal Anthropological Institute*, **86**, no. 2, pp. 39–80.

——, 1960. *Government in Zazzau, 1800–1950*, The International African Institute, London.

'South Vietnam's Chinese problem' (by a special correspondent), *Far Eastern Economic Review*, **xxxiii**, no. 3, pp. 146–48, 1961.

TAN, GIOK-LAN, 1963. *The Chinese of Sukabumi: a study in social and cultural accommodation*, Modern Indonesia Monograph Series, Ithaca.

TAO, L. K., 1915. 'The town administration', in *Village and town life in China* by Y. K. Leong and L. K. Tao, Monographs on Sociology (L. T. Hobhouse and E. Westermarck, eds.), no. 4, London.

THOMPSON, VIRGINIA, 1937. *French Indo-china*, London.

T'IEN, JU-K'ANG, 1953. *The Chinese of Sarawak, a study of social structure*, London School of Economics Monographs on Social Anthropology, no. 12, London.

TOPLEY, MARJORIE, 1961. 'The emergence of social functions of Chinese religious associations in Singapore', *Comparative Studies in Society and History*, **iii**, no. 3, pp. 289–314.

——, 1963. 'The Great Way of Former Heaven, a group of Chinese secret religious sects', *Bulletin of the School of Oriental and African Studies*, **26**, no. 2, pp. 362–92.

TSIEN TCHE-HAO, 1961. 'La vie sociale des Chinois a Madagascar', *Comparative Studies in Society and History*, **iii**, no. 2, pp. 170–81.

UCHIDA, NAOSAKU, 1956. 'Economic activity of the Chinese in southeast Asia', *Far Eastern Economic Review*, **xxi**, no. 19, no. 590–3.

VAN DER KROEF, JUSTUS M., 1953. 'Chinese assimilation in Indonesia', *Social Research*, **xx**, pp. 445–72.

VIGIER, DANIEL, 1936. 'Le statut juridique des Chinois en Indochine', *Asie-française*, no. 341, pp. 176–86.

VU QUOC THUC, 1955. 'Les villes vietnamiennes', *Recueils de la Société Jean Bodin*, Librairie Encyclopédique, **vii**, pp. 207–18, Brussels.

WANG WEN-YUAN, 1937. *Les relations entre l'Indochine française et la Chine, étude de géographie économique*, Paris.

WARD, BARBARA E., 1954. 'A Hakka kongsi in Borneo', *Journal of Oriental Studies*, **I**, no. 2, pp. 358–70.

WARD, J. S. M., and STERLING, W. G., 1925-26. *The Hung Society or the Society of Heaven and Earth* (3 vols.), London.

WEIGHTMAN, GEORGE HENRY, 1960. *The Philippine Chinese: a cultural history of a marginal trading community* (unpublished Ph.D. dissertation), Cornell University.

WERTHEIM, W. F., 1964. 'Trading minorities in southeast Asia', in *East-West parallels: sociological approaches to modern Asia* by W. F. Wertheim, The Hague, pp. 39-82.

WICKBERG, EDGAR BERNARD, 1961. *The Chinese in Philippine Economy and Society, 1850-1898* (Ph.D. dissertation), University of California at Berkeley.

——, 1965. *The Chinese in Philippine Life 1850-1898*, New Haven.

WILLIAMS, LEA E., 1960. *Overseas Chinese nationalism, the genesis of the pan-Chinese movement in Indonesia, 1900-1916*, M.I.T. Center for International Studies, Glencoe.

——, 1961. 'The ethical program and the Chinese of Indonesia', *Journal of Southeast Asian History*, **2**, no. 2, pp. 35-42.

WILLMOTT, DONALD E., 1960. *The Chinese of Semarang: a changing minority community in Indonesia*, Ithaca.

——, 1961. *The national status of the Chinese in Indonesia, 1900-1958* (revised edition), Modern Indonesia Project Monograph Series, Ithaca.

WILLMOTT, W. E., 1963. Review of *Overseas Chinese in Southeast Asia – a Russian study* by N. A. Simoniyam, *Pacific Affairs*, **xxxvi**, no. 3, pp. 317-20.

——, 1964a. 'Chinese clan associations in Vancouver', *Man*, **lxiv**, no. 49, pp. 33-7.

——, 1964b. *Chinese society in Cambodia, with special reference to the system of congrégations in Phnom-Penh* (Ph.D. dissertation), University of London.

——, 1966. 'History and sociology of the Chinese in Cambodia prior to the French protectorate', *Journal of Southeast Asian History*, **7**, no. 1, pp. 15-38.

——, 1967. *The Chinese in Cambodia*, Vancouver.

WYNNE, MERVYN LLWELYN, 1941. *Triad and tabut, a survey of the origin and diffusion of Chinese and Mohammedan secret societies in the Malay peninsula, A.D. 1800-1935*, Singapore.

Xin Bao (Chinese language daily newspaper), Phnom-Penh.

YANG, LIEN SHENG, 1952. *Money and credit in China, a short history*, Cambridge, Mass.

YANG, MARTIN, 1948. *Chinese village, Taitou, Shantung Province*, London.

INDEX

achar, 132n
administrative leaders, 39, 114
adoption, 106n
age, 175
ai-si-ting, 90
alcohol, 146, 150
aliens, 60
Alor Janggus, 158n
American aid, 130
American occupation of Philippines, 156
Amoy, 6, 98
ancestors, 56
ang-bang, 38n
Ang-Eng, 27n, 54, 55, 68, 103
Angkor, 127, 130, 135, 137
Annam, 9, 13–17, 22n, 100n. (See Vietnam)
Annamese emperors. (See Vietnamese emperors)
anomie, 167
apex leader, 121, 138, 140
Arabs, 18
assimilation, 62, 172
associational structure, 85, 111, 113, 114, 118ff, 122ff, 126, 141, 159
  in Bangkok, 146f
  in China, 164–9
  in Siemréap, 138
  in Vancouver, 148, 159
associations. (See Chinese associations)

bai, 92
bakery, 93, 107, 132
baku, 96n
Banam, 133n

bang, vii, 12, 15. (See *congrégation*, speech group)
bang-hui, 34, 36, 38, 39, 40, 50, 128
Bangkok, 49, 93, 94n, 126, 128, 143, 145–7, 148, 149, 159, 160
bang-zhang, vii, 38n, 127. (See *chef de congrégation*)
banking, 44, 162
Bao-an, 90n
Bao-sheng Da Di, 97
Bao Xing, 106
Barom Reachea V, 9f
Batavia, 149, 150, 151n, 152
Battambang, v, 6, 7, 19, 20, 28, 31, 75, 76, 96n, 131, 139, 140
Ba Xian Jia Xi, 89
Ben-tou Gong, 35n, 54, 95, 179
betrothal, 86f
Billiton, 156n
Bo-lo, 90n
Borneo, 143, 156ff, 159. (See Sarawak, Kuching, Pontianak)
Brahmins, 96n
British, 144, 146, 147
British Columbia, 147n, 160
Bureau des Contributions des Asiatiques Etrangers, 24
Burmese, 10
business licences, 27, 110
businessmen (See Chinese businessmen)

Cambodia, v, vii, viii, 2, 5, 6, 7, 8, 9, 10, 12, 13, 16, 17, 18, 19, 20, 21, 26, 28, 29, 31, 34, 39, 40, 43, 46, 48n, 49, 51, 52, 54, 58, 60, 62, 63, 64,

LONDON SCHOOL OF ECONOMICS
MONOGRAPHS ON SOCIAL ANTHROPOLOGY

Titles marked with an asterisk are now out of print. Those marked with a dagger
have been reprinted in paperback editions and are only available in this form.
A double dagger indicates availability in both hard cover and paperback editions.

†20. L. H. PALMIER
    Social Status and Power in Java, 1960.
†21. JUDITH DJAMOUR
    Malay Kinship and Marriage in Singapore, 1959.
†22. E. R. LEACH
    Rethinking Anthropology, 1961.
★23. S. M. SALIM
    Marsh Dwellers of the Euphrates Delta, 1962.
†24. S. VAN DER SPRENKEL
    Legal Institutions in Manchu China, 1962.
 25. CHANDRA JAYAWARDENA
    Conflict and Solidarity in a Guianese Plantation, 1963.
 26. H. IAN HOGBIN
    Kinship and Marriage in a New Guinea Village, 1963.
 27. JOAN METGE
    A New Maori Migration: Rural and Urban Relations in Northern New Zealand, 1964.
‡28. RAYMOND FIRTH
    Essays on Social Organization and Values, 1964.
 29. M. G. SWIFT
    Malay Peasant Society in Jelebu, 1965.
†30. JEREMY BOISSEVAIN
    Saints and Fireworks: Religion and Politics in Rural Malta, 1965.
 31. JUDITH DJAMOUR
    The Muslim Matrimonial Court in Singapore, 1966.
 32. CHIE NAKANE
    Kinship and Economic Organization in Rural Japan, 1967.
 33. MAURICE FREEDMAN
    Chinese Lineage and Society: Fukien and Kwantung, 1966.
 34. W. H. R. RIVERS
    Kinship and Social Organization, reprinted with commentaries by David Schneider and Raymond Firth, 1968.
 35. ROBIN FOX
    The Keresan Bridge: A Problem in Pueblo Ethnology, 1967.
 36. MARSHALL MURPHREE
    Christianity and the Shona, 1969.
 37. G. K. NUKUNYA
    Kinship and Marriage among the Anlo Ewe, 1969.
 38. LUCY MAIR
    Anthropology and Social Change, 1969.
 39. SANDRA WALLMAN
    Take Out Hunger: Two Case Studies of Rural Development in Basutoland, 1969.
 40. MEYER FORTES
    Time and Social Structure and Other Essays, 1970.
 41. J. D. FREEMAN
    Report on the Iban, 1970.
 42. W. E. WILLMOTT
    The Political Structure of the Chinese Community in Cambodia, 1970.
 43. I. SCHAPERA
    Tribal Innovators: Tswana Chiefs and Social Change 1795–1940, 1970.
 44. E. R. LEACH
    Political Systems of Highland Burma: A Study of Kachin Social Structure, 1970.